Voices on the Margins

Voices on the Margins

Inclusive Education at the Intersection of Language, Literacy, and Technology

Yenda Prado and Mark Warschauer

The MIT Press
Cambridge, Massachusetts
London, England

© 2024 Massachusetts Institute of Technology

This work is subject to a Creative Commons CC-BY-NC-ND license.
This license applies only to the work in full and not to any components included with permission. Subject to such license, all rights are reserved. No part of this book may be used to train artificial intelligence systems without permission in writing from the MIT Press.

The MIT Press would like to thank the anonymous peer reviewers who provided comments on drafts of this book. The generous work of academic experts is essential for establishing the authority and quality of our publications. We acknowledge with gratitude the contributions of these otherwise uncredited readers.

This book was set in Stone Serif and Stone Sans by Westchester Publishing Services. Printed and bound in the United States of America.

Library of Congress Cataloging-in-Publication Data

Names: Prado, Yenda, author. | Warschauer, Mark, author.
Title: Voices on the margins : inclusive education at the intersection of language, literacy, and technology / Yenda Prado and Mark Warschauer.
Description: Cambridge, Massachusetts : The MIT Press, 2024. | Includes bibliographical references and index.
Identifiers: LCCN 2023035584 (print) | LCCN 2023035585 (ebook) | ISBN 9780262548021 (paperback) | ISBN 9780262378598 (epub) | ISBN 9780262378581 (pdf)
Subjects: LCSH: Inclusive education—United States. | Inclusive education—Technological innovations. | Mainstreaming in education—United States. | Children with disabilities—Education (Elementary)—United States.
Classification: LCC LC1201 .P73 2024 (print) | LCC LC1201 (ebook) | DDC 371.9/0460973—dc23/eng/20230920
LC record available at https://lccn.loc.gov/2023035584
LC ebook record available at https://lccn.loc.gov/2023035585

10 9 8 7 6 5 4 3 2 1

From Yenda

For my beloved son, Attillio Andrés. You are my universe and the catalyst for this work.

For my students—past, present, and future. To you, I owe everything.

To my faithful mother, Nelida, for being the first to fight for me, and to my extended family and friends for setting a strong foundation of love.

Finally, to my teachers and mentors for believing and challenging me to shoot for the stars.

From Mark

For Danny

Contents

A Note about Authorship   ix
Acknowledgments   xi
Foreword: A Note about the Writing of This Book during
the Pandemic   xiii

I

1 **Introduction**   3
2 **Contested Models of Inclusive Education**   17
3 **Technology-Supported Language and Literacy**   31

II

4 **Future Visions Academy: An Inclusive School**   49
5 **Amplifying Student Voice: LLT Practices at FVA**   81
6 **Technology as Connection**   115
7 **Reflections on Technology and Inclusion in a Changing World**   149

III

8 **Interdependence: A Relational Framework for Exploring Inclusive Education**   161
9 **Looking to the Future**   179

Appendix A: Methods for Investigating Inclusive Education   195
Appendix B: Technologies Used at FVA   215
Notes   221
Bibliography   259
Index   285

A Note about Authorship

The genesis of this research lay in a research-practice partnership between the University of California, Irvine School of Education, and Future Visions Academy, with the first author, Yenda Prado, as the graduate student researcher and the second author, Mark Warschauer, as the faculty supervisor. It later expanded into Yenda's dissertation, for which Mark served as advisor and chair. Following the dissertation, the two of us continued to collaborate closely on all aspects of the book manuscript, from developing the initial prospectus, to revising the dissertation and adding additional material, to responding to feedback from reviewers and MIT Press editors. However, while the analysis and interpretation of data and the conceptualization and planning of the book have been a highly collaborative effort, all of the data gathering and most of the writing was done by the first author. For that reason, unless otherwise specified, we use first-person singular pronouns in this manuscript to refer to Yenda as the first author.

Acknowledgments

We are immensely grateful to the students, parents, teachers, and paraprofessional staff at Future Visions Academy who introduced us to the possibilities of fully inclusive schools and whose commitment to interdependent community inspires us on a daily basis. This book builds upon research we conducted at Future Visions Academy, under the auspices of the Orange County Education Advancement Network.

A number of colleagues provided feedback for the ideas that inform this book. In particular, we extend our thanks to Dr. Elizabeth Peña and Dr. Stacy Branham, whose interdisciplinary work in the space of disability and language, and interdependence and inclusion, respectively, demonstrated to us the need for intersectional approaches to the study of technology for social inclusion; Dr. Penelope Collins, for engaging with us as a fellow reading specialist and cultivating our interests in language and literacy for differentially abled students; and Dr. Steve Graham, whose research has transformed how we support the literacy practices of students with disabilities.

A great deal of gratitude also goes to Kaitlyn Koo and Ricardo Hernandez. This work would not have been possible without their dedicated assistance and meticulous attention to detail. Dr. Sharin Jacob and Dr. Melissa Dahlin also provided helpful comments and support.

Finally, we would like to thank the editors and reviewers at the MIT Press, particularly our acquisition editor Susan Buckley, for understanding and championing our vision for this book.

Foreword: A Note about the Writing of This Book during the Pandemic

As social scientists, it is easy to get lost in the day-to-day phenomena of what we study and to miss the bigger picture of how and why these things matter. This was supposed to be a book about technology and literacy, but as the pandemic forced us to engage in new and digitally intimate ways, it also became a book about connection and the ways that we could choose to use digital technologies to mediate that connection inclusively. As we reflected on our uses of digital technologies, both before and during the pandemic, we couldn't help but extrapolate the broader impact social uses of digital technologies have had on people's access and inclusion in this historical moment in time.

Nor could we ignore how the need for interdependent collaboration and engagement, always relevant, had magnified. As a result, the events of the past four years have illuminated the importance of working together and the disastrous effects of not doing so. Our handling of crises, including how we choose to engage—or not engage—with the digital technologies at our disposal, bears direct consequence on our ability to mitigate impact.

What the past four years have taught us, more than anything, is that the problems of the future will continue to be of a global, and interdependent nature. This means that solutions must come forth from a place of interconnection. Our increasingly digitized lives will center more and more on the ways that we can use technology to engage collaboratively in both problem solving and communication. Global problems require an interdependent framing to generate global solutions.

The physical isolation precipitated by the pandemic afforded a unique window in time to experience technology's potential to bring people together, whether it be to share a meal together virtually, say a final FaceTime goodbye, or to teach a Zoom class of fourth graders how to use a protractor. Through various digital technologies, we came together to celebrate and mourn both the quotidian and the extraordinary moments of our lives. If there was ever a time to understand and to act upon the power of digital technologies to amplify or to minimize our interconnection, that time is now.

As countries and states across the world reflect on their responses to the pandemic, the transition of educational programs to collaborative hybrid environments for teaching, learning, and working has created a context entirely distinct from what came before. Acknowledging this reality entails not shying away from examining how digital technologies can be used to cultivate and maintain inclusive communities that make learning maximally accessible for the diversity of students in today's schools.

Alongside extraordinary challenges, the pandemic has presented an opportunity of sorts: a forced revisioning of the role of digital technologies in inclusive education. Of particular concern in this context are those students most likely to face significant barriers to meaningful learning opportunities: young students, students with learning differences and disabilities, students who are linguistically and culturally diverse, and students living in poverty. By centering the needs of these students in the adaptation of digital technologies for inclusive education, this book aims to support educators and policymakers in the pursuit of maximizing the integration and engagement of *all* students across diverse learning contexts.

I

1 Introduction

> An inclusive approach to education is a universal human right and focuses on all children learning and socializing together . . . acknowledges our shared humanity, and respects the diversities that exist in ability, culture, gender, language, class, and ethnicity.
>
> —Matthew J. Schuelka and Suzanne Carrington, "Innovative and Global Directions for Inclusive Education in the 21st Century"[1]

In an era of integrated schools, one group remains segregated: children with disabilities. This book takes an in-depth look at a school that is breaking the mold.

We do this through the lens of language, literacy, and technology (LLT)—the three media of communication that most define our twenty-first-century lives. In particular, we examine how new digital tools are used in a school not only to reshape how individual students communicate, read, and write but also to foster a larger community of social and educational inclusion among teachers, children, and families. We learn about children such as Tammy, a nonspeaking fourth grader with Down syndrome who enthusiastically uses the software Proloquo2Go on her iPad to collaborate with her classmates, and Finn, a second grader with autism who uses interactive digital writing tools to mediate his writing experiences and give voice to his thoughts. Through these stories and others, we catch a glimpse of both what is possible and what is yet to be done.

In the remainder of this introductory chapter, we offer a brief overview of the landscape of inclusive education and then discuss how we approach inclusion in relation to LLT both in our work and in this book.

The Landscape of Inclusion in Education

Educators, policymakers, and communities are increasingly charged with advocating for inclusion in all aspects of life. Toward this endeavor, organizations such as the United Nations Educational, Scientific and Cultural Organization (UNESCO) and the National Council on Disability (NCD) in the United States have increasingly invested in supporting institutional cultivation of inclusive education practices critical to developing equitable education systems fundamental to increasingly diverse nations. Global initiatives supporting inclusive education include Education for All and the Convention on the Rights of Persons with Disabilities.[2] These global initiatives built upon the Salamanca Statement developed in 1994 at the World Conference on Special Needs Education and signed by more than one hundred countries.[3] In the United States, the movement toward inclusion is historically grounded with the passing of *Brown v. Board of Education*, which made segregated school environments (i.e., the separation of students based on their race and ethnicity) unconstitutional and led to the passage of the Individuals with Disabilities Education Act (IDEA).[4]

However, despite advancing efforts, the segregation of students with disabilities from their nondisabled peers persists. In the United States, for example, 63 percent of all students with Individualized Education Programs (IEPs) spend approximately 20 percent of their instructional time in segregated classrooms. In response, the NCD pushed for full desegregation of children with disabilities in their 2018 report *Segregation of Students with Disabilities*.[5] Additionally, they have called on the US Department of Education to support research identifying practices that improve educational outcomes for students with disabilities educated in inclusive environments. More broadly, UNESCO reports that 258 million children in low- and middle-income countries have limited access to schooling, and those without access receive their education in segregated settings.[6]

Accordingly, as countries and states begin shifting toward inclusive models of education, understanding technology's role in this process will be critical to the success of inclusion efforts aimed at creating educational access and equity. Technology matters in the context of inclusive education in part due to a shared history between assistive technologies and the education of students with disabilities.[7] This history affords examples of how accessibly designed technologies, including but not limited to assistive

Introduction

technologies, could be used to create access to information and activities for people with disabilities.[8] More broadly, research to date indicates that students with disabilities benefit from inclusive instructional supports, including those mediated by technology, that scaffold students' learning and engagement. Inclusive uses of technologies, particularly those informed by universal design principles, afford visual, auditory, and tactile scaffolds that all students, including those with disabilities, can use to engage with content.[9]

In this context, research specifically targeting inclusive uses of mainstream, educational, and assistive technologies to include and scaffold disabled students' language and literacy practices have emerged. Inclusive supports for literacy are those that create access to the reading and writing curriculum and bolster the development of fluency and comprehension for all students.[10] As such, examining the social uses of digital technologies to support students' inclusion and engagement with language and literacy practices has become increasingly salient.[11]

However, this research has not been conducted in full inclusion environments in which students with and without disabilities are educated together in the general classroom setting with supports being pushed in rather than students being pulled out.[12] Moreover, in the majority of research in the area of disability, LLT has been conducted with students either partially included in the general education setting or in a special day-class placement.[13] Furthermore, this research has primarily focused on clinical uses of assistive technologies as interventions to support individual student functioning rather than the broader social uses of digital technologies to support inclusion and access in education.[14]

Purpose

Where we are in our quest for inclusive education begs several questions. What does it mean to be inclusive in today's schools? How do we approach the increasingly pervasive use of digital technologies in schools from an inclusive perspective that supports access for all students? What does inclusive education look like at the intersection of language, literacy, and technology? *Voices on the Margins* is about how Future Visions Academy (pseudonym, hereafter FVA), an extraordinary full inclusion public charter school in the Western United States, engaged, and sometimes grappled with, these questions. In this book, we seek to examine the ways that digital technologies support inclusion and language and literacy practices for culturally and linguistically diverse children with and without disabilities. Based on a wide range of qualitative data collected during our case study of FVA, we illuminate three central themes: (1) the social organization that allowed a fully inclusive environment for children with disabilities to thrive, (2) the ways that digital technologies were used in the program to help students express their voice and agency while developing language and literacy skills, and (3) the ways that digital technologies were used to foster stronger networks and connections within the school.

The impact of this work supports an improved understanding of technology's role in operationalizing a full inclusion model, as well as of how integrating digital technologies into language and literacy practice can support student inclusion. As a result, this book is also about how insights gleaned from our work with FVA can lead to broader understandings of approaches for supporting inclusion in schools on a wider scale. This is achieved through a discussion of social inclusion and technology, a review of extant literature topics, and an examination of school community engagement across sociocultural context.

Voices on the Margins centers on an ethnographic case study of FVA, incorporating participant observations across in-person, hybrid, and remote schooling environments; interviews with a culturally and linguistically diverse group of teachers, staff, parents, and children; and collection and analysis of a variety of school-, teacher-, and student-produced documents. While the argument could be made that a case study of a single school may not be representative, our purpose was not to examine typical practices but rather to illuminate the possibilities of what *could be*. Baines beautifully makes the argument for the value in studying unique schools in her examination of another outlying institution: "It is tempting to write off the case of Pathways Academy as a unique and singular case impossible to replicate . . . it is important not to let 'yes, but . . .' statements act as excuses to ignore cultural ideals that can be actionable or disregard such as culture as a valuable aspiration."[15]

Finally, we seek to understand how learning takes place through multilayered development, examining both the unfolding of events and the transformation of school community members over time. This work is situated in sociocultural theories of education, learning, and literacy[16] and

Introduction

associated new literacy studies,[17] disability studies,[18] and a novel theoretical perspective of interdependence—a framework that makes human collaboration central to understanding the ways that inclusion occurs within communities.[19] In adopting these perspectives, *Voices on the Margins* takes a student-centered, assets-based approach to exploring how FVA engages with technology in the context of creating community in relation to disability and inclusion. As such, this book explores the wide range of overlapping and plural practices that students, teachers, and parents engage in at FVA. This includes examining the role digital technology use plays within the broader school ecology in relation to students' inclusion, engagement, and practice. It also examines the varying attitudes, tensions, and competing priorities among FVA's parents, teachers, and staff regarding the value and use of digital technologies to inform and mediate instruction, particularly during the transition to remote learning in the spring and fall of 2020.

Argument

To our knowledge, few ethnographic works present in-depth case studies of teacher, student, and parent day-to-day inclusive education practice at the intersection of language, literacy, and technology in schools using a full inclusion model of instruction. We preview here the foundational works upon which we built our study of inclusive education, language, literacy, and technology to situate, complement, and differentiate our work within current academic literature.

Prior academic works examining the use of digital media by children with disabilities include Meryl Alper's *Giving Voice: Mobile Communication, Disability and Inequality* and *Digital Youth with Disabilities*, as well as Sue Cranmer's *Disabled Children and Digital Technologies: Learning in the Context of Inclusive Education*. Similar to this book, both take an intersectional approach to examining issues of disability, technology, and inclusion. However, what differentiates this work is our focus on students' language and literacy practice vis-à-vis the mediating impact of mainstream, educational, and assistive uses of digital technologies in a fully inclusive school integrating students with and without disabilities. Another differentiating factor is that much of the emerging literature is set in contexts outside the United States, making this research a complementary US-based addition to international contributions.[20]

Moreover, *Voices on the Margins* is intentionally intersectional in response to the tendency for research addressing technology, inclusion, language, literacy, or disability to do so in silos (i.e., with a principle focus on one, sometimes two, of these topics). Examples include ethnographic investigations of culturally diverse children's use of digital media but without a focus on disability and inclusive practice, such as Sonia Livingstone and Julian Sefton-Green's *The Class: Living and Learning in the Digital Age* and Antero Garcia's *Good Reception: Teens, Teachers, and Mobile Media in a Los Angeles High School*. Alternatively, work in education anthropology that looks at disability and inclusive education practices, but not necessarily the mediating impacts of digital technology use, includes Matthew J. Schuelka and Suzanne Carrington's *Global Directions in Inclusive Education*, Federico Waitoller's *Excluded by Choice: Urban Students with Disabilities in the Education Marketplace*, and AnnMarie Baines's *(Un)Learning Disability*. This book is meant to situate, and extend, the utility of such academic works in understanding the multiple socio-technical factors that preclude or support students' inclusion and practice.

While *Voices on the Margins* does not center on clinical, interventionist, or specialist uses of assistive technologies, as is sometimes the norm for works examining the dual topics of disability and technology, we do discuss assistive uses of digital technologies for social engagement and inclusion within a well-known body of assistive technology literature. These foundational works include Sumita Ghosh's *Technology for Inclusion: Special Education, Rehabilitation, for All*, Elina Beltrán, Chris Abbott, and Jane Jones's *Inclusive Language Education and Digital Technology*, and Mike Blamires's *Enabling Technology for Inclusion*.

This work intends to continue the tradition occupied by the aforementioned works by taking an in-depth assets-based approach to examining the ways that children engage with technology in the context of creating community—but with a specific focus on issues related to disability and inclusion. In these ways, *Voices on the Margins* both fits and extends these empirical bodies of literature pertaining to inclusive education practice at the intersection of language, literacy, and technology.

Author Positionality

We were not neutral observers in our research and writing for *Voices on the Margins*, given our holding of specific beliefs about the potential and

Introduction

affordances of using digital technologies to support inclusion and language and literacy practices within school communities. These beliefs informed our analysis and writing. For example, as a disabled person, I situate my disability as an inextricable part of who I am. This intersects with both my, and Mark's, personal experiences as parents of children with disabilities—all of which inform our orientations toward social perspectives of disability and inclusive school practice.

Professionally, our backgrounds as researchers are precluded by our backgrounds as educators and practitioners. In these capacities, we have taught and provided services and programs across socioeconomically diverse school community settings. These experiences inform our individually developed beliefs about children with disabilities and the potential of using digital technologies to support student agency and voice inclusively.

As a result, we adopt a social model of disability, grounded in the critical view that identity is intersecting and multiple, to interrogate the social-contextual impacts of school practices on disabled children's lives.[21] As social constructivists, we also adopt the perspective that knowledge is co-constructed and is interdependent on a variety of individual and group processes that position schooling as a cultural process.[22]

Approach to Disability, Language, and Inclusion

Voices on the Margins adopts a social model of disability, affording a more nuanced way to interrogate contextual impacts of inclusion and exclusion on disabled children's lives and education. As such, we look to seminal academic works, such as Alper's *Giving Voice*, Cranmer's *Disabled Children and Digital Technologies*, and Schuelka and Carrington's *Global Directions in Inclusive Education*. We also look to the disability community's positioned use of language in our framing of disability and inclusion. This includes the writings of culturally diverse disability rights activists, such as Mia Mingus, whose liberatory conceptualization of interdependence inspired this book, as well as Alice Wong and Emily Ladau, whose works *Disability Visibility* and *Demystifying Disability*, respectively, critically informed our approach to writing this book.[23]

As a disabled person, I use identity-first language to take terms typically deemed pejorative and reappropriate them as a source of identity and strength—a common practice among many marginalized folk.[24] As a result, when discussing disability, we may interchangeably use identity-first ("disabled students") in addition to person-first ("students with disabilities") language, in recognition of the fact that language preferences vary within and across disability, advocacy, and research communities. We also differentiate between our use of "inclusion" (i.e., inclusion model) and "inclusive" (i.e., inclusive practice), with the first referring to structures of access and participation and the latter referring to integrative actions.

Furthermore, we adopt Schuelka and Carrington's conceptualization of inclusive education as requiring a reimagining of schools as ecosystems where all children learn together and are respected for the diversity of abilities and backgrounds that they bring.[25] In this context, we define inclusive instructional practices as those that address the needs of students with a variety of abilities and support a sense of belonging.[26] Inclusive classrooms are those that support an integrated environment in which all students' contributions are equitably supported and valued.[27] Non-inclusive classrooms are those that privilege specific ranges of ability and need deemed normative and exclude or segregate students who fall outside these externally prescribed norms.[28]

Approach to Investigating Digital Technologies

Complementing our adoption of a social model of disability, *Voices on the Margins* takes a social use approach to the study of digital technology use. This contrasts with determinist approaches that center the premise that technologies place positive or negative impacts on society. Determinist perspectives privilege the technology itself and tend to obscure the mediating impact of human characteristics on technology use, including class, gender, race, and disability.[29]

In contrast, views that center the social uses of technology privilege the role of people in mediating technology use.[30] This is an important distinction that affords a study of technology in context, as well as more balanced views of technology use vis-à-vis wider systems of influence.[31] The social use approach is consistent with sociocultural perspectives that view human development and learning as social, collaborative, and interdependent, mediated by a variety of tools best understood in their unity rather than as separate components. Thus, we frame our approach in terms of how digital technologies might help change the broader ecology of learning. Specifically, *Voices on the Margins* outlines the impact of sociocultural dynamics at

Introduction

play in students', teachers', and parents' meaning making across in-person, remote, and technology-mediated contexts.

Approaches that consider "the social shaping of technology" reflect the influence of social group designation and consider the sociocultural factors that inform technology use.[32] These approaches support analysis of inclusive uses of digital technologies in schools. In taking a social use approach to investigating technologies, we hope to demonstrate how new uses and forms of digital technologies provide a powerful means for children with disabilities to amplify their voice, thus enhancing their educational and social inclusion.

It is important to note that *Voices on the Margins* focuses attention on the social, educational, and assistive uses of digital technologies and applications, rather than on clinical or specialist uses of assistive technologies. The technologies studied include laptop and tablet computers such as Chromebooks and iPads, software with features that support accessibility such as those found in Google Suite, and assistive communication applications such as Proloquo2Go for iOS.

Approach to Intersectionality and Diversity

Voices on the Margins situates technology use as mediated by sociocultural context, including the impact of culture and disability. Similar to Livingstone and Sefton-Green's *The Class* and Alper's *Giving Voice*, this work engages in a richly descriptive ethnographic study of linguistically and developmentally diverse children's engagement across a sociocultural context. This includes the impact of sociocultural dynamics at play in students', teachers', and parents' meaning making across technology-mediated contexts.

We present the origin story of FVA as a county public charter school codeveloped by multiple community constituents, including parent advocates, to serve the needs of culturally and linguistically diverse students with and without disabilities. As such, this case study centers on marginalized voices of families of color—a departure from prior research on disability, technology, and education centering majority white, higher-resourced families.

We intentionally recruited family interviewees with racially, linguistically, culturally, and developmentally diverse children who reflect the demographics of the school and community (e.g., high- and low-income immigrant families from rural and urban Mexico, working- and middle-class mixed race and second-generation families, as well as families whose children had a variety of disabilities or, in some cases, no disabilities). Our analysis focuses on how these families' diverse life experiences, combined with the school practices, shaped the education and development of their children and how they draw on their funds of knowledge to address challenges.

Narrative Organization

As discussed above, chapter 1 front-loads the aims and, along with chapters 2 and 3, makes up part I of the book to provide an introductory framing for case-study findings, synthesis, and recommendations. Part II, consisting of chapters 4, 5, 6, and 7, is the heart of the book and details case-study findings from our ethnographic work at FVA. Chapters 8 and 9 compose part III and provide final syntheses and recommendations for using digital technologies to support students' language and literacy practices inclusively in schools. Below, we outline the subsequent chapters in detail:

Chapter 2, "Contested Models of Inclusive Education," presents a brief history of inclusion in the United States within the context of global initiatives in inclusive education. The chapter outlines models of inclusive education leading up to current approaches aimed at benefiting the maximum number of students with and without disabilities in which each student is seen as a permanent member of the general education classroom.[33] The chapter then juxtaposes this movement toward inclusive models of education with the continued and persistent segregation of disabled students from their nondisabled peers. The chapter discusses the movement's contested nature—including challenges faced by inclusion advocates in the design and implementation of inclusive practices—as being centered in the varied, and often contentious, perceptions held toward inclusion.[34] Questions of equity and access—essentially, who are general education settings made for and who has the right to share space within such settings—are presented in this chapter as being at the heart of the struggle to normalize the inclusion of all students into general education settings.

Chapter 3, "Technology-Supported Language and Literacy," starts with a brief overview of the language and literacy needs of disabled students before diving into the uses of digital technologies to support disabled students' language and literacy needs specifically. While several research syntheses of technology-based solutions for promoting literacy instruction

Introduction

exist,[35] few specifically outline the impact of technology use on supporting interdependent language and literacy practices between students with and without disabilities. A more common approach over the past decade has instead been for empirical studies to present the use of specific technology tools to support the development of specific components of literacy, such as decoding or comprehension.[36] This chapter presents the argument that digital technologies hold a broader potential to be used collaboratively to support inclusion, language and literacy practices, and shared meaning across school contexts. This concept will be reiterated and made evident in the subsequent chapters "Amplifying Student Voice: LLT Practices at FVA" and "Technology as Connection," where an essential value of the social use of digital technologies lays in their affordances for bringing school communities together.

Chapter 4, "Future Visions Academy: An Inclusive School," descriptively introduces results from the two-year case study at FVA, a full inclusion public charter school in the Western United States, which form the basis for the remaining chapters in the book. This chapter presents a detailed discussion of the particular ways in which FVA strove to ensure that the social organization of the school facilitated a fully inclusive environment for students to thrive. We detail the origins and context of FVA as the only fully inclusive public charter school in its county, discuss how this case study centers on marginalized voices of families of color, and elaborate our intentional recruitment of family participants who reflect the demographics of the school and community. Analyses focus on how these families' diverse life experiences, combined with the school's practices, shaped the education and development of their children and how they draw on their funds of knowledge to address challenges. Observations of classroom learning and interviews with students, parents, teachers, and staff are all used to document inclusive practices across the school.

Chapter 5, "Amplifying Student Voice: LLT Practices at FVA," discusses how FVA families and staff used digital technologies across school and home environments to engage students in language and literacy practices. This includes an examination of LLT practices, defined here as an integrated approach to examining LLT as interconnected practices and literacies.[37] The chapter includes student, staff, and parent observations and perceptions of LLT practices at FVA, while exploring the uses of digital technologies to support disabled students' language and literacy practice across contexts.

This chapter also analyzes how FVA used digital technologies to afford alternative modes of expression for students to express their agency and voice while developing their language and literacy skills. Vignettes—such as the case of Tammy, a nonspeaking fourth grader learning to use Proloquo2Go to engage with her classroom community—are used to illustrate potential uses of digital technologies to embody and empower student voices.

Chapter 6, "Technology as Connection," chronicles FVA's shift to remote learning at the onset of the COVID-19 pandemic during the spring of 2020. The chapter specifically documents the historical moment when schools were forced to pivot to emergency remote learning—essentially turning our original one-year ethnographic study of FVA's school practices into an (un)natural two-year experiment. This chapter documents how the transition to emergency remote learning precipitated novel shifts in how FVA used technology to mediate and cultivate connection during a period of significant isolation brought on by the pandemic. Combining analysis of remote interviews and observations collected during the pandemic, the chapter explores how motivations for technology use during the pandemic gravitated toward bolstering family support, connection, and inclusion within the FVA school community. The chapter also includes exploration of FVA's use of synchronous platforms such as FaceTime, Zoom, and instant messaging, as well as asynchronous uses of platforms such as Google Classroom and YouTube content, to scaffold instruction inclusively during the transition to emergency remote learning.

Chapter 7, "Reflections on Technology and Inclusion in a Changing World," provides a snapshot of FVA's return to hybrid and in-person instruction during the latter portion of the 2020–2021 school year. The chapter chronicles that transitory space during the mid-pandemic period when quarantine restrictions began to lift and schools, including FVA, started to take tentative steps back toward in-person instruction. The chapter focuses on the residual effects of surviving the first year of the pandemic and explores future hopes and dreams at FVA. This shift resulted in a revision to FVA's hybrid program, consisting of on-site in-person instruction coupled with a real-time synchronous remote learning option for approximately 30 percent of FVA families who opted to remain fully remote.

Chapter 8, "Interdependence: A Relational Framework for Exploring Inclusive Education," fully explicates the theoretical perspective presented in *Voices on the Margins* and builds an argument for using interdependence

Introduction

as a frame for (1) assessing the moves that participants make to support inclusion, (2) interpreting current aims in the intersectional study of inclusive education and LLT practices, and (3) interrogating the notion that independence is the most important goal of assistive uses of digital technologies. We discuss interdependence in relation to sociocultural theory, new literacies, and disabilities studies, arguing that the true social value of technologies—those designated as both assistive and mainstream—is their mediational power to promote interdependence between users. This argumentation is illustrated with examples taken from the preceding chapters to provide further analysis of the meaning making and actions that took place among students, parents, teachers, and staff at FVA.

Finally, chapter 9, "Looking to the Future," synthesizes the preceding chapter content to offer suggestions, policy, and best practices in bringing a fuller vision of inclusive education to fruition. In this concluding chapter, we discuss how a comprehensive vision of inclusive education requires a substantive paradigm shift by policymakers, district and school leadership, teachers, and parents in understanding and mitigating how principles of inclusion have historically played out in public schools. Using FVA as a case study, this chapter identifies key factors and recommendations for realizing a fuller vision of inclusive education in schools. Finally, the chapter suggests a rethinking of the way that digital technology use can contribute to the inclusive education of students with disabilities, arguing for a perspective of interdependence.[38] We highlight how a framework of interdependence can support the development of policies, practices, and pedagogies that foster full inclusion of *all* students across schools and society.

2   Contested Models of Inclusive Education

Inclusive education refers to educating *all* students, regardless of their differences, within the same school community. In this context, inclusion necessitates providing students of all ability levels with the necessary supports to achieve full access to a school's curriculum.[1] Inclusion as it is operationalized today is built on the premise that all students are valued and included in the school community, an entitlement broadly supported by global initiatives, including current federal disability law in the United States.[2] As a result, this book takes the position that the implementation of inclusive educational practices is a matter of equity and social justice. However, this view has not always prevailed, as the integration of students with disabilities into general education contexts has historically been marked by contention.[3]

Research to date indicates that students presenting with diverse instructional, developmental, and linguistic needs benefit from inclusive instructional supports that scaffold students' engagement. Inclusive instructional supports are those that enable access to the curriculum and bolster the development of academic and social skills for all students.[4] Within this context, there is an emerging body of research specifically targeting inclusive practices, technologies, and tools—particularly those informed by universal design principles (see chapter 3)—to scaffold students' engagement and participation in general education or special day-class placements.[5] For example, data from the National Longitudinal Transition Study-2 suggests that students with disabilities primarily placed in general education settings were twice as likely to enroll and persist in postsecondary education compared to their peers with a greater degree of placement in specialized education settings.[6] Other research has found that inclusive education practices promote academic performance, social inclusion, and continued postsecondary and employment trajectories for children both with and without disabilities.[7]

However, little of this research has been conducted with students with disabilities integrated into full inclusion classroom environments. Full inclusion environments are those in which all students are educated together in the general classroom setting with services and supports being pushed in rather than students being pulled out.[8] As a result, most research at the intersection of education, technology, and disability has been conducted with students with partial inclusion in the general education setting or special day-class placement.[9]

This chapter presents a brief history of the US classroom as situated within the broader international inclusive education movement, outlining models of inclusive education leading up to current approaches aimed at benefiting the maximum number of students. The chapter then presents the movement's contested nature, including challenges faced by inclusion advocates in the design and implementation of inclusive practices. Within this context, we differentiate between our use of "inclusion" (i.e., inclusion model) and "inclusive" (i.e., inclusive practices), with the former referring to structures of access and participation and the latter referring to integrative actions. Moreover, we define inclusive education as schooling systems and practices intentionally designed to enable children of diverse abilities and backgrounds to participate and learn together.[10] Our discussion is a US counterpoint and complement to Cranmer's discussion of inclusive practice within the international context.

History of Inclusion in US Classrooms

The movement toward inclusion in US classrooms is historically situated in the passing of US federal civil rights legislation aimed at eradicating race-based segregation—specifically *Brown v. Board of Education*, which struck down the false premise of "separate but equal." *Brown v. Board of Education* made segregated school environments unconstitutional, setting the tumultuous stage for school integration efforts across the United States in the 1960s and 1970s.[11]

Brown v. Board of Education also opened the doors for parents, educators, and communities to advocate for equal educational access for students with disabilities and to question segregation of students according to disability status. As a result, *Brown v. Board of Education* set the stage for the social justice protests of the 1960s that spurred parental activism and court challenges to the practice of denying students with disabilities a free public education.

These advocacy efforts culminated in the passage of the Education for All Handicapped Children Act in 1975, which mandated that every child be entitled to a Free and Appropriate Public Education in the least restrictive environment (LRE), setting the legal standard by which all special education cases that go before the courts are tried.[12] Prior to the passage of this act, students with disabilities, particularly those with intellectual differences, were largely excluded and denied a free public education.[13] The legal requirement that *all* students be educated in the LRE set the stage for advocacy that would eventually lead to approximately 60 percent of students with disabilities being educated alongside their already mainstreamed peers in regular classroom settings at least 80 percent of the time as of 2008.[14] Prior to this law being passed, only one in five students with exceptional needs were educated in regular public school environments, and usually in segregated classrooms.[15]

In 1997, the Education for All Handicapped Children Act was renewed as the IDEA. The IDEA reinforced the concept of inclusive education as a matter of civil rights and additionally required that school districts develop IEPs to ensure that students receive an education program appropriate to their particular needs in the LRE.[16] IEPs are legally binding documents under US law developed by a team of school professionals, teachers, and parents for children identified as having a disability or impairment who qualify to receive specialized instruction and services.[17]

The passage of the IDEA had the profound effect of mainstreaming students who had previously been kept at home or who were institutionalized in US public schools.[18] In 2004, the reauthorization of the IDEA mandated educators implement evidence-based practices (EBPs) in their work with students with disabilities. The reauthorization of the IDEA further opened the gateway for increased levels of funding toward educational research for students with disabilities.[19] Reauthorization of the IDEA, coupled with the No Child Left Behind Act of 2001, challenged school districts to integrate EBPs into their instruction of students with disabilities.[20] This mandated the inclusion of additional personnel, such as school psychologists, supplemental aides, and services to be included in the provision of EPBs deemed necessary to support all students within the LRE.[21]

More recently, the movement toward inclusion in US classrooms has been informed by global policies on the development of inclusive education, which, as Schuelka and Carrington detail, were amplified with the Salamanca Statement and Framework for Action on Special Needs Education.[22] That statement was adopted by the World Conference on Special Needs Education in 1994, when more than ninety-two governments and twenty-five international organizations met to consider needed policy changes to promote inclusive education to ensure schools serve all students, including those with disabilities. It presented a call for education for all, as well as a call for governments to develop inclusive schooling.[23]

The Salamanca Statement and Framework for Action also set the stage for future global initiatives such as Education for All and the Convention on the Rights of Persons with Disabilities.[24] These initiatives have supported the great strides that have been made in ensuring access to education for a larger proportion of the world's child population.[25] However, as Schuelka and Carrington explain in their analysis of UNESCO's 2015 Global Monitoring Report, the focus on unequal access to education has overshadowed the need for more focused efforts on improving the quality of education to include all children more fully once that education is obtained.[26] It is against this backdrop that more contemporary school efforts to support inclusive education practices, including those observed at FVA (see chapter 4), have shifted focus to practices that promote the integration of students with and without disabilities from diverse backgrounds in culturally responsive and inclusive ways.[27]

History of Inclusion in Relation to Disability Models and Justice Movements

The history of inclusion in schools is also informed by perceptions regarding the nature of disability. While disability can be categorized a multitude of ways, a common approach to understanding and discussing disability is to do so in relation to disability models and movements.[28] In this subsection, we preface the specific discussion of inclusive education in schools with a broader discussion of inclusion across disability models and movements.

Inclusion in Relation to the Medical Model of Disability

The medical model of disability centers disability as a diagnosis to be managed or cured.[29] From this viewpoint, medical intervention is necessary to diminish the impact of the disability on an individual's quality of life. The medical model of disability positions the disabled person as a dependent and passive, rather than active, participant in their own care, with service providers positioned as the active agents in remediating the disability.[30] In these circumstances, inclusion is seen as being afforded with the provision of interventions and tools to remediate the perceived deficits of the individual with the goal of increasing their ability to function. As such, the individual is positioned as dependent on external supports—including reliance on interventions provided by teachers, parents, clinicians, and other significant people in the disabled person's life.[31]

Inclusion in Relation to Social Models of Disability

Advocacy from the disability community led to the formation of social models of disability whose goal was to afford a differing perspective from the medical model of how disabled people actually live and organize their lives.[32] The focus of social models of disability places agency for action, access, and support within disabled individuals themselves with the goal of collectively creating independence and self-advocacy within the disability community.[33] Social models of disability place a greater emphasis on the identification of external rather than internal barriers to access and inclusion—a significant premise being that people are disabled by barriers in their environment rather than personal characteristics or impairments.[34] A social view of disability therefore centers inclusion on the need for structural changes to systems to minimize barriers to access.

Inclusion in Relation to the Independence Movement

The shift toward social models of disability led in part to the independence movement, which sought to promote the independence of people with disabilities.[35] This movement was important because it positioned people with disabilities as independent and capable of making their own decisions.[36] The history of the independence movement has its roots in the disability community's countering of the medical model of disability.[37] As pushback to the decision-making power that the medical model bestows on practitioners, the disability community moved toward seeing the short-term curative objectives of the medical model as incompatible with the long-term nature of disability.[38] Moreover, the independence movement situates the problem not within the body but rather within the environment. It also situates problems encountered by the disability community as being caused by overdependence on service providers and caregivers.[39] To overcome issues of dependency, the independence movement advocated for supports that enabled disabled individuals to make their own choices about their own care.[40]

Inclusion in Relation to Other Social Justice Movements

While we emphasize the independence movement due to student independence being a central goal in education, perceptions of inclusion in schools are also informed by additional movements undertaken by the disability rights community. These include the disability justice movement, which centers on recognizing the multiple forms of prejudice and discrimination that marginalized people face; the self-advocacy movement, which was started by people with intellectual and developmental disabilities to fight the harm perpetuated by the notion that it is better to institutionalize those with disabilities; the neurodiversity movement, which rejects the concept of "abnormal" brains to embrace the natural occurring diversity and variation in human cognition and development; and the psychiatric survivors movement, which aims to remove stigma from mental illness.[41] While beyond the purview of this book, the extensive works of disability rights activists (e.g., Mia Mingus, Alice Wong, Steve Silberman, Naoki Higashida, Emily Ladau) provide diverse and detailed accounts of the histories and perspectives held across the various disability rights movements.[42]

Redefining the Meaning of Inclusion in the Classroom

While disability models and movements inform how inclusion is conceptualized in schools (see chapter 8), they do not directly account for how inclusion is operationalized in the classroom. To do this, we now turn to a brief detailing of inclusion in the classroom. Inclusive education had its origins in the development of "ungraded classrooms" for the special education of children with disabilities under the auspices of New York City's early iterations of free public schooling in the 1900s.[43] Eventually the movement for compulsory education for all children, including those with disabilities, would lead to the passage of the Education for All Handicapped Children Act, as well as the eventual passing of the IDEA of 1990, as detailed earlier in this chapter.

Contested Models of Inclusive Education

The passage of these acts—also propelled by the values generated by President Lyndon B. Johnson's Great Society and the Civil Rights Movement in the 1960s—created an environment ripe in the 1970s and 1980s for further considerations into the equitable education of children with disabilities.[44] From this arose the mainstreaming movement as a precursor to today's modern inclusion movement. In his seminal book, *Achieving the Complete School: Strategies for Effective Mainstreaming,* Biklen moved beyond the question of whether to mainstream to make the case that the decision to mainstream children with disabilities was a moral one: "It is a moral question. It is a goal, indeed a value, we decide to pursue or reject on the basis of what we want our society to look like."[45] Much as Biklen does, we too approach the necessity for inclusive education as a moral imperative.

More recent iterations of inclusive education have begun to move from deficit-based perspectives of special education toward social constructivist–based perspectives of fully inclusive schooling.[46] Social constructivists argue that "it is the educational environment that must adapt to the child, not the other way around."[47] As a result, inclusive education has continued to be redefined, with an emphasis on each student being seen as a permanent member of the general education classroom.[48] Toward this end, Wayne Sailor and Blair Roger have outlined key principles for inclusive schools.

- All students attend their regularly assigned school, are considered general education students, and are taught within the general education context.
- Parent input and participation is sought and promoted as an integral part of creating an inclusive school community.
- General education teachers are responsible for all students and engage in collaborative team teaching with special education teachers and paraprofessionals.
- All students benefit from an inclusive school's configuration, are included in all school events, and have access to school resources.
- Positive behavioral supports are integrated at the individual, group, class, and school level to support all students' participation and inclusion as full citizens of their school.
- Inclusive schools use data to inform teaching and learning processes and solve problems.[49]

The vision of the fully inclusive school supports social justice, values students, and encourages collaboration.[50] A commitment to this view of inclusion positions students with disabilities as normative, valued, and included members of the school community. This vision of inclusion requires a substantive paradigm shift by policymakers, district and school leadership, as well as teachers and parents in how principles of inclusion have historically played out in public schools. The burden of creating inclusive school environments should be shared at school, district, state, and national levels rather than falling solely on specific subsets of the school community, as sometimes happens when the onus for change is primarily placed on teachers and service providers. In the same way that the burden should not rest on teachers and service providers alone, neither should it rest on individual students needing to "prove" their "belongingness" in the general education classroom.[51] The placement of responsibility on individual students, as opposed to the educational system itself, usually derives from deficit perspectives on the education of students with disabilities.[52]

Models of Inclusive Education

While the movement toward inclusive models of education continues to be juxtaposed with the continued and persistent segregation of students with disabilities from their nondisabled peers, multiple models of inclusive education have emerged over time to inform current approaches aimed at benefiting the maximum number of students with disabilities as permanent members of the general education classroom.[53]

Inclusion models range from full inclusion, in which all instruction takes place in one setting and where services and supports are pushed in, to partial inclusion, in which students are pulled out of the classroom to receive services.[54] Classroom implementation of inclusive practices typically utilizes a variety of instructional services and support.[55] These services are usually outlined in detail in the IEP and may include one-to-one or small-group individualized academic instruction, speech or occupational therapies, reading or writing interventions, or applied behavior analysis services.[56]

Regardless of the level or model used for implementing inclusive practices, the primary goal is to have most core instruction take place within the general education classroom setting. However, how this is implemented,

Contested Models of Inclusive Education

and to what degree, has historically been left up to individual school districts' interpretation of the LRE guidelines as outlined in the IDEA.[57]

Inclusion often, although not always, takes place within a co-teaching framework consisting of a general education teacher and a special education teacher coordinating instruction to varying degrees, typically determined by individual districts and schools.[58] As a result, co-teaching is often operationalized loosely and diversely from school to school and from district to district. With that said, several evidence-based models of co-teaching have surfaced as the most commonly used by schools implementing inclusive models of education.[59]

One teach, one assist This model involves one teacher, usually the general education teacher, providing instruction for all students, while the other teacher, usually the special education teacher, circulates the classroom, providing individual assistance to students requiring additional support. This is one of the most common models of co-teaching due to its relative ease of implementation and minimal level of coordination required between the two teachers.

Station teaching In this model, students are divided into small groups. The groups rotate between teachers, aides, and possibly community or parent volunteers as they move from station to station as a group. This model is also popular because it allows for students to receive individualized small-group instruction across a variety of mediums in a relative short span of time with only moderate coordination involved.

Parallel teaching This model is more time and resource intensive, and thus it is not as common, as it requires teachers to plan lessons together ahead of time. Students are split into two groups and provided with either the same, or complementary, lessons in their smaller groups within the same classroom. This model allows students to receive small-group instruction and affords teachers the opportunity to learn from each other.

Alternative teaching This model is also more time and resource intensive. However, it allows one teacher to assume responsibility for teaching the core lesson, while the other teacher assumes responsibility for pre-teaching and reteaching content to students needing additional support.

Team teaching This co-teaching model is the most time intensive but, when done well, can be quite effective in promoting a full inclusion model.

In this model, both general and special education teachers coordinate and plan together to provide instruction together to students within the same classroom. The benefit of team teaching is that all students have equitable access to both teachers simultaneously in the general education classroom.

As can be seen, inclusive education models, particularly those integrating co-teaching practices, are varied in the differing levels of coordination, planning, staffing, and participation required for implementation.[60] This leaves much room for interpretation of what inclusive practices might look like in the general education classroom. Variability in implementation and approach presents both affordances and challenges for general and special education teachers' efforts, and the schools and districts mandated to support them, in coordinating and implementing educational programming that addresses the needs of all students. Herein lies potential opportunities, and challenges, for educators and practitioners striving to realize fully inclusive schools.

Challenges Faced by Advocates of Inclusion

Many of the challenges faced by inclusion advocates in the design and implementation of inclusive school practices focus on the varied, and often contentious, perceptions held toward inclusion.[61] This section outlines several of the more common concerns and controversies put forth by different constituents regarding the inclusion of students with disabilities in general education classrooms.

To get to the heart of many of the concerns and fears involved in including students with disabilities within general education settings, we start with Armstrong et al.'s assessment of the situation: "Despite the simplicity of its message, inclusion is highly contestable . . . The key questions raised by the concept of inclusion are not definitional, despite of, or perhaps because of the difficulties of framing a meaningful definition, but are rather questions of practical political power which can only be meaningfully analyzed with reference to the wider social relations of our increasingly globalized world."[62] In other words, questions of equity and access—essentially, *who* are general educations setting made *for* and who has the *right* to *share space* within such settings—are at the heart of the struggle to normalize the inclusion of all students, regardless of ability level or developmental need, into general education settings. We address the challenges faced by advocates of inclusion across three reoccurring themes reported within the literature as well as across our interviews and interactions with schools: deficit-based beliefs about disability and special education, perceptions regarding the feasibility of fully inclusive school environments, and barriers in teacher professional development and support.

Deficit-Based Beliefs about Disability and Special Education

Deficit-based beliefs about the nature of disability and special education services often center on the idea that placement in general education settings is only appropriate for students who have "earned" this placement by falling within a range of what is considered normative achievement and development.[63] As a result, students who are not able to progress academically without the need for curricular modifications or structural supports are viewed as either requiring placement in a special day class or partial removal from the general education setting to receive specialized academic services.[64] Moreover, it is only when students can "prove" that they can fit in, essentially by performing within predetermined constraints of what is considered normal, that they are "released" from segregated specialized environments and permitted into the general education classroom.

Deficit-based beliefs about special education have also traditionally centered on remediation of the individual student rather than on addressing structural deficits within educational institutions themselves.[65] Perspectives of fully inclusive schooling, as detailed above, place the onus of reform on restructuring school environments rather than centering reform on the remediation of individual students,[66] the central premise being that learning is situated in cultural practices and activities, not solely in the minds of students.[67]

These structural shifts in countering deficit-based beliefs about students requiring services and instruction under the label of "special education" support changing attitudes toward the inclusion of students with disabilities in the general education classroom. Rather than focusing on differences as deficits, social constructivists begin with a *presumption of competence*: the idea, also discussed in chapter 4, that all children, with all their differences, are competent students.[68] Thus, instead of focusing on the teaching of low-level skills aimed at remediation, social constructivist perspectives seek to challenge all students with "the sort of rich, engaging content, common in classrooms serving the most academically successful students."[69]

Perceptions Regarding the Feasibility of Fully Inclusive Environments

Deficit-based beliefs about the nature of special education services often position placement in general education settings as conditional, rather than as a right, based on whether students meet the threshold for what a district or school considers "normal" progression. As a result, deficit-based beliefs about the nature of special education services also inform perceptions and opinions regarding the degree to which provision of specialized services, and the students who need them, should be integrated into the general education classroom. As such, there has been mixed reaction regarding the implementation of fully inclusive practices aimed at integrating students with and without disabilities in the general education classroom.[70] For example, some researchers have found positive effects on social development and esteem, sense of belonging, increased peer modeling, and improved academic motivation for all students,[71] while others have suggested that the general education classroom is not equipped to afford inclusion for students with disabilities.[72]

Perceptions about inclusion among parents also tend to be mixed, with parents of students with disabilities being more supportive of inclusion than parents of students in mainstreamed general education settings.[73] While research on parent perceptions of inclusion is still a developing field, it suggests that parents of students with disabilities tend to believe that most disabled students would be best served learning alongside their peers in general education settings.[74] Social interaction with peers, in fact, is a principal reason given by parents who wish for their disabled children to be placed in the general education classroom.[75] As we explore in chapter 4, parents believe that the ability to raise their disabled children in mainstream environments and participate in neighborhood life is important for their children's social development.[76]

Student perceptions of inclusion have generally been found to be positive, as the premise of inclusion taps into children's ideals of fairness.[77] Students overwhelmingly believe that all students should be given the same work and be exposed to the same education content. For example, Klingner and Vaughn's synthesis of twenty studies investigating the perceptions of more than 4,659 K–12 students found that students with disabilities overwhelmingly wanted to learn the same material, use the same books, and enjoy the same homework and grading practices as their mainstreamed peers. Klingner and Vaughn also found that students with and without disabilities understood the concept of learning differences and modifying instruction accordingly.[78]

With that said, research also indicates that students with disabilities are at increased risk of being teased, rejected, or ostracized compared to their mainstreamed peers.[79] Research on social acceptance consistently demonstrates that students with disabilities educated in regular classrooms tend to be less accepted, have lower social status, and be more socially isolated than their mainstreamed peers.[80] Thus, inclusion of students with disabilities in the general education setting may require additional supports to bolster positive social interactions.[81]

Similarly to students, teachers tend to have positive attitudes toward inclusion in the general classroom setting.[82] Scruggs and Mastropieri found that approximately 50 percent of general education teachers and 65 percent of special education teachers surveyed believed that inclusion for at least part of the school day benefited students.[83] However, teachers' attitudes toward inclusion are mitigated by multiple factors, and only a small percentage believed that full-time inclusion provides more benefits than pullout programs.[84] Teachers' support of inclusion is principally related to the perceived nature and severity of the needs presented by students in the classroom.[85] Avramidis and Norwich found that teachers tended to have more positive attitudes about including students with physical and sensory needs and less positive attitudes about including students with learning or behavioral needs. They also found that teachers' attitudes toward inclusion tended to be more positive for younger students in the elementary grades than for older students in the upper grades.[86]

Barriers in Teacher Professional Development and Support

Finally, the level of perceived competency and preparation, including institutional supports offered by the school and district leadership, impacted teachers' attitudes towards inclusion.[87] Surveyed teachers have indicated concerns that the inclusion of students with disabilities in the general classroom setting creates the potential for significant instructional challenges.[88] For many teachers, the need for substantive modifications to the general education environment to support the inclusion of students with disabilities is compounded by a lack of resources, professional development, and institutional support.[89] These challenges present both practical and philosophical obstacles for inclusion advocates and widen gaps in teacher professional development, often resulting in the segregation of professional development for general education and special education instructional practice. This has led to a dearth of teachers trained to support students with disabilities within general education classrooms.[90] It has also resulted in a dearth of teachers and service providers trained to provide pushed-in special education services to students with disabilities within general education classrooms.[91]

The lack of professional development for teachers, particularly those securing credentials in general education settings, includes a lack of training on the implementation of inclusive instructional models and practice, as well as a lack of pedagogical support by school leadership.[92] The lack of professional development is often coupled with a lack of institutional resources, infrastructure, and support—such as the provision of co-teachers and aides—that are needed for fully inclusive models to thrive.[93] Finally, a philosophical understanding of the value and need for full inclusion (see chapter 4) needs to be integrated into teacher professional development to support assets-based beliefs, perspectives, and approaches to inclusive education.[94] Teachers who expressed the view that the responsibility for teaching students with diverse needs should fall on general education teachers tended to have more positive attitudes and be more successful in creating an inclusive classroom.[95] Finally, barriers in teacher professional development and support also present as infrastructure challenges in the form of restrictive reporting requirements and processes that prioritize documentation aligned with segregated pullout and one-to-one models of service delivery.

Just as students have the right to learn together to the maximum extent possible, so do teachers have the right to be supported in the implementation of effective inclusive practices.[96] Research on teacher concerns regarding inclusion points to a need for institutional supports and professional development.[97] Strategies for supporting teacher professional development—including the cultivation of positive attitudes, beliefs, and practices—include providing additional planning time and ongoing professional development, promoting collaboration and team teaching, and supporting assistive uses of digital technologies and tools to support student learning and engagement.[98] With this, we now turn to chapter 3 to discuss the mediating role that digital technologies play in supporting students' language and literacy practices, learning, and engagement.

3 Technology-Supported Language and Literacy

While several research syntheses of technology-based solutions for promoting individual students' language and literacy skills exist,[1] few outline the social impact of technology use for supporting students' interdependent language and literacy practices with peers across school contexts. A more common approach for empirical studies is to explore the use of individual technology tools to support the development of specific components of literacy, such as decoding or comprehension.[2] As a result, the focus of research to date on the uses of assistive, educational, and mainstream digital technologies by students with disabilities has primarily centered on building students' independent access to content across instructional settings while minimizing the need for external supports.[3]

This chapter argues that students' use of digital technologies can broadly mediate and support their collaborative engagement in language and literacy practices with peers across school contexts to create shared meaning. Moreover, while children with differing disability designations present with diverse language and literacy needs, this chapter does not necessarily seek to categorize specific needs by specific disabilities. Our aim is to provide examples of language and literacy needs that students with diverse disability designations might encounter—setting the stage for later discussion of universal LLT practices that inclusively support a wide range of learners in chapters 4–7. This approach aligns with Schuelka and Carrington's recommendation that inclusive education professional development moves beyond a focus on specific disability designations to a more expansive needs assessment of the whole child:

> Teacher preparation for inclusion and diversity must move beyond the weekly focus on a different category of disability or difference, because this perpetuates

a special education model of categorization and intervention that assumes that young people with disabilities need to "be fixed." Focusing on categories of medical disability diagnosis and so called "best-practices" for each category universalizes disability and difference—which, as we have already argued, runs counter to "disability" as a constructed, relational, contextually defined, and social experience. This kind of teacher training prepares teachers not to look at the child in front of them, but rather to only look at the disability or difference.[4]

This chapter starts with a brief overview of salient language and literacy needs of students with disabilities, particularly in the areas of reading and writing, before diving into assistive, educational, and mainstream technology use in schools. Finally, we preview how inclusive uses of these digital technologies can support students' language and literacy needs.

Language and Literacy Needs of Students with Disabilities: Reading Acquisition

Students with disabilities present with extended language and literacy needs, particularly in reading. Strong reading skills are predictors of academic and occupational success, and quality reading interventions, especially those designed to be accessible to a wide range of students, can support academic achievement.[5] Students with disabilities often experience reading difficulties related to the structure and content of reading, particularly academic reading, which is often marked by challenging features such as lower-frequency vocabulary content, higher lexical density, and increased syntactic and semantic complexity.[6] Students with disabilities may also rely more heavily on visual cues and scaffolding to comprehend complex text.[7]

Reading acquisition tends to occur in two phases: learning to read and reading to learn.[8] Learning to read general commences at the start of the elementary years, with reading goals focused on using sound units (phonemes) to create words, make letter–sound connections, and decode words. Reading to learn tends to start around the fourth-grade reading level, with the shift from decoding to using text to gain information and extract meaning for academic purposes. Emerging readers must master learning to read before moving on to reading to learn.[9]

In a landmark review and analysis of the literacy research titled *Preventing Reading Difficulties in Young Children*, the National Research Council found that successful readers:

Technology-Supported Language and Literacy

- Have prerequisite knowledge in phonological and syntactic awareness, ability to name letters rapidly, and knowledge of the alphabetic principle at the time of entry into first grade.
- Can rapidly and automatically identify written words (known as fluency and critical to memory retention and comprehension of texts).
- Use word knowledge and sight vocabulary to comprehend texts, thus moving away from decoding over time.
- Independently monitor their own reading.[10]

Emerging readers tend to have less knowledge of topics, structural and functional knowledge of reading, and practice engaging in extensive reading activities. For students with disabilities, this may lead to not getting sufficient practice reading connected text, potentially leading to what Stanovich refers to as the "Matthew effect." The Matthew effect, in reference to the New Testament phrase "The rich get richer, and the poor get poorer," asserts that for students with reading difficulties, the gap in reading skill tends to snowball over time.[11]

In their compilation of reading research, including a synthesis of the seminal work of Adams and Snow, Byrnes and Wasik outlined areas of need that students with disabilities face when reading: phonological processing, understanding of the alphabetic principle, automaticity, and working memory[12]:

Phonological processing Students with disabilities in reading often require additional instruction in parsing individual phonemes, the distinct units of sound in a specified language. This ability to understand the sound structure of words is known as phonological awareness.

Understanding of the alphabetic principle Mapping phoneme (sound) units onto grapheme (letter) units is referred to as the alphabetic principle. Students with disabilities in reading often require additional support learning to relate the graphic representations of sounds (letters) with their corresponding phonemic representations (sounds).

Automaticity The ability to recognize words quickly is referred to as automaticity. Automaticity impacts the fluency, or rate, of reading directly and of reading comprehension indirectly. Decoding rapidly and fluently can be difficult for students with disabilities in reading due to syntactic features in text and increased strain on cognitive processing.

Working memory As students progress through the elementary years, texts become more syntactically complex, placing increased strain on students' working memory, the ability to retain information in the short term. Students with disabilities tend to be overburdened with reading processes that should become automatic over time. As a result, students with disabilities in reading may have difficulties retaining what they just read.

Students with disabilities, particularly those with developmental differences, may also have a higher need for controlled learning environments free from the social demands imposed by face-to-face or verbal communication.[13] Integrating inclusive uses of digital technologies into reading interventions, materials, and the curriculum has great potential for engaging students with disabilities, including those that impact reading.[14]

Language and Literacy Needs of Students with Disabilities: Writing Development

Despite the IDEA's call for research dedicated to the exploration of evidence-based language and literacy practices, not enough research has been devoted to the study of writing instruction interventions for students with disabilities, particularly those with profound developmental needs such as autism or Down syndrome.[15] With that said, a body of research on effective writing instruction and intervention does exist for students with writing difficulties, notably the work of Karen Harris and Steve Graham.[16]

Students with disabilities often face a concordance of fine- and gross-motor coordination needs that make the writing process particularly taxing.[17] Handwriting difficulties may lead to decreased legibility and shorter, less complex pieces to reduce handwriting burden.[18] Difficulties with self-regulation can present as distractibility and impede planning processes critical to producing coherent writing.[19] As a result, such challenges can result in writing becoming a physically laborious and potentially demotivating task.[20]

The work of Asaro-Saddler, Pennington, and Delano identifies six areas of need that students with developmental disabilities, particularly those who identify as autistic, face when presented with writing tasks: challenges in the ability to plan and write a story, writing for absent audiences, writing about non-preferred topics, attending to language, the transcription process, and self-regulation during the writing process[21]:

Technology-Supported Language and Literacy

Ability to plan and write a story Students with developmental disabilities can engage in literal thinking and may need support understanding abstract concepts, developing organizational skills, and imagining future scenarios.[22] Literal thinking and difficulty imagining future scenarios may limit the number of story paths students envision for their writing.[23] Weak organizational skills impede the planning process involved in organizing the components and trajectory of a story, and difficulty understanding abstract concepts might impede the ability to visualize the story during the planning process.[24]

Writing for absent audiences Difficulties conceptualizing other people's mental states and perspectives may present cognitive challenges for students with developmental disabilities who are expected to write for absent audiences.[25] Writing for absent audiences requires anticipating the needs and expectations of an audience, and engaging in such anticipatory planning is made difficult if the writer does not understand that their audience may have needs and expectations that differ from their own. Difficulties with perspective taking may also present difficulties understanding that writing may be read by an audience with differing perspectives.[26]

Writing about non-preferred topics Students with developmental disabilities may be more likely to exhibit specific scopes of interest on a select number of topics. This could result in less background knowledge about non-preferred topics, a necessary component of effective writing.[27] Students are often asked to write about non-preferred topics, and a desire to only write about preferred topics can result in a reluctance to engage with writing prompts and assignments focused on non-preferred subjects.[28]

Attending to language Students with developmental, language, or learning disabilities may require additional support attending to language.[29] Receptive language needs, such as not understanding task directions or providing inappropriate responses, as well as expressive language needs, such as writing needing a clear focus, transitions, or organization, are potential barriers for disabled students.[30]

The transcription process Students with disabilities, particularly those with physical or developmental disabilities, often face a concordance of fine- and gross-motor coordination needs that make the transcription process particularly taxing.[31] Handwriting difficulties may lead to decreased legibility and shorter, less complex pieces to reduce handwriting burden.[32] Such challenges can result in writing becoming a physically laborious and potentially demotivating task.[33]

Self-regulation during the writing process   Students with developmental and physical disabilities, often need additional supports to maintain attention toward tasks and self-regulate during the writing process.[34] Difficulties with self-regulation can present as distractibility and underdeveloped self-management and planning skills. These difficulties can impede students' planning and execution processes that are critical to producing clear coherent pieces of writing.[35]

Using Digital Technologies to Support Language and Literacy

Over the past fifty years, technology has played an increasing role in supporting the education of students with disabilities. During this time, practitioners and researchers have been challenged with evaluating technology interventions and ensuring that their use in schools promotes learning outcomes for all students.[36] To date, several lines of research have sought to investigate the uses of technology to support language and literacy instruction, particularly among students with disabilities. A focus of this research has been to build students' capacity and independence across instructional settings while minimizing the need for ongoing external supports.[37]

However, few research syntheses of technology-based tools focus on the broader social impacts of using digital technologies to support language and literacy instruction among students with disabilities.[38] A more common approach has traditionally been to present the use of specific technology tools aimed at supporting specific academic components, such as decoding or comprehension within the realm of reading instruction.[39] Edyburn found reading to be one of the most common applications of technology in his comprehensive review of the state of special education technology research.[40] Moreover, in Okolo and Bouck's review of assistive technology literature, 39 percent of studies addressed the use of technology to improve students' academic skills, of which 32 percent were in the area of literacy. The next highest category focused on technology implementation, accounting for 23 percent of studies reviewed.[41]

The research community's focus on the assessment of specific technology tools to support discrete literacy skills mirrors teachers' own perceptions and uses of digital technologies in the classroom. As such, the extent of technology use in many US classrooms primarily focuses on its use as instructional tools to support the functions of the classroom.[42] This contrasts with more transformative and intentional uses of digital technologies for personal expression, inclusion, collaboration, and content creation.[43]

Despite somewhat limited uses and views of technology, teachers have expressed interest in using technology as a tool to support effective literacy instruction. For example, in their survey of special education teachers' attitudes toward education uses of technology, MacArthur and colleagues found that 85 percent used technology to support literacy instruction, and 97 percent believed that technology could be used to help students acquire literacy skills.[44] Below, we briefly describe ways in which teachers might use digital technologies to support development of literacy skills among students receiving literacy intervention services as a result of intellectual, learning, or developmental disabilities.

Uses of Technology for Reading

Students with reading difficulties present with needs in the areas of phonological awareness, decoding, word recognition, reading fluency, and comprehension that could lend themselves to the use of digital reading applications to support reading instruction.[45] Digital technologies that support reading instruction can be used to develop phonological awareness, decoding, and word-recognition skills by providing extended opportunities to practice decoding text.[46] These technologies can fall within the category of universally designed educational technologies, which we discuss in greater detail below. Mainstream technologies designed with accessible features and tools, such as screen readability features for eye tracking, electronic text enhancements for text comprehension, and computer-assisted instruction (CAI) and speech feedback for decoding and word identification, also support reading and are discussed in greater detail below.

Uses of Technology for Writing

Students who find writing difficult, including those with reading, learning, and developmental disabilities, need support with multiple aspects of writing.[47] These include supporting the ability to plan, execute, and revise their writing, as well as mitigating difficulties with the transcription process.[48] Digital technologies can be used in various ways to support the development of writing skills in developing writers, particularly in the areas of word processing and spelling.[49] There is also some indication within the research that as students begin writing more fluently, usually in the mid to upper elementary grades, they are in an improved position to take advantage of the affordances of digital technologies for writing. This can be particularly true and impactful for students who require additional scaffolds or supports for their writing. Research indicates that for these students, writing with digital tools can support improvements in both the quantity and quality of writing content.[50]

While specific technology-based literacy interventions, programs, and tools have been a primary focus of prior educational and assistive technology research,[51] the remainder of this chapter is dedicated to providing a broader overview of digital technologies to support language and literacy. We provide this overview across three categories, with a focus on technology's social use within the classroom to support inclusion: assistive technologies specifically designed to support students with disabilities, educational technologies universally designed to support all students, and mainstream technologies designed with features that facilitate student access. In the sections that follow, we will focus on highlighting the distinguishing technology features of each category. Specific technologies commonly used across US schools, including FVA, are briefly introduced here and are described in greater detail in appendix B.

Assistive Technologies Designed to Create Access

Technologies designed for use by students with disabilities have typically been referred to as assistive technologies.[52] Most definitions of assistive technologies date back to the passage of the Technology-Related Assistance Act for Individuals with Disabilities, known as the Tech Act.[53] The Tech Act, first passed in 1988 and reauthorized in 1994, was instrumental in laying the groundwork for future policy that defined and contextualized the use of assistive technologies.

Assistive technologies are of two types: assistive technology devices and assistive technology services. As defined within the IDEA, assistive technology devices are items, equipment, or systems that are used to "increase, maintain, or improve the functional capabilities of a child with a disability." Assistive technology services refer to any service that assists a student with a disability "in the selection, acquisition, or use of an assistive technology device."[54]

Assistive technologies have traditionally been used to support students with disabilities in independently accessing academic content and classroom participation. Central to these goals are the objectives of selecting appropriate assistive technologies to use with individual students, as well as using assistive technologies to operationalize universal design principles to support accessible educational environments.

Assistive systems of support for students with disabilities fall along the range of low-, mid-, and high-tech tools.[55] Low-tech tools are simple, do not require extensive training, and are the most commonly used assistive tools in classrooms. These can include the use of behavior charts and visual calendars to support and reinforce positive classroom behavior. Mid-tech tools straddle the line between low- and high-tech and include, for example, the Picture Exchange Communication System (PECS). Finally, high-tech tools are complex, require substantial training, and tend to be much more expensive.[56] These can include augmentative and alternative communication (AAC) applications typically downloaded onto dedicated tablets, such as Language Acquisition through Motor Planning (LAMP) and Proloquo2Go (see appendix B).

In this book, we will focus on assistive technologies that create access to the curriculum and support students' language and literacy practices. These include assistive technologies and tools for communication (e.g., AAC) that support students' linguistic expression, which we define as a person's use of language, whether articulated by that person or through an intermediary, to share thoughts and feelings, make requests, and solicit or give information.[57] These often incorporate text-to-speech and speech-to-text software, as well as synthetic speech feedback.[58]

Originally designed for people with developmental disabilities such as autism, assistive technologies that support communication are now used by minimally speaking people across a range of disabilities.[59] Assistive technologies that transform speech and text are critical to the facilitation of classroom engagement for students who require alternative means to respond verbally or physically to prompts.[60] Text-to-speech software, such as LAMP or Proloquo2Go, allows students who are minimally speaking to type a message that can be shared verbally, facilitating their participation in classroom discussion.

LAMP speech-to-text software can be used by students with manual dexterity needs who could benefit from support composing written responses.[61] Digital tablets and iPads equipped with synthetic speech feedback software, such as Proloquo2Go, afford minimally speaking students the opportunity to communicate via their device (see appendix B). The use of synthetic speech feedback paired with digital texts has also been found to support word recognition, comprehension, and fluency in students with language-related disabilities.[62]

Also common in schools is the use of low- to mid-tech assistive tools, such as PECS, to support functional communication (see appendix B). PECS uses pictures of preferred and high-frequency objects and actions as exchange items that students can use with a communicative partner to comment, make requests, and answer questions. The goal of PECS is to teach functional communication, with more advanced users often transitioning to AAC applications and speech-generating devices, such as Proloquo2Go.

While a primary aim of assistive technologies is to support independent learning in the classroom, we maintain that independence should not be the only goal for students' uses of assistive technologies. In chapters 5 and 6, we use an interdependent perspective to present cases of students using assistive technologies in ways that promote social collaboration and inclusion. In chapter 8, we use interdependence—a frame emphasizing collaborative access as complementary to independence—to argue that a true social value of assistive technologies is their mediational power to promote collaboration between users.[63]

Universally Designed Educational Technologies

Broadly defined, educational technologies, also sometimes known as EdTech, are technologies that are designed to facilitate learning.[64] In its broadest definition, the field of educational technology includes any of the actual tools, processes, and theoretical foundations that may be used to support classroom learning.[65] Because the expansive field of EdTech is beyond the scope of this book, we focus our discussion of educational technologies on actual uses of these tools and media to support students' language and literacy practices in the classroom.

Many of today's educational technologies for the classroom, such as Epic, IXL, and Lexia (see appendix B), are developed to be adaptive by design and are grounded in principles of universal design for learning (UDL). The principles of UDL were first laid out by Anne Meyer and David Rose in collaboration with colleagues at the Center for Applied Special Technology (CAST).[66] UDL affords a constructivist framework for the design of educational technologies that can be used to support inclusion within general education settings.[67] Social constructivist theory states that knowledge is constructed from human experience and interactions with others, and that it is informed by sociolinguistics, cultural psychology, and anthropology.[68]

Central to the social constructivist perspective, as well as to fully inclusive schooling, is the use of frameworks, systems, and tools that build on the competencies of all students.[69] Within the context of educational technology design, UDL is used as a framework to address student variability in the classroom through intentional design that supports multiple ways to access academic content and curricula.[70] The adoption of UDL by educational technology designers does this by encouraging flexible curricula, materials, and tools with customizable options, allowing students to "progress from where they are and not where we would have imagined them to be."[71]

Universally designed educational technologies are developed with digital infrastructures to reach the widest spectrum of students, providing appropriate and adaptive levels of challenge for these students.[72] UDL is guided by three principles that outline that materials, tools, and curricula should provide multiple means of representation (the "what" of learning), action and expression (the "how" of learning), and engagement (the "why" of learning).[73] The ways in which universally designed educational technologies could be used to promote a wide range of students as readers and writers are briefly outlined below in the context of providing multiple means of representation, action, expression, and engagement.

Provide multiple means of representation This principle states that students differ in the ways that they perceive and comprehend information. Students with a variety of needs, including those with disabilities, may require differing ways of approaching content. Thus, providing multiple options for the representation of material in educational technologies is critical for engaging a variety of students. Educational technologies incorporating UDL features afford alternative means of visual, textual, and auditory representation, such as closed-captioning or audio voice-over, and support students seeking multiple ways to access content.

Provide multiple means of action and expression Students differ in their approaches to navigating learning environments. Students' approaches to learning tasks can be impacted by additional needs in the areas of movement, executive function, and language. The scaffolding afforded by educational technology features—such as visual animations, word prediction and text-to-speech software, spellcheckers, and adjustable font sizes—afford multiple options for action and expression by providing alternatives to how students access, navigate, understand, and express content.[74]

Provide multiple means of engagement Affect is an important factor in learning. Students differ in how they become motivated to learn, requiring multiple modes of engagement. The use of features—for example, those supporting open-ended play, descriptions of non-text content, and sound-effect modifications in educational technologies—meets this criterion by presenting content in alternative ways to increase students' engagement.[75]

Mainstream Technologies Designed with Accessible Features

We define mainstream technologies as being accessibly designed when their features support a wide range of users. At this point, we would like to reiterate a difference in our discussion of digital technologies to distinguish between assistive technologies and mainstream technologies whose features are assistive, or accessible, in nature. While both can be used to facilitate and enable inclusion and access, assistive technologies are specifically designed to be used by people with disabilities. Mainstream technologies can be assistive in nature when designed accessibly to support a wide range of users. Below, we specifically discuss the qualities and features that make mainstream digital technologies accessible and how these can be used to engage students inclusively in cultivating their language and literacy practices.

Burgstahler identified three basic forms of accessible mainstream technologies and how they could support the literacy engagement of students with a wide range of needs, particularly those with disabilities. These include web pages that allow students with diverse reading skills to engage with written content; software that allows students to collaborate with their peers and complete assignments in the classroom, and which reduce the need for individual accommodations; and accessible telecommunications technologies that enable communication for a wide range of students.[76] Particularly with the advent of the COVID-19 pandemic (see chapters 6 and 7), accessible mainstream technologies—such as Google Suite, YouTube, and Zoom—are being increasingly used in US classrooms. These mainstream technologies are equipped with various accessibility features that lend themselves to use within schools, which we describe below.

Mainstream Digital Technologies for Academic Instruction

Assistive uses of mainstream digital technologies support fuller participation and engagement in the classroom.[77] Academic uses of mainstream technologies, such as word-processing software and electronic keyboards, can play an essential role in creating access to reading and writing practices for students with disabilities. Assistive uses of mainstream technologies can also be used to support students in developing their academic skills and performance in the areas of reading and writing.[78] For example, Asaro-Saddler identified the use of technology-aided instruction as an effective instruction best practice that can be integrated into writing instruction of students with developmental disabilities such as autism. She specifically pointed to benefits in relieving handwriting fatigue, a known challenge for autistic children engaging in the transcription process.[79] Online tools that incorporate text highlighting and captioning can be used to support access to instruction. In their examination of classroom projects created by students with hearing impairment, Ok and Rao found that text highlighting and supportive captions, coupled with digital instructional materials, helped these students access academic content.[80]

Mainstream Technologies to Facilitate Writing Production

Assistive uses of mainstream digital technologies create opportunities for students with sensory support needs to mediate the writing experience positively, freeing students to focus on content generation and expression of voice rather than the mechanics of writing.[81] Assistive uses of digital technologies for writing can include the use of speech-to-text and spell-check functions in word-processing applications such as Google Docs. Assistive uses of digital technologies for reading can include the use of text-to-speech and "read to me" functions integrated into digital software and applications (see appendix B).

Word processors such as Google Docs support emerging writers by facilitating the editing and revision process and alleviating handwriting strain.[82] Desktop publishing features make writing less tedious and more expeditious for emerging writers and also facilitate possibilities for peer collaboration through applications such as Google Docs.[83] Finally, assistive use of mainstream digital tools, such as spell-check and text-to-speech, afford benefits for emerging writers engaged in the production and revision processes of writing.[84]

Research on writing strategies for students with disabilities has also demonstrated that word-processing features can assist students with disabilities in the writing process.[85] Spellcheckers vary in their ability to select correct word choice and spelling. However, they could afford benefits for emerging writers engaged in the production and revision of writing.[86] For example, in their study of spellchecker use with middle school age children with learning disabilities, MacArthur and colleagues found that students were able to self-correct 37 percent of spelling errors using a spelling checker as opposed to 9 percent without the aid of spell-check.[87]

Mainstream Technologies to Support Reading Comprehension and Fluency

Screen readability features in computer software can be used to alleviate problems with eye tracking, a matter of frequent concern for emerging readers who have difficulties tracking text. Screen readability refers to the graphical layout of text on the screen, and research in this area relates to how students perceive the layout of text on a screen. Screen readability software can be used by students to change text layout and highlight text during reading.[88] Digital text augmented with electronic enhancements such as speech synthesis, definitions, graphics, dictionaries, features that allow for changes in font size and color, and supplementary text can be used to support access to text and promote reading comprehension.[89] Speech feedback may be used to strengthen reading comprehension by engaging the communicative aspects of reading.[90] Using speech feedback in conjunction with word highlighting can also be used to support students' phonological awareness.[91]

The Future of Technology-Supported Language and Literacy Research

Research to date demonstrates that digital technologies can be used to support language and literacy practices among students with disabilities.

Technology-Supported Language and Literacy

However, much of this research has focused on the technical features of specific technologies rather than on socially inclusive approaches to integrating digital technologies into the classroom.[92] As such, integration of digital technologies into literacy practice needs to take into account not only the technical aspects of the technology but also the relational, social, and task-specific aspects, particularly as they relate to creating access and inclusion.[93] As noted in chapter 1, prior work in this area includes that of Alper and Cranmer.[94]

In part II of the book, consisting of chapters 4–7, we use findings from our FVA case study to add to this emerging body of literature by detailing the ways that assistive, educational, and mainstream technologies can be used in schools to support both inclusion and literacy engagement in classrooms integrating students with disabilities. We now turn to chapter 4, where we explore the inclusive practices that FVA used to support disabled students' inclusion in the general education classroom.

II

4 Future Visions Academy: An Inclusive School

During the 2019–2020 and 2020–2021 school years, our research team collaborated with FVA to cultivate a research-practice partnership committed to exploring the school's inclusive education program and use of digital technologies to engage students and support language and literacy practices. This research-practice partnership work was initiated through a mutual connection between the research team and the school's executive director as an alumna and community partner of the university. Beyond the implementation of this study, our collaboration with FVA also resulted in the regular sharing of thoughts, ideas, and plans for supporting mutually held research-practice partnership objectives, including dissemination of research findings through conferences as well as the implementation of teacher professional development.

Originally, this was going to be a yearlong study focused on conducting classroom observations of in-person instruction, interviews with families and staff, and collection of physical and digital artifacts during the 2019–2020 school year. However, the pandemic-related closure of schools, including FVA, in the spring of 2020 precipitated the continuation of our field study into the 2020–2021 school year. Our fieldwork was conducted primarily in person during the fall and winter months of 2019–2020 and shifted to remote fieldwork in spring 2020. As such, we present findings resulting from in-person instruction in chapters 4 and 5, and findings resulting from the shift to remote and hybrid learning in chapters 6 and 7. Analyses, lessons learned, and reflections for the future are discussed in chapters 8 and 9, and we provide a comprehensive description of the research methodology used to develop the case study in appendix A.

In this chapter, we introduce FVA as a case-study to discuss the particular ways in which the social organization of the school facilitated a fully inclusive learning environment for students to thrive. Using FVA as a case study of a well-established full inclusion public charter school, we first situate FVA's charter school status within the broader discussion of public charter schools' realized and unrealized potential as sites for inclusive education.

Public Charter Schools as Sites for Inclusive Education

The ethnographic research on which this book is based is situated in the practices observed at FVA, a full inclusion public county charter school. Charter schools are publicly funded schools independently managed under a contract (charter) between the school and a local or state education authority. Though not necessarily the norm in charter school education, FVA found the charter school avenue to be a natural one for inclusive education. The original aims of charter schools as sites of inclusion and choice align with FVA's aims as a charter to provide inclusive classroom instruction for children with disabilities who would otherwise have been placed in specialized classroom settings in their neighborhood school. The creation of a choice for families to enroll their children in an inclusive educational environment tailored to their needs encapsulates the National Alliance for Public Charter Schools' described vision for charter schools: "Charter schools are independently operated public schools that have the freedom to design classrooms that meet their students' needs . . . Charter schools aim to provide a range of options so that parents can choose the public school that best fits their child."[1]

This vision of equity and choice, while embraced and operationalized at FVA, contrasts with the reality for some charter school students, particularly those with disabilities and other marginalized identities, for whom charter schools have not necessarily been considered inclusive.[2] As described by Waitoller, charters were originally established to release teachers from bureaucratic mandates in support of creating environments conducive to pedagogical innovation.[3] However, with the exception of individual charters and states that intentionally design their charter programming to be inclusive, a number of charters today invoke corporatized approaches to education that are counter to the original ethos of charter schools as potential sites for equity and inclusion.[4]

As such, there are mixed results regarding the efficacy of charter schools, with some research indicating positive academic gains for students of color and students with disabilities who attend charters.[5] whil other research

Future Visions Academy

points to charter schools as being less likely to enroll English learners and students with disabilities, further exacerbating segregated schooling.[6] In our description of practices observed at FVA, we hope to illuminate possibilities for both public and charter schools as potential sites for equity and inclusion—particularly for students with disabilities and other marginalized identities. We now turn to describing how FVA intentionally strove to meet inclusive ideals in its efforts to serve culturally and linguistically diverse students with and without disabilities.

Instruction at FVA

FVA is a full inclusion public charter school located in the Western United States serving 150 students with a variety of disability designations from culturally and linguistically diverse families. Founded in 2018 as a model of inclusive education, it was codeveloped by community members and parent advocates with the hope of becoming an exemplar of inclusive education practice for both charter and public schools. Students at FVA are linguistically and developmentally diverse, given the lottery system that the school uses to enroll families from across the county. At the time of this study, 80 percent of FVA's families self-identified as BIPOC, 67 percent had at least one child with a disability and identified as working or middle class, 50 percent spoke a language other than English at home, 63 percent qualified for free/reduced-price meals, and 37 percent had an English Learner designation.

All families lived within the county parameters of FVA's charter and had at least one child enrolled in K–5 at FVA, of whom approximately 21 percent have an IEP to address needed supports and accommodations for a variety of disability diagnoses. These include learning/reading disabilities, autism, Down syndrome, cerebral palsy, language delays/impairments, and physical/mobility needs. Many of the parents arrived at FVA because they were not happy with their children's previous placements, usually in special day classes. These parents typically enrolled at FVA precisely to afford their children an opportunity to be educated alongside their mainstreamed peers. As a result, many of the selected child participants in our study had previously been in Special Day Classes at their prior schools and were now acclimating to learning in an integrated general education setting.

FVA used a team-teaching model (see chapter 2) in which five general education teachers and two special education teachers collaboratively planned together to provide instruction to students in their shared classroom. Grades were organized in the following combo-grade configurations: TK/K, K, 1/2, 2/3, and 4/5. All general education teachers had earned their elementary teaching certification, and all special education teachers had additionally completed an Education Specialist Instruction Credential in the area of special education.

The teachers were supported by a team of four full-time and five part-time paraprofessionals, with two to three paraprofessionals in each classroom at any given time. In addition to providing one-to-one support for individual students, paraprofessionals engaged in station teaching in which groups of students rotate between staff as they move from station to station (see chapter 2). Additionally, part-time speech and occupational therapists rotated among the classrooms providing push-in services. FVA also contracted with outside agencies to provide physical therapy, nursing, counseling, psychology, and adaptive physical education as needed.

Inclusion at FVA

FVA's diverse-by-design classrooms brought students with and without disabilities together in an interest-based learning environment and was a key feature of the school. FVA emphasized the diversity of its campus in its description of the school's mission, as outlined here in an excerpt from the FVA Parent Handbook, which parents were asked to review and sign as a condition of their child's enrollment in the school:

> FVA is grounded in an inclusive vision of education, and a schoolwide learning community cultivated intentionally to promote friendship, empathy, and the joy of new discovery. Students at FVA are active students who engage in group problem-solving, critical thinking, creativity, communication and collaboration. All members of the FVA community—students, staff, and families—honor and celebrate the diverse range of socioeconomic and cultural backgrounds, abilities, languages, perspectives, and interests students bring to the learning setting. FVA aims to maximize every child's learning potential within an atmosphere of caring and belonging. The FVA instructional philosophy rests upon the concepts of hands-on learning, meaningful instructional activities, systematic instruction, and a collaborative group of professionals working together to make the learning environment exciting for students.

FVA is a tight-knit school community bonded over a shared need to support families and teachers in meeting their students' exceptional needs. As a result,

Future Visions Academy

the social organization of the school centered on learning practices that prioritize the cultivation of peer-to-peer socialization and inclusion of students with and without disability across shared school spaces, as indicated by Dina, a primarily English-speaking working-class mother of Mexican descent to James, a third grader with Down syndrome, and Daniel, a first grader not identified as having a disability: "It matters to me that inclusion is part of their daily focus and that the entire staff—from the front office to the teachers to even the volunteers—really, really have an example of what that looks like. It's not something that they just talk about. They have play structured around it. They have activities in the classroom that support inclusion."

With this focus in mind, FVA strove to ensure that the social organization of the school facilitated a fully inclusive environment for students to thrive. This organization included the use of collaborative team-teaching configurations to facilitate learning; combo-grade level groupings to encourage peer modeling between older and younger students; and active parent volunteerism and participation. Critical to the team-teaching structure was the integration of service providers (e.g., speech and language therapists and occupational therapists) into the classroom. This integration included the provision of push-in services—a distinct deviation from how services are typically delivered as segregated pullout sessions in other schools. Notably, paraprofessionals were fully integrated into the operation of the school's full inclusion model and went beyond a traditionally auxiliary role in the classroom to serve as cultural brokers between teachers and families, helping to create social skills content centered on cultivating inclusive communication practices within the school.

Observations of classroom learning and school-wide practices, as well as interviews with students, parents, teachers, and staff, were all used to document inclusive practices within the school community (see appendix A). These observations led us to identify four principles that guided how FVA sought to facilitate a fully inclusive environment: creativity and innovation, autonomy and choice, culture of kindness, and an intersectional vision of inclusion.

Creativity and Innovation

FVA's inclusion model drew on several key features, including its focus on creativity and innovation in its team-teaching model of inclusion;

54 Chapter 4

philosophical differentiation of the meaning of inclusion; and intentional recruitment of staff and families with inclusive orientations. Also key was Dr. Tully's unique and extensive background as an experienced instructional leader, founder, and executive director of FVA, with more than twenty years of practice as a general education teacher, special education teacher, and teacher educator at inclusively modeled schools (see Instructional Leadership below); and FVA's intentional recruitment of staff.

FVA Team Teaching: Collaboration as Ecosystem

Team collaboration at FVA is a constant and telltale sign of FVA's innovative approach to teaching and learning. Ecological in nature, collaboration is integrated into classroom lessons, activities, and interactions between immediate and extended members of the FVA community. In chatting with Ms. Carina, a Spanish-English bilingual paraprofessional of Latina descent in her second year, she indicated that constant communication made teaching at FVA a team effort. Continual communication across team members allowed Ms. Carina to feel connected to the work of inclusion, as well as informed about approaches the team took to support students: "When something new starts, I don't feel completely lost because we're all learning together. So, I think one of the biggest best surprises of [FVA's inclusion model] would be how everybody is pouring into each other like, 'Hey, we're all in this together.'" The symbiotic nature of Ms. Carina's description, "pouring into each other," alludes to FVA's interdependent approach to inclusion. This interdependent approach to team teaching is ecological and involves the paras and teachers sharing happenings continuously via walkie-talkies, even as they float past each other, as Ms. Sandy, a first-year English-speaking paraprofessional of European descent, describes:

> Me and the paras, we're always communicating. We're always looking at each other like "You need me to jump in?" Like talking about what's worked for us [in collaboration meetings] at the end of the day—that's what helps the most because we get to hear feedback from each other and hear what works . . . The way that Dr. Tully has it set up is that we're constantly moving. She wants us all to be able to be in any classroom working with any kid at any time. So that not only that we don't get comfortable, but also that the kids aren't just attached to one person, you know?

In this excerpt, Ms. Sandy discusses the role Dr. Tully plays in shaping the nature of collaboration at FVA—including supporting interdependence at

Future Visions Academy

FVA by not restricting specific staff to specific classrooms—as is often the case in special day classes.[7] Here, Ms. Sandy cautions a consequence of one-to-one support staff assignments: students become overly dependent on individual staff, effectively limiting students' ability to be fully included and integrated across general education settings and staff.

Ms. Sandy, as well as other paras and teachers, regularly commented that they appreciated Dr. Tully's hands-on approach with their professional development. Ms. Sandy explained that Dr. Tully made it a point to discuss pedagogical decisions and strategies individually and during staff meetings. However, this collaborative approach did not always extend to include contracted part-time service providers, such as Ms. Alexa, a first-year English-Spanish bilingual speech–language pathologist assistant (SLPA) of Latina descent tasked with providing speech and language services according to students' goals as outlined in their IEPs. Ms. Alexa indicated sometimes feeling out of the loop within the team teaching dynamic due to her part-time contract status: "It's hard when you are an outsider coming in. You don't know what to say or how much feedback to give. I kind of feel it's not my place." Ms. Alexa's sentiments are indicative of the continuous work that is required of schools to equitably include all staff as key constituents in collaborative teaching endeavors.

The IEP Development Process

Collaboration, a constantly evolving process at FVA, also permeated the IEP writing process. IEPs, integrating goals and services aimed at supporting education in the least restricted environment, are typically written by a special education teacher. This delegation can have a myopic or segregating effect on how curricula are taught.[8] At FVA, writing IEP goals was collaborative, with the general education teacher playing a significant role in identifying goals for students that could be extended within the general education classroom. Ms. Severin, an experienced special education teacher of European descent, describes her deeply collaborative approach with general education teachers at FVA:

> I use my lens to say, "Okay, how do we create that access bridge for the kids?" And that's very personalized based on where the kids are at. "Okay, so here's the bridge, here's the access, here's what we're going to do." And then we go, "Okay, that's helpful for everybody." So, then we just roll it out to the whole class [laughs]. So that's what collaboration looks like, and also planning how we're

going to co-teach . . . So even though it's in my job description to write the IEP, I really can't write a quality IEP without their input. I'll bounce goals off them and I'll say, "Okay, so the student is here in math, what's coming up next year in the next grade? How do we write a goal that is not only relevant to the kid but that's relevant to the curriculum coming up?"'Cause it's useless to write a goal that's not going to be taught in class.

One purpose of this deep collaboration between the general education and special education teachers is to develop student IEP goals that support the integration of students into general education settings and key content beneficial to all students.

Push-In Services

Providers' push-in of services to students at FVA was another unique aspect of FVA's full inclusion model in contrast to school programs that either place students with IEPs in special day classrooms or pull students out of general classroom settings to receive services. For Ms. Davis, an experienced, primarily English-speaking SLP of multiracial descent contracted by FVA on a part-time basis, FVA's service approach afforded students the benefit of peer-to-peer modeling: "I've enjoyed getting to know and build rapport with all the students. The students who aren't on my caseload get to see how we help students with SLI, and in turn become great peer models for the students on our caseload."

A notable benefit of pushing services in was the transformative effect it had on FVA students as peer models. In traditional pullout services, particularly for speech, a challenge is that the adult provider is often the speech model for the child. This could have limiting effects on students' progression toward speech goals, including ability to generalize skills learned across multiple social settings.[9] Engaging all students in the provision of speech services affords service providers opportunities to better understand how classroom and peer dynamics can be used to support students' IEP goals. At the same time, implementing a push-in model of service delivery is not without its challenges, as described here by Ms. Davis: "Planning therapy to meet everyone's needs is challenging. You really have to be creative in working to address the student's IEP goals but still be engaging enough for the students who don't have a disability, since no pullout is allowed. It's important to be open-minded and flexible, writing goals to be measurable may need to be different than in a traditional setting. A must is finding time

Future Visions Academy

to collaborate with the staff." Ms. Davis explains, both here and in other conversations, the tensions that exist between the push-in model of service delivery at FVA and the ways most service providers—herself included—are trained and mandated to deliver services and report progress toward goals in the IEP. These points of tension form a major source of challenge at the heart of a lack of training and institutional support for service providers and schools attempting to implement a push-in model of service delivery.[10]

As such, a significant revision of policies addressing delivery of services is needed, outlining a more inclusive definition of "what counts" as provision of service. This includes institutional revision and support in (1) the development of IEP goals conducive to push-in service provision, (2) extended collaboration between teachers and providers, and (3) how progress toward goals is defined, documented, and reported. Ultimately, challenges to these needs endanger the feasibility of push-in services and can become obstacles to implementing integrated models of inclusive programing.

Presumed Competence: A Paradigm Shift in Being Inclusive

In addition to a unique service implementation structure, how inclusive education is defined and operationalized at FVA differs fundamentally from other schools we have observed. First, inclusion at FVA is positioned as a moral imperative. Inclusion is strongly felt as a prerequisite for all interactions and educational endeavors, the seeking of which should compel people to act in ways that are supportive of the full integration of people with disabilities. This nonnegotiable stance at FVA centers on presuming competence—that is, centering behaviors and intentions on the belief that all students can learn and engage, as explained by Ms. Gomez, an experienced English-Spanish bilingual fourth-/fifth-grade combo teacher of Latina descent at FVA: "We welcome every single child and that is very firm. No child will ever be removed from our classroom for services. So just knowing that—and how much even all the paras, the teachers, we all believe in the ability of every single student—is very refreshing. And you know, we always presume competence with everyone." Ms. Gomez expresses the unequivocal stance at FVA that nobody gets removed and nobody gets left behind. Everyone is included. She also emphasizes the point that all staff adhere to this belief—an important distinction touching on the need for successful school programs to have a unified school culture with intentional messaging.[11] Moreover, Ms. Gomez touches on presumed competence as an important aspect of FVA's inclusion model. The premise of centering inclusion on presumed competence is central to a social justice perspective of disability and is a prerequisite for creating opportunities for participation and inclusion within school communities.[12]

Ms. Gomez's commentary points to the bedrock of how FVA defines and implements inclusive education. The commitment to never removing a student from the general education classroom creates impetus and rationale for engaging in multiple forms of modification. Integrating students of diverse ability levels and needs requires substantial content differentiation and modification. Content modification thus becomes a prerequisite for creating participatory access to the classroom curriculum.

Another fundamental component of presuming competence is the belief that educators must give students opportunities to succeed.[13] Ms. Wezner, a primarily English-speaking second-/third-grade combo general education teacher of European descent in her first year of teaching, explains the necessary relationship between opportunity and presumed competence, integral to how staff sought to operationalize inclusion at FVA:

> Coming [to FVA] after a whole semester of teaching in a learning center, I was like, "I don't know how this is going to work." For the first couple of weeks, I thought "this place is my dream and I don't know how the kids are making progress here." Then, after a month or so of getting in the groove, I was like, "Oh my gosh." There was this insane difference of how much the kids were growing. I was like, "I cannot believe how much more all these kids are doing when they do have those typically developing peers with them." In our ESI classes, it was almost like no one had a place to look for a peer model . . . And those kids that never get the chance to even try doing a general ed assignment . . . I think about it often with more severe disabilities in the class who participate in such a great way on a gen ed assignment, and then think "they would never have that chance at a different school."

Ms. Wezner echoes Ms. Gomez's sentiments on the importance of presuming competence and shifting one's mindset to believe that all students must be given a chance to participate. She reflects on the rarity of seeing students designated as having moderate-to-severe disabilities integrated into general classroom settings.[14] She also cites the common perception that students designated as having moderate-to-severe disabilities are best served in segregated classroom environments—a belief prevalent in education.[15]

This desire for a presumption of competence when teaching students with disabilities was reiterated by parents we interviewed, particularly those with children identified as having significant needs due to a disability designation such as autism or Down syndrome. For example, in describing her reasons for enrolling her daughter Star, a second grader of Filipino and European descent with Down syndrome, at FVA, Madeline, a middle-class, primarily English-speaking mother of Filipino descent, alluded to the aversion school districts have in allowing general classroom placements of children identified as having significant needs due to a disability: "I was thinking about asking [Star's prior school] to change her education goals 'cause I noticed that she was very bright. I took her to tutoring, and they all said, 'You know what, Star doesn't belong in a moderate-to-severe classroom.' Everyone pretty much said that . . . I had never even heard of FVA, and I was just thinking, 'Oh my gosh' because I heard horror stories about trying to advocate for kids to get into mainstream."

Madeline describes a common battle that parents of children with disabilities face in trying to get schools to integrate their children into the general education setting. For Madeline, Star's potential as a student should be what guides the choices surrounding her inclusion in a general education setting. However, as she notes above, schools are reticent to do so, in part because of an inability to presume competence: "So, I think here [at FVA], from the get-go, there was already that foundation built in that we're going to work together. Whereas, like I said, I've talked to people on the outside and it's always like they feel like the teacher is kinda frustrated because they don't know. It's like, 'Okay, here's a kid. Help them and help your other twenty-five kids too.' So, they don't have, I don't think, that support. So, I think that's the main difference here." Like Ms. Wezner, Madeline believed that this lack of presumed competence was related to insufficient training and experience, coupled with inadequate support and resources—all of which were partly to blame for schools' reticence to integrate disabled students into the general education classroom. In these discussions, it became clear just how difficult this shift in thinking was, with staff and parents themselves indicating the difficulties, frustrations, and doubts that come with advocating for presumed competence.

In many ways, the staff and family commentary we encountered pointed to the leap of faith that families and staff at FVA had to take in supporting a full inclusion model of schooling. This leap of faith included presuming competence and believing in students' abilities to achieve levels of success that went beyond pre-prescribed notions of what disabled students can and cannot do.

Instructional Leadership

An understanding of FVA's history and trajectory as a full inclusion school would be incomplete without a discussion of founder and executive director Dr. Tully's background and instructional leadership. Dr. Tully's background as an experienced general and special education teacher and leader at both typical and inclusively modeled schools—was critical to understanding both the philosophy and execution of how inclusive education was operationalized at FVA. During many discussions and interviews, Dr. Tully circled back to how her personal histories as a teacher, school leader, and parent informed FVA's origins and founding principles:

> My [childhood school], it's an elementary school and a graduate school on site. It's part of the progressive education movement from John Dewey times. So, my elementary learning experiences were in this very integrated, intentionally open, classroom project-based environment. I grew up with a real justice commitment related to that.
>
> I went into special ed because I was really interested in people that were different than what the norm said you should be. I went into special education to understand what's being normed and what's being called abnormal . . . So, I studied special education.
>
> I just had a real interest in flipping the script in a justice-oriented way. I just always did. That was my early childhood. And I did that as a gen ed teacher. And I would really look for ways to highlight the strengths of kids that were marginalized as a teacher. Right? Like, "What is it about this person who has a reading disability that's going to be featured as awesome in front of all their friends? What are we going to do to move this around?"
>
> I did that for about two years. Then when I came to the West Coast, I taught at [an inclusive model school]. So, then I got experience in the practices of inclusion that you see at FVA. I've been working with teachers for many, many years on universal design, differentiated instruction, strength-based teaching—all the kinds of mindsets and strategy approaches that we use at FVA. It's all built on my whole history of that.

Dr. Tully's commitment as an instructional leader was clearly apparent to staff at FVA, manifesting in the ways that she supported teachers and paraprofessionals in modifying their instruction. Dr. Tully's beliefs in how instruction should be differentiated also informed the delivery of professional development. As a result, professional best practices, such as formative classroom observation with feedback and modeling, were quite common at FVA. This level of professional support contrasted with what several of the more experienced teachers at FVA had experienced in prior

Future Visions Academy

school placements, echoing a common concern among educators that not enough time or support is dedicated to teacher professional development.[16] Ms. Gomez cited the need for comprehensive professional development in her description of Dr. Tully's support for her teaching at FVA: "Our principal is an instructional leader. There've been times throughout these two years that I've been at FVA where she will sit with me and help me lesson plan. And when she gives us feedback from observations, it's just so helpful. You know, helping with modifications, how to include everyone in the classroom. That has been beyond beneficial. Unfortunately, I haven't really had that in my other twelve-plus years of teaching."

A major aspect of Dr. Tully's instructional leadership involved preparing teachers and staff for the challenges in adapting to teaching at a school that uses a full inclusion model. This level of insight and support would not have been possible without Dr. Tully herself having prior experience implementing full inclusion programming as a teacher. Consequently, all staff, except for Ms. Severin, were new to the full inclusion model and needed substantial support from Dr. Tully in this. Ms. Wezner shares a fundamental lesson in successfully adopting a "full inclusion mindset" that Dr. Tully gave her:

> Dr. Tully said to me in the beginning, "You have to let go of closing that gap completely." Especially in the older grades, they're going to make a ton of progress, but they're not necessarily going to be at grade level by the end of the year if they were already so behind. I think in the beginning of the year, that was really beating down on me. Like, "How am I going to get this kid who's barely counting to now be multiplying? How can I do that?" And feeling so much pressure from myself to make that happen. Being able to just let go of that and be like, "Progress is progress."

Ms. Wezner touches here on a core point of tension in teaching: that student progress is synonymous with grade-level standards. Adherence to, and measurement of, student performance via the meeting of grade-level standards is the bedrock of most teacher professional development programs.[17] This positioning of student achievement is further extended into the world of standardized achievement as markers of student success and attainment.[18]

This tension between adherence and letting go is particularly strong in environments with diverse ability levels where many of the students are identified as being "below grade level." The question at FVA is "By whose standards?" A shift to "progress is progress" that allows for greater variation and flexibility in how we define student achievement is an essential leap for teachers and staff to make in the adoption of a fully inclusive framework.

Intentional Recruitment and Onboarding of Staff

The intentional recruitment and onboarding of staff was another critical factor in FVA's development of a full inclusion program. Dr. Tully strategically recruited staff that had at least one of the following: a social justice perspective and commitment to full inclusion (e.g., Ms. Gomez), training in both general and special education (e.g., Ms. Wezner), or prior experience teaching or providing services at another full inclusion program (e.g., Ms. Severin). Dr. Tully was also particularly interested in hiring staff new to education who demonstrated openness, flexibility, and strong socio-emotional intelligence and communication skills during their interviews (e.g., the paraprofessionals).

Above all, Dr. Tully indicated that the most important quality she looked for while recruiting staff was a commitment to inclusion and a willingness to learn in a novel environment. She also indicated that, in some ways, it would have been more of a challenge to start with staff who had multiple years of experience in non-inclusive settings with incompatible mindsets and that she wanted staff who would be willing to "start fresh" in their professional development and learning:

> We're organized intentionally as a learning organization for adults. So, the way that the staff works with students, but also with each other, is very intentional. It's all designed to give teachers agency, give support staff a loud voice, and reflect the values of honoring and respecting diverse perspectives among the staff as well as among the students.
>
> So that's just really different than what I've seen in other places. The goal and purpose of the entire staff is to work as a team with a shared kind of effort for an inclusive school, as opposed to "doing my part and then going home."
>
> One thing that I've been surprised by is the unfamiliarity with how radically different this approach is from what people have experienced . . . It's been an interesting journey of recognizing that what I'm asking of people is outside of what they've seen.

Willingness to work as a team toward a shared vision of inclusion required staff to shed preconceived and preestablished notions of the nature of schooling. For many, this "starting over" constituted a radical departure from prior

Future Visions Academy

understandings of inclusion in schools. Mr. Gabriel, an English-Spanish bilingual first-year paraprofessional of Latino descent, shares his experiences at FVA as a paraprofessional as being replete with transformative growth and learning:

> It's been just an amazing experience. Life changing. Everything was new for me. I've never worked at a school setting, but I was able to learn a lot from my peers, teachers, especially Sped teachers, you know. The paras that were already here prior to me, because I came in a little bit after the school year started, taught me. They showed me how to do certain things, how to deal with situations. And so, I was so excited to work because I was learning so much and I was making a difference, educating.

Mr. Gabriel points to the importance of support and mentorship among FVA staff as integral to his professional development at FVA. This deeply collaborative engagement was endemic to the inclusive culture of FVA. Mr. Gabriel's experiences are also an example of Dr. Tully's interest in recruiting staff with flexible attitudes and openness to FVA's philosophy of inclusive education.

Autonomy and Choice

Another distinguishing factor in FVA's inclusive education program was the focus on autonomy and choice. In the context of inclusion, we define autonomy as the freedom to make decisions and choice as access to multiple opportunities. The acquisition of autonomy and choice in the disability space are typically centered as desired outcomes for interventions and supports afforded to people with disabilities.[19] Historically, autonomy and choice have been closely tied to the independence movement (see chapter 2) and can be viewed as a source of social capital that enables inclusive interactions between disabled and nondisabled communities.

At FVA, autonomy and choice are seen as prerequisites for full inclusion and essential components of a fully participative school community. Autonomy and choice were made possible through the allowance of multiple forms of participation and content modification to increase engagement in FVA's classroom communities. Our view of classrooms as communities is ecological and supports an interdependent framing of relations and interactions at FVA (see discussion in chapter 8).[20]

Supporting Autonomy and Choice through Teacher and Student Agency

The centering of autonomy and choice in FVA's inclusive classroom communities reveals a commitment to agency. This commitment is in line with the philosophy and ethos of what it means to include students fully in schools. Toward this end, in-person classroom observations afforded a firsthand look at the strategies teachers and paraprofessionals undertook to support student autonomy and choice.

For example, during an English language arts (ELA) lesson, Ms. Wezner and Ms. Severin adopted a team-teaching approach to aid students in monitoring their own self-regulation. Self-regulation is a crucial skill for all students to develop for school success and has also been tied to students' ability to maintain autonomy and choice within the classroom.[21]

During this observation, Ms. Severin read Numeroff's illustrated storybook *If You Give a Mouse a Cookie* to the class while Ms. Wezner monitored students' behavior from the back of the classroom, marking it as "on-task (+)" or "off-task (–)" on a handheld whiteboard.[22] Upon finishing the book, Ms. Wezner asked students to reflect on their self-regulation:

Ms. Wezner: How do you think you did paying attention?

Students: So-so.

Ms. Wezner: That's right. I was listening for positives and quiet. There was a lot of talking. The reason we are doing it without a [visual] reminder is so that we can give ourselves feedback.

From the perspective of supporting autonomy and choice, several aspects make this interaction interesting. First, we see a strong example of Ms. Wezner and Ms. Severin being afforded autonomy in their instructional approaches through their choice to engage in team teaching using a one teach/one assist model—in this case Ms. Severin, the special education teacher, conducting a reading lesson while Ms. Wezner, the general education teacher, collected behavioral data to share with the class later.

The reversal of general education and special education instructional roles and practices also makes this interaction novel. Historically, special education teachers have been relegated to supportive or auxiliary roles, if they are included at all, in the general education classroom.[23] The inclusion of special education teachers in primary lesson implementation and planning is indicative of the autonomy and choice that FVA staff have in

Future Visions Academy

implementing their team-teaching instruction. This supports the message that all staff play an important role in the classroom community.

The second aspect that makes this interaction unique is that Ms. Wezner's transparent approach supports student autonomy and choice in monitoring their own behavior. The students are informed in real time of their performance with the self-regulation exercise. In other words, there is full transparency in terms of Ms. Wezner's processes and strategies for supporting students' growth toward autonomy vis-à-vis the cultivation of their self-regulation strategies. We see these strategies made visible when Ms. Wezner asks, "How do you think you did paying attention?" To which the students respond, "So-so." Ms. Wezner then confirms their assessment when she says, "That's right. I was listening for positives and quiet. There was a lot of talking."

Centering Autonomy and Choice in Peer-Directed Leadership

Involving students in their own self-regulation and monitoring was not the only strategy for promoting choice and autonomy at FVA. Another strategy, exemplified by Ms. Gomez in her fourth-/fifth-grade combo class, was peer-directed discussion during activity share-outs. In the following example, Ms. Gomez promotes student autonomy and choice by encouraging students themselves to select fellow classmates to share activity designs:

Ms. Gomez: Erica, who are you calling on to share?

Erica: I call on Lisette.

Lisette: [Shares activity design idea]

Ms. Gomez: Great! Lisette, who are you calling on?

Lisette: I call on Zach.

Ms. Gomez could have chosen the students herself—it would have been quicker—but instead promoted students' classroom participation and inclusion using practices that support student autonomy and choice. The success of this peer-directed discussion was evidenced by students' engagement in calling upon their disabled and nondisabled peers alike. That classroom members called on each other equitably, regardless of disability, was notable because in typical school settings children designated as having moderate-to-severe support needs tend to be less frequently called upon.[24]

Students' inclusion was also supported through the voluntary designation of leadership opportunities, such as being designated homework checker for the day. This is significant because active opportunities for leadership are not often given to students with disabilities, many of whom tend to be "acted upon" and seen as passive vessels for support (see chapter 2).[25] Thus, ascribing autonomy and choice through assigned community leadership roles positions students with disabilities as active participants within their classroom communities.

Supporting Autonomy and Choice in Student Expression

Finally, FVA staff supported student autonomy and choice by allowing multiple forms of expression, affording students various ways to articulate ideas, including through nonspeaking forms. Nonspeaking forms of communication include use of facial expression and physical signing or gestures, and can be supported through the use of assistive technologies and visual aids (see chapters 3, 5, and 6).[26] We intentionally use the terms "nonspeaking" and "minimally speaking" throughout this and subsequent chapters, rather than "nonverbal," to describe alternative forms of communication as still possibly including verbal utterances. While these terms are sometimes used synonymously to describe verbal communication, they are *not* interchangeable. "Nonverbal" as a descriptor of communication practice ignores the various nonspeaking—but very verbal—ways that we communicate. These can include, for example, the variety of verbal utterances we use to mark joy, frustration, or anger, such as laughter, sighs, and shouts. The terms "nonspeaking" and "minimally speaking" more precisely embody the notion that while a person may not use verbally articulated words to communicate, they may still use verbalizations for expressive and communicative purposes.

At FVA, supporting nonspeaking forms of communication encourages students' autonomy and choice as equally participating members of their classroom communities. We saw this in Ms. Gomez's class during a speech push-in lesson in which Ms. Davis supported the participation of Carissa, a minimally speaking student. When it was Carissa's turn to engage with classmates during the lesson, she was allowed to write her responses on an individual whiteboard, which were then read aloud by the speech therapist to her classmates. The fact that Carissa was intentionally included in classroom discussion and allowed alternate forms of expression is significant because it respects her bodily autonomy and choice of self-expression while also going against the grain of practices that center oral language

Future Visions Academy 67

production as the optimal, or only, acceptable form of communication during discussions.[27]

Other accepted forms of self-expression and participation at FVA included allowing students to pass on an activity if they did not want to share or respond to requests. Flexible allowances for student expression promote autonomy and choice by releasing students from needing to express themselves in prescribed ways and by broadening criteria for acceptable participation. For example, in another observation of Ms. Gomez's class, students who did not have enough time to name their dinosaur during a science classification activity were allowed to share their work anonymously. When student work is shared, regardless of completion status, multiple forms of participation are supported. In this example, allowing students to share their work in multiple ways supports the extension of students' knowledge and modes of expression.

Autonomy and Choice within Classroom Placements

In our discussions of what inclusive education means at FVA, families and staff repeatedly expressed that, for them, it meant helping students build autonomy and the life skills needed to make good choices, cultivate social capital, negotiate relationships, and engage in their communities. These objectives are aligned with social models of disability where a principal purpose of rehabilitation programs is promoting independence.[28] However, the full inclusion model at FVA went beyond the centering of independence as a means to an end and instead sought to help students learn to live interdependently with others.

Cultivating social capital, relational negotiations, and an ecological view of community centers on affording students the opportunity to be autonomous and make their own choices. This view aligns with interdependence as a relational frame for understanding the ways that inclusion occurs in school communities (see chapter 8). The centrality of giving students a chance to achieve their potential is echoed by Ms. Wezner as she explains how her experiences in a prior school placement inform her views on autonomy and choice:

> Coming from a different perspective at a different school, we just have so many kids that a typical school would never think to include in a gen ed setting. I have a friend who teaches an SDC class in [district name] and she fully believes that the kids in her class could not be in a gen ed setting. And it's so crazy to me to

think, "I have kids just like that who are in my class and doing so great." They just wouldn't have had that opportunity to try in a different school. I think that has been a big shift in my thinking because when I first came [to FVA] I was like, "This is crazy."

Here, Ms. Wezner points out the stark differences in the level of presumed competence and autonomy often afforded to students designated as having moderate-to-severe disability.[29] Her mention of teachers' attitudes also alludes to the importance of teacher mindset and institutional support in cultivating student autonomy and choice within the classroom (see chapter 2). As such, a differentiating factor for students at FVA is an assumption of competence, and resulting autonomy, afforded as an outcome of their integration into the general education classroom.

A growing desire for autonomy and choice for students with disabilities was reiterated by parents we interviewed, especially those with children identified as having significant needs due to a disability such as autism or Down syndrome. In describing the family's reasons for enrolling Daniel, a first grader with Down syndrome, at FVA, Dina points to a change in her understanding of autonomy and choice, and how that relates to her perspective of her school districts' refusal to allow Daniel into a general education classroom setting:

Earlier on, I never questioned the segregation of the students. I just assumed that was the way it was and that there was no choice. When I had Daniel, a whole new perspective came based off his development and progress. We craved for him to be in an inclusive setting, especially because he has an older brother, James, and was mimicking everything that his older brother did. So, my experiences with the school district that we were living between the ages of three and five were difficult. Including him in an inclusive setting, at even a pre-K setting, I got an immediate "No." So, because I wanted him to have schooling, I obviously stuck with that. But I knew that before kindergarten hit, I would, if necessary, move to a different city to enroll him in a school that was inclusive.

Like Ms. Wezner, Dina came to believe in the right of her son Daniel, and students with disabilities in general, to have the choice to be educated in an integrated setting with access to typically developing peers. Dina came to see integration as necessary for the development of her son's autonomy and potential—the developmental benefits of which she witnessed firsthand in Daniel's engagement with his older brother James.

Future Visions Academy

Culture of Kindness

At FVA, a culture of kindness was positioned as community social capital essential to students' engagement and integration. The modeling of kindness as a critical social skill, crucial to a unified school community, was one of the key outcomes FVA hoped to accomplish with its full inclusion model and philosophy.

Para Power! Making Social Skills Visible to Cultivate Kindness

Paraprofessionals held a substantial role in modeling kindness at FVA. As an example, during a structured math lesson using a team-teaching approach, I observed Ms. Carina, a paraprofessional in Ms. Gomez's class fourth-/fifth-grade combo classroom, modeling what it means to be kind by sharing her noticing of behaviors and feelings with Santiago, a minimally speaking student with Down syndrome. Santiago stubbed Ms. Carina's finger, and Ms. Carina immediately made visible the impact of his actions: "Ow! You hurt me, Santiago. That hurts. Please be gentle." Ms. Carina's reaction was important and intentional, modeling for Santiago, and the surrounding students who had taken notice, how to check in with others and make alternative requests. Ms. Carina's modeling of her feelings and requests points to the focus that FVA sought to place on consideration for others—a key feature in how the school defined kindness.

FVA sought to ensure that modeling social skills—particularly in relation to kindness—was presented as imperative to being fully inclusive. In another example of social skills modeling, Ms. Carina supports cooperation between a small group of girls, consisting of Carissa, Margo, and Tammy, in an independent reading activity. Minimally speaking to varying degrees, the girls are working on modified versions of the activity. Carissa and Margo are giggling and chatting with each other when Tammy says, "Shhh!" Ms. Carina turns to the talkative pair and says, "That's Tammy's way of telling you to please be quiet. She is trying to work."

This interaction is significant for two reasons. First, Tammy advocates for herself in a manner that is recognized and accepted by Ms. Carina. Moreover, Tammy is not asked to "use her words" as is sometimes the case with providers tasked to support minimally speaking students.[30] The acceptance of Tammy's verbal exclamation as legitimate communication positions her as an equally participative member in her group. The second reason this is significant is that Ms. Carina uses Tammy's communication as an opportunity to make visible people's feelings and to model considerate behavior. These interpersonal interactions between students and staff exemplify modeling kindness to support student inclusion while cultivating social skills.

"Let Me Help You Help Me": Peer-to-Peer Modeling of Culture of Kindness

At FVA, we also noticed substantial peer-to-peer modeling of considerate behaviors that supported a culture of kindness. Peer-to-peer modeling is associated with positive socio-emotional outcomes in social skills development, ability to make friends, and greater community integration.[31] We observed the affordances of peer-to-peer modeling firsthand during a whole-class art activity in Ms. Gomez's classroom. James and Tammy, both identified as having IEPs, were working independently at a shared table when Tammy suddenly grabbed the scissors from James to which James responded, "Give them back. If you want my scissors, you need to ask for them." Tammy returned the scissors to James after a pause, and they continued working. With his request, James effectively uses his social skills to model considerate behaviors and to redirect Tammy in a prosocial way. These kinds of student interactions were common at FVA and served both to build students' social capital within the classroom and to support a culture of kindness.

Another example of peer-to-peer modeling occurred during a speech push-in activity facilitated by Ms. Alexa, a SLPA in the first-/second-grade combo classroom of Ms. Ohlin, an English-speaking general education teacher of European descent in her second year of teaching. Ms. Alexa turned to Jake, a boy who presented as being autistic. Jake had lost track of his place in the visual story the group was using for the activity and was alternating between covering his face with his activity sheet and holding it upside down. Jonathan, another autistic student sitting next to Jake, responded, "That's the wrong side," and helped Jake to orient his activity sheet correctly. Annie, a student presenting as neurotypical, also leaned over and used a sheet of paper to guide Jake visually to where he should read. In this example, neurodiverse students model and engage in helpful prompting behaviors, mimicking what they have seen staff do at FVA.

Engaging in kind and helpful behavior is presented as what everyone should do for each other and disrupts a common presumption that nondisabled students are more capable of serving as behavioral models

Future Visions Academy

than disabled students.[32] Another notable aspect of this interaction was the normalization of neurodiverse behaviors. For example, the students were not bothered by Jake's autistic stimming and displayed a high level of acceptance for human diversity than what might otherwise be seen in general education settings.[33] Examples such as these directly counter arguments against full inclusion programs that students with "atypical" behaviors create distraction within the general education setting.[34]

Time and time again, we witnessed students' acceptance of neurodiversity at FVA. This was, in part, a testament to the "kindness as culture" work that the staff at FVA strove to undertake. As a final example, one day before school, fourth grader Luigi approached Jonathan, his classmate, who was sitting upset and alone on the floor. "What's wrong?" Luigi asked. "You wouldn't care," replied Jonathan. "I *do* care!" replied Luigi, who firmly stood by Jonathan and patiently waited for his response. Luigi's commitment to helping Jonathan reflected FVA's intensive cultivation of kindness, a behavior integral to FVA's inclusive school culture. It is often the case that students with disabilities in distress are ignored or avoided by their classmates, who may not have been exposed to, or shown how to engage in, supportive behaviors.[35] These examples demonstrate the interdependent approach FVA students and staff take in negotiating social encounters with each other.

Perceptions of Culture of Kindness at FVA

Creating moments of unity and loving kindness within the school community was an integral part of supporting FVA's culture of kindness. This commitment to kindness was philosophically essential to fulfilling FVA's mission of inclusion. Mr. Gabriel describes students' evolution toward a "kindness as culture" mindset:

> Kids who started going to school [at FVA], especially our special needs kids, they came in being shy and not really wanting to interact with different friends. And over time, we just were patient, and we loved them, and we took care of them, and we were just waiting for that sprout to happen. And when it did happen with a lot of kids, and even now looking back, so many kids have made so much progress. Not just Sped students, but also our typical students, just accept the loving and caring and leave that hard side aside.

Mr. Gabriel points to developing kindness as being an incremental process. He illustrates how initially the students, most of whom came from segregated school environments, were not accustomed to a more diverse school community and did not know how to engage with what Fabien describes as "different friends." Mr. Gabriel compares the concerted cultivation of kindness to the cultivation of a sprouting shoot, the resulting growth blooming as inclusion and acceptance of peers. "Leaving that hard side aside," in this case, refers to what Mr. Gabriel earlier revealed to be difficult aspects of human nature: prejudice, fear, and segregation. "The kids [with disabilities], we know that they tend to get picked on. So, I think our community has created this barrier to walk all of that and allow that love and sense of empathy and care in our family and our community. They've been nurtured at a great school, so I know they're going to be successful. And I hope that they just always care for their friends and their families." Here, Mr. Gabriel discusses the protective factors FVA's community promotes as both a "barrier" to negative behaviors, such as bullying, as well as a protective circle of "empathy and care." Mr. Gabriel description of FVA's protective factors aligns with research demonstrating the socio-emotional health benefits, including an improved sense of belonging, that come with being part of a community.[36] Mira, a middle-class English- and Tagalog-speaking Filipina mother to kindergartener Maddox, second grader Marco, and fourth grader Maya, all of whom she identified as not having a disability, echoed Mr. Gabriel's perspective on kindness as it related to empathy and care:

> I want my kids to grow up knowing everyone is equal. I want them to know how to interact with all kinds of children. You have to learn to work with different people.
>
> So, the benefit is they're making friends, they're learning how to work with all kinds of kids. When I was dropping the kids off at school, there was another child that [has a disability]. And she called my daughter, and they ran to each other and hugged and embraced, "Good morning." It warmed my heart because we don't see that every day.
>
> I want them to come out of FVA with a big heart, knowing how to accept other people, how to work with other people, especially because in the real world, that's what it's all about . . . I talk to them every morning about helping other people, having empathy for other people, and giving yourself to others.

Mira, in describing her decision to place her nondisabled children in a full inclusion school, emphasized the necessity of kindness as integral to learning how to engage comfortably with a diverse range of people and to engage outside oneself. Moreover, she reiterated a commitment to kindness as philosophically essential to being inclusive. Mira sees the skills her children learn at FVA as protective factors critical to navigating life successfully.

Ms. Carina echoes the commentary regarding the development of prosocial skills as protective factors in the context of navigating change and

Future Visions Academy

friendship, connecting both to inclusiveness and kindness. Regarding change, Ms. Carina alludes to children as naturally inquisitive and willing to try new things, including FVA's inclusive school model: "With all the inclusion, I was surprised how it didn't really [negatively] affect the kids. They're unfazed about it. So, it was really cool to see that from the beginning they're like, 'Oh, these are my friends.' You know, 'We're all friends.'" Ms. Carina points out how quickly the children grew accustomed to new ways of "doing school." This includes new ways of "doing friendship." This is in contrast to the development of cliques, in-groups, and out-groups, which tend to be a common schoolyard phenomenon.[37] At FVA, it was more often the case that students would invite other children at the margins into their play. These inclusive schoolyard behaviors, modeled from the start by FVA staff, align with findings from Paley's (1993) playground culture studies, which placed great value on play as "the most usable context" for children's academic and social growth.[38]

A culture of kindness also includes caring for the success and well-being of others. From this viewpoint, cultivating an inclusive school culture requires producing citizens that care for each other. Ms. Yadira, a Spanish-English bilingual second-year paraprofessional of Latina descent, reiterates the premise that kindness and inclusion are necessarily intertwined, and she expresses a belief that inclusion naturally leads to kindness: "[Inclusion] makes everybody kind. It makes everybody understand things that we wouldn't if we weren't in that setting. I see students being kind to each other. I don't see them making fun of each other. That helps us [the staff] be that person to adults as well." In FVA's school community, a major product of kindness is thus an expanded ability to engage with people as they are. Inclusiveness, and the kindness that results from it, allows us to acquire a wider lens of acceptance. Ms. Yadira alludes to the "contagious" nature of inclusivity and kindness: once someone starts being inclusive and kind, it spreads to others, including adults being kind to each other.

Intersectional Vision of Inclusive Education

Finally, adherence to FVA's mission was expressed as a commitment by families and staff to an intersectional vision of inclusive education. Adopting an intersectional approach to the cultivation of inclusion is essential in an increasingly globalized society where people identify across multiple identities, including those that intersect with language, disability, and race.[39]

Dr. Tully iterated the necessity of adopting an intersectional perspective of inclusion in her description of FVA as an inclusive school community in the school handbook: "Our school community understands that the diverse experiences, cultures, languages, abilities, and skills students bring to the classroom are assets for learning. School-wide values of empathy and respect are promoted through cooperative learning experiences in our diverse and inclusive classrooms, and through attention to each student's social emotional learning and growth." In this section and the remainder of the book, we connect the ways in which FVA families and staff strove to consider students' multiple identities in the implementation of FVA's inclusion model. We found that staff and families' own multiple identities, and perspectives, inform their view and approaches to inclusion. We explore how families' diverse experiences and perspectives, combined with FVA's school practices, shaped the students' experiences at FVA.

Intersecting Needs across Language and Disability

Examples of students' intersectional identities influencing delivery of services were particularly evident in the speech and language therapy work that took place with multilingual children at FVA. The influence of children's intersectionality manifested as a tension between supporting both their IEP and their language needs.

To date, strategies for comprehensively serving students at the intersection of language and disability are few.[40] Adding to the complexity of serving children with IEPs who are also multilingual is the fact that most therapy providers are not bilingual, as was the case with the service providers at FVA. This is a common phenomenon across the service provider industry, including the fields of speech–language pathology, occupational therapy, and behavior interventionists, with profound ramifications for how best to support multilingual students requiring services.[41] This scarcity in the face of great need behooves intersectional considerations in the implementation of inclusive programming that center a students' multiple identities in the provision of services.

At FVA, we observed the impact students' intersecting language and disability identities had on provider decisions, specifically services to support students identified as being both multilingual and disabled. As an example, Ms. Davis was observed providing speech push-in services to multilingual students during small-group literacy centers in the kindergarten classroom of Ms. Macias, an experienced English-Spanish bilingual teacher of Latina descent. Ms. Davis was supporting Cindy, one of three children in the class with IEPs who was also designated as emerging Spanish-English bilingual. Ms. Davis worked with Cindy on her /r/ sounds using the *Little Mermaid* storybook. While the focus of the lesson was /r/ sounds, Ms. Davis also improvised to address the /sh/ sound.

Ms. Davis later told me that working on /sh/ was not part of Cindy's IEP. However, because the *Little Mermaid* storybook had many /sh/ sounds, as in the word "shell," it afforded Ms. Davis an opportunity to support Cindy's emerging language needs as a Spanish-English bilingual. Ms. Davis understood that for many emerging Spanish-English bilinguals, the distinction between the English /sh/ and /ch/ is a tricky one. Accordingly, she used Cindy's language status to justify the service addition: "As a Spanish-speaking English-language learner, she needs to practice /sh/."

While this was an improvised service decision, it demonstrates Ms. Davis's awareness of her students' multiple identities and needs across disability and language. In Cindy's case, this meant addressing her needs as a Spanish-English bilingual in tandem to the needs associated with her language delay. It also speaks to an often unanswered need to support service providers in their intentional integration of strategies that support both language and disability needs, particularly for providers who are not proficient in the heritage languages of the children they serve.[42] Moreover, this example demonstrates why adopting intersecting approaches to support both students' language and disability needs is so important: to not do so makes effective service delivery difficult for the significant number of students who have service needs related to both disability and language status.[43]

Intersecting needs across language and disability were also evident in FVA's attempts to include multilingual language support for students. This was evident in the language choices that were made during school-wide celebrations, performances, and events that brought FVA's linguistically diverse families and staff together. As an example, FVA's winter celebration included multiple songs across languages, including American Sign Language (ASL), Spanish, and English across all class performances. Usage of ASL across contexts at FVA is significant because ASL is not always supported as a second or foreign language in school settings, despite its common usage to support students with disabilities.[44] At FVA, this was not the case, with ASL being frequently observed during school events and classroom instruction. Moreover, ASL usage was observed in students both with and without disabilities and both general and special education teachers, not only service providers. As a result, ASL use at FVA came to signify one of the intersecting ways in which disability and language informed communication and instruction at FVA.

Paraprofessionals as Cultural Brokers

The positioning of paraprofessionals, who were mostly multicultural and multilingual, as cultural brokers within the school community was another way in which FVA attempted to support the inclusion of diverse students with disabilities. We use the term "cultural broker" to signify persons who use their multiple identities to facilitate the bridging of cultures and communication.[45] We focus on paraprofessionals as cultural brokers at the classroom community level.

One such relationship that centered paraprofessionals as cultural brokers within the classroom setting involved Ms. Wezner, who is monolingual in English, and Ms. Carina, a Spanish-English bilingual paraprofessional assigned to support the classroom. Ms. Wezner and Ms. Carina were tasked with serving emerging Spanish-English bilingual students with and without disabilities in her second-/third-grade combo class. Toward this endeavor, Ms. Wezner broadly described the immense support Ms. Carina provided, outlining the ways that Ms. Carina used her multilingual status to help Ms. Wezner support students and parents: "I think especially with our demographic of so many Spanish speakers, I lean on Carina a ton for translating and helping families that I don't think feel as comfortable talking to me because I don't speak Spanish. She makes it more of a comforting feeling for them." In this commentary, Ms. Wezner explicitly positions Ms. Carina as a cultural broker in several ways. First, Ms. Wezner supports Ms. Carina by using her multilingual status to bridge the language barrier that is sometimes present between monolingual teachers and multilingual students and parents.[46] As Ms. Wezner explains, language disconnect can result in alienation or feelings of discomfort between parents and teachers.[47] Ms. Carina serves as a cultural broker by bridging language gaps between her and parents to create connection and "comfort" for parents, facilitating their participation in the classroom community.

Second, Ms. Carina also acts as a cultural broker within the classroom by helping bridge the language gap between Ms. Wezner and her students through translation of academic content and support of language learning.

Future Visions Academy

Here, Ms. Wezner describes how Ms. Carina uses her Spanish-English language skills to support the inclusion and instruction of multilingual students:

> She played a huge part in integrating more Spanish into our class. She would write our morning meeting message in Spanish, and then I would read it in class to the kids, as best as I can, and they would all laugh . . . Half or more are [multilingual], so they translate after I read it. We started doing that every Wednesday, and it was such a fun thing in class. For the first time, I let the kids step into "I'm learning with you." And they were like, "What? How can you learn new things? You're our teacher." So, I thought that was a really cool aspect of using our paras and using each other as resources.

Ms. Wezner's description of Ms. Carina's facilitative role in supporting student-driven language learning illustrates how paraprofessionals use their intersecting identities to broker connections between multilingual and disability communities. In Ms. Wezner's classroom, Ms. Carina facilitated language cultivation by supporting Ms. Wezner in making language invitations to students and using student-driven language modeling to support classroom engagement, all of which affirm students' intersecting identities and cultural capital.[48]

Family Perspectives on Intersectionality

The multilingual families we interviewed also had specific perspectives about the intersecting needs of multilingual and disabled students. This included discussion of how the needs of their multilingual children were being addressed via FVA's full inclusion model. In this subsection, we focus on discussions we had with Hilda and Sara, two first-generation Mexican mothers with diverse backgrounds and experiences.

Hilda, a working-class Spanish monolingual mother from a rural village in Mexico, indicated that she primarily relied on her two multilingual children, Leonardo, a first grader identified as having a learning disability, and Luigi, a fourth grader not identified as having a disability, to relay classroom information to her. For school matters, she relied on the front office staff and the paraprofessionals assigned to her children's classrooms. Somewhat indicative of the fact that she was willing to be interviewed but not audio-recorded, Hilda was somewhat wary of the systems she had encountered thus far in the United States, with the US education system being no exception. Her own experiences with formal education had been mediated by economic disruption and the need to work. Hilda's experiences with schooling carried over into her perspectives of FVA's inclusion model and what it meant for her children to be enrolled at FVA:

> La forma de ensenar es diferente. Tratan bien a los niños. Se enfocan en ellos. No los enseñan lo mismo porque su nivel es diferente. Es una escuela chiquita y les ponen más atención en sus necesidades . . . En una escuela mas grande, si no entienden se pasan . . . Aquí, si no entienden, tratan de explicar otra vez.

> The education is different. They treat the children well. They pay attention to them. The teaching is not the same because the [children's] levels are different. It's a small school where they attend to their needs . . . At a larger school, if you don't understand, you get left behind . . . Here, if you don't understand, they try again to explain.

The positive treatment of her children, which included school staff meeting children at their "level" and children not being "left behind," were important aspects of FVA's inclusive school model for Hilda as a first-generation immigrant to the United States. This could be in contrast to prior schooling experiences where perhaps Hilda, or her children, may not have been as well supported. Hilda was hesitant to criticize directly and only alluded at these sentiments indirectly—a communicative approach in line with Hilda's rural upbringing.

Hilda's comments also illustrate her understanding of a defining goal of inclusive education: to ensure comprehension across diverse ability levels using differentiated instruction. In Hilda's view, the use of differentiated instruction to support children with disabilities at FVA also supported the needs of her multilingual children. The view of inclusion, care, and support of diverse students as a community value at FVA was also echoed by Sara, a college-educated monolingual Spanish-speaking woman from an urban area of Mexico, mother to kindergartener Leon and third grader Isla, both designated as English language learners without disability:

> Me habían dicho que era inclusiva, pero no visualizaba hasta ya estar aquí, qué tan inclusiva es ¿No? Ya el poder de tener con ellos como compañeros a niños con educación especial y con ciertas necesidades me hace entender todavía más. Y sobre todo, que ellos puedan sentirse parte de una comunidad tan diversa . . . Porque aquí se van a encontrar de todos los estratos económicos, sociales, culturales, ideológicos, y ahora también de habilidades o disabilidades.

> I had been told that the school was inclusive, but I didn't realize it until I saw it for myself. You know? Seeing them engage with classmates that receive special education and have additional needs helps me understand this even more. And

Future Visions Academy

what's more, to see them feel like they are part of such as diverse community . . . Because here, you'll find all the socioeconomic, cultural, and ideological statuses, as well as abilities and disabilities.

Sara's perspective of intersectionality at FVA was also evident in her framing of the diverse backgrounds and needs of multilingual and disabled children as analogous in their shared necessity for community and support:

> Creo que desde un principio los maestros pudieron hacer sentirlos como parte de una comunidad. Que llegaron sin saber inglés y que están aprendiendo el idioma, es una habilidad menos como el que a lo mejor no puede caminar o como él que no puede comer por sí mismo. Osea, cada uno tiene diferente tipo de necesidad.

> From the beginning, the teachers have helped them feel part of a community. That they are here without speaking English, in the process of learning the language, is one less ability as someone who perhaps cannot walk or perhaps cannot feed themselves. In other words, each of us has a different type of need.

Sara's reframing of language status and disability as distinct but potentially interrelated and interconnected designations points to the commonalities they share in the context of inclusion. In this sense, both multilingual and disabled students require resources to integrate into the classroom, including curricular adjustments to gain access to the curriculum. Finally, Sara reiterated a perspective that was shared by both Mira and Mr. Gabriel in their discussion of kindness, empathy, and inclusivity as social capital:

> El beneficio creo que va a ser el poder hacerlos conscientes desde chicos de las necesidades que hay a su alrededor . . . Y de lo importante que es poder compartir y convivir con el resto del mundo, porque aquí en Estados Unidos habemos de todo tipo de personas.

> The benefit is that from an early age they will be aware of the needs that exist around them . . . As well as the importance of being able to share and engage with the world, because here in the United States, we have many kinds of people.

Parents' shared perspectives of inclusion supported a belief in the necessity of promoting an interdependent community. In the following chapters, we will continue to explore parent, staff, and student perspectives on inclusion as they relate to LLT practices at FVA across in-person and remote learning contexts. Specifically, chapter 5 will pivot to a descriptive discussion of FVA's in-person LLT practices during the 2019–2020 school year, while chapters 6 and 7 will document the shifts to remote and hybrid learning commencing in the spring of 2020.

5 Amplifying Student Voice: LLT Practices at FVA

In this chapter, we highlight the social affordances—and challenges—of using digital technologies to support children's inclusion across language, literacy, and technology (LLT) practices in diverse school communities. As discussed in chapter 1, we use the term "LLT practices" to describe an integrated approach to examining language and literacy practice in the context of technology use. This interdisciplinary view of literacy practice across dimensions aligns with twenty-first-century sociocultural conceptualizations of literacy and differs from prior examinations looking at LLT practices as relationally distinct.[1] Applying an interdependent lens (see chapter 8), we examine the sociocultural context of inclusive technology use at FVA as they strove to support students' LLT practices.

In the second half of the chapter, we also explore how students' and teachers' use of assistive technologies can be used to embody, empower, and give agency to students as creators and participants in the classroom. Our focus is broadly centered on communication and connection and the ways in which LLT practices support student agency and expression. The chapter also details how experiences with digital technologies had a profound mediating impact on how parents and staff come to understand students' voices and competencies.

Our study of digital technologies at FVA revealed LLT practices that aligned with those often found in other schools, as well practices that diverged from typical uses of technology in the classroom. First, we discuss LLT practices, perspectives, and preferences at FVA, including how they align with and differ from LLT practices often seen in schools. Then, we discuss LLT practices in the home with a focus on supporting the LLT practices of children with disabilities. Finally, we take a closer look at how assistive technologies can be used to support and empower students' linguistic expression and voice.

Throughout, we use FVA as a case study to provide analysis for how LLT practices might be used to support students' agency and voice within and beyond the classroom.

A Walk through of LLT Practices at FVA

This section provides a descriptive overview of LLT practices in the FVA school community. This includes a description of LLT practices in the classroom and supporting LLT practices for children with disabilities. Connections will be made to how LLT practices align and diverge from practices generally seen in schools and how they might be used to support inclusion, engagement, and learning in school communities.

LLT in the Classroom

In discussing LLT practices, we use the term "physical technologies" to refer to hardware, tools, instruments, and machines, and we use the term "digital technologies" to refer to applications of data and code, such as software, data storage systems, and the Internet. The use of physical technologies as instructional tools (e.g., Elmo projectors, television screens, and digital whiteboards) for a review of core subjects during whole-group lessons was common in all the classes we observed at FVA. These technologies were primarily used as visualization and scaffolding tools for teaching and lesson review. Often, these uses were coupled with physical manipulatives as in the following observation of a whole-group math lesson reviewing mathematical thinking and vocabulary in Ms. Macias's kindergarten classroom:

> Ms. Macias combines her use of the Elmo projector with physical manipulatives, including Post-it notes, stickers, and worksheets. Shapes are projected using the Elmo. Ms. Macias asks, "What does 2D and 3D mean?" as she places a whiteboard next to the Elmo, divided in half and labeled "2D" on the left and "3D" on right. Students clap their hands twice or thrice to demonstrate understanding as shapes are sorted into their respective columns. Ms. Macias finishes the lesson by reviewing geometric vocabulary, including "vertices," "diagonal," "parallel," "acute," "obtuse," and "straight." Students stand and model each vocabulary item, using their arms to motion the direction and angle of lines.

Additional uses of physical technologies in Ms. Macias's classroom, observed across all classrooms at FVA, included the use of digital alarms to cue and direct students from activity to activity. The integration of physical technologies

Amplifying Student Voice 83

with visual manipulatives and tools is typical of well-scaffolded classrooms and was critical to maintaining classroom flow and order, aligning with the need for physical cues and supports written into many students' IEPs.[2]

The following observation of guided reading and computer small-group literacy centers in Ms. Ohlin's first-/second-grade combo class was also typical of the integrated use of physical technologies, manipulatives, and tools used at FVA to support students' LLT practices:

> A digital alarm goes off, and students stop their activity. When all students are quiet, they rotate to their next center. At the guided reading station, Ms. Severin chats with students: "How was your weekend? I missed you guys." Then, she pulls out a book: "This book is called *Can You Go Here?* What do you think it's about? Do you guys want pointers?" Ms. Severin hands out plastic pointers that students can use to guide their reading. They begin choral reading, and when they get to the end of the page, Ms. Severin says, "Turn the page." They continue reading page by page together. She waits for all students to finish reading each page before providing the verbal prompt, "Turn the page."

In this example, Ms. Ohlin uses a digital alarm as an audio cue for students to move to their next literacy station, supporting students' ability to self-regulate and remain on task with their literacy activities. Once at the guided reading station, led by Ms. Severin, pointers are offered as physical tools to support students' choral reading.[3] This is a simple example of the interplay between physical tools and technologies commonly observed across FVA's classrooms.

Functional Uses of Digital Technologies in the Classroom

The use of physical technologies as tools to support classroom function often extended to how digital technologies were used in the classroom. We saw this primarily with how digital technologies, specifically education applications and websites, were used to engage students during small-group centers. Based on our observations of classroom LLT practices, and confirmed by interviews with staff, educational game applications, such as Smarty Ants and Lexia, were used to support early language and literacy goals—for example, letter sound identification and blending CVC words. Prior to the period of pandemic-induced remote learning (see chapter 6), digital technology use, including educational game applications, centered on facilitating self-guided literacy skills review during small-group centers, as described by Ms. Wezner: "We had one station during reading that was on computers, and I was starting to have them do guided reading on the Read Works website—kind of like a test-prep skill. They have little passages that you can go answer questions on and go back to the passage. So more of that skill of going back into the text and finding the answers to the question."

In this example, Ms. Wezner alludes to test-prep skills as auxiliary or supplemental skills suitable for delegation to self-guided computer center stations. This delegation was in contrast to direct reading and writing instruction using physical technologies and tools. With exception of assistive digital technologies, which we detail later in the chapter, and assistive uses of mainstream technologies, such as Google Workspace (formerly G Suite) on a Chromebook, for supporting writing, it wasn't until the pandemic that we saw a more expansive shift in the use of digital technologies as integral instruments for transforming and informing students' reading and writing practice.

Ms. Yadira reiterated the limited use of digital technologies in the pre-K and early-grade classrooms that we saw in the upper-grade classrooms. As Ms. Yadira describes, uses focused primarily on supporting student autonomy during independent study, freeing staff to facilitate what were perceived to be more instruction-intensive centers, such as guided reading: "In TK, we didn't have a lot of technology. We did literacy stations. They would have iPads, so they could use an app and then work on that. And then, Ms. Jarvis had a reading station."

In these ways, digital technologies in the classroom served as holding spaces for students, allowing staff to work more intensively with students needing additional support, affording flexibility in how teachers and staff organized literacy instruction for students. Ms. Severin also reiterated the functional use of digital technologies for facilitating classroom management: "I think if anything, tech is great for us when we do small groups because from a classroom management standpoint, we need a fourth, or a third, or half the class to just be quiet. So, plug and play is fantastic for that. I can manage the other ten kids." As described by Ms. Severin, and corroborated by several staff interviewees, a central purpose of digital technologies was to support classroom management functionally by keeping a portion of the class autonomously occupied. In this way, the primary benefit of integrating digital technologies into classroom instruction centered on their use as freestanding activities, allowing staff to focus on targeted one-to-one and small-group literacy instruction. These uses, while simultaneously practical and limited, are representative of the functional approaches to integrating digital technologies as instructional tools observed across US classrooms.[4]

LLT Perspectives and Preferences at FVA

Perspectives and preferences regarding reading and writing with digital technologies also surfaced during classroom observations and interviews with staff and families. Considering the impact of perspectives and preferences for LLT practices (1) informs our understanding of observed practices, (2) illuminates potential areas for supporting LLT practices in schools, and (3) provides useful information for designing inclusive instructional approaches for students with diverse literacy needs.[5] In this section, we discuss teacher and student perspectives and preferences for LLT practices in the classroom.

Teacher Perspectives

When we asked teachers to describe student reading preferences with and without the use of digital technologies, most indicated that they had not noticed a preference but ventured to guess that students preferred reading with physical books rather than reading digitally on a computer or tablet. It became apparent in asking teachers about student preferences that this had not been a question they had considered before, perhaps as a result of digital technologies being relegated to functional applications in the classroom. This ambivalence was evident in Ms. Wezner's description of student preferences for reading with digital technologies:

> I think that when I first introduced doing reading on the computer, they were really excited about it 'cause it's new and different. But [the reading website] was only informational articles. So, I don't think it was quite as fun as reading books that are stories. I don't know what they would prefer for themselves, but my class loved read-alouds, and when Ms. Severin would read a picture book, they could ask questions for an hour. So, I think in that sense, real books, but I don't know.

Ms. Wezner's commentary was typical of the responses we received during interviews, with teachers themselves indicating a preference for reading with books. This led us to wonder whether teachers' own preferences colored how they viewed reading with digital technologies.

We would later learn, in discussions with Dr. Tully, that historically the school had not had an opportunity to focus on intentionally integrating digital technologies more holistically into classroom practice. Rather, the focus of FVA's piloting years had been on getting the full inclusion model off the ground. Ms. Davis, who was tasked as the SLP collaborating with the special education teachers to integrate assistive technology use into classrooms, confirmed that the prioritization of the full inclusion model's push-in structure sometimes made it challenging to use technology-enabled strategies to engage students with IEPs. She shared the case of Chandler, an autistic kindergartener in Ms. Macias's classroom as an example: "Chandler really responds better with the iPad. He loves animals. So, do we or do we not incorporate iPad work into a storybook reading center? I think I'll try to incorporate that the next time I go into the classroom because I didn't get a chance to work with him today."

Ms. Davis described how she has to balance what will motivate individual students with IEPs while keeping the push-in content as close to the broader general education activity as possible. These tensions illuminate the philosophical differences in approaches to serving students found between the worlds of inclusive education and special education. They also illuminate how competing instructional priorities—so common in schools, with FVA being no exception—are major factors in decisions about whether, and how, to integrate technology use more intentionally into classroom practice.[6]

Pivoting the discussion to student preferences for writing with and without digital technologies, teacher perceptions were less ambivalent. Teachers indicated a preference for writing with paper in both the lower and upper grades. Ms. Wezner describes student preferences for writing in her second-/third-grade combo class:

> Typing is challenging for a lot of them, so they would prefer by hand. But then, for our first publishing of stories, I called them one by one during centers, and they read me their piece, and I typed it for them. I think they like seeing it all typed up, official. But they're not able to type it themselves yet. At least, not fluently. So, I think that it took so long that they would prefer to handwrite if they had to.

At second- and third-grade levels, Ms. Wezner indicated that students still preferred writing with pencil and paper because, as emerging writers, they had more fluency and speed writing by hand. In her view, this corresponded with fewer frustration points compared to typing, which can be very "hunt and peck" in the early stages of learning to type.[7] This relationship between writing and typing fluency, frustration thresholds, and preferences supports

Amplifying Student Voice

prior findings indicating these as factors informing students' digital technology use to support writing (see chapter 3).[8]

In the upper-grade levels, both usage and preference for writing with digital technologies seemed to change. As an example, Ms. Gomez had the following to say regarding her fourth and fifth graders' perspectives of writing with digital technologies: "I think they enjoy writing on technology, but because I think they enjoy being able to manipulate their font . . . how big it is, what color it is. Those kinds of things are very new and fun for them. And so, it made it exciting to type and they want it to be on the computers in that respect." According to Ms. Gomez, there is a shift in upper-grade students realizing, and exploring, the affordances of writing with digital technologies. These include the ability to select and manipulate font size and style, use spelling and grammar check functions to improve writing accuracy, and take advantage of speech-to-text and text-to-speech functions to support writing fluency (see chapter 3). While Ms. Gomez did not mention writing proficiency as a factor in students' preferences for using digital technologies, there is an indication within the research that as students begin writing more fluently, usually in the mid to upper elementary grades, they are also in an improved position to take advantage of the affordances of digital technologies for writing.

Student Perspectives

In interviews with students, we found a positive interest in using technology for both reading and writing, particularly in the upper grades engaging with educational technology gaming applications. This positive interest is typical of that found in studies of student preferences and uses of digital technologies.[9]

LLT practice in lower grades: Marco and Maddox Reiterating staff responses, students indicated that their preferred uses of digital technologies included using their Chromebook computers to access educational game applications and websites while at centers. In the lower grades, literacy practices incorporating digital technologies focused on using educational game apps to engage working memory and information recall of literacy and mathematical concepts (i.e., Lexia and Kahoot; see appendix B), as Marco, a second grader in Ms. Wezner's class describes:

Interviewer: So, Marco, I want to start by asking you to tell me a little bit about what you like about your school.

Marco: I like it because we can do fun stuff like Kahoot. It's really fun.

Interviewer: Can you tell me more about Kahoot? What is that?

Marco: It's a website on your laptop. You have to try and figure out what is the answer.

Marco's positive response to using educational technology applications such as Kahoot on his Chromebook as fun and a highlight of his school day was typical of student interview responses given regarding the use of digital technologies to support LLT practices at FVA. For the youngest students, using digital technologies to support LLT practices extended to engaging with educational technology applications downloaded onto one-to-one iPads to support phonological and alphabet awareness. For example, Lexia was used to develop students' phonological awareness, as Maddox, a kindergartener in the class of Ms. Jarvis, an experienced English-speaking teacher of European descent, describes here:

Interviewer: How do you use computers for reading?

Maddox: I play Lexia.

Interviewer: You play Lexia? What do you do? Can you tell me what Lexia is?

Maddox: It's about rhyming words.

Interviewer: And what's your favorite thing to do in Lexia?

Maddox: To rhyme words.

Maddox's response to this, and additional questions about his LLT practices, was typical of the younger elementary-aged children we interviewed at FVA. In addition to the phonological uses of educational technology applications such as Lexia to support LLT, Maddox indicated that he enjoyed reading student-produced writing:

Maddox: What I like about my school is the library.

Interviewer: The library. What do you like about the library?

Maddox: 'Cause they have books.

Interviewer: Yeah, do you have favorite books? Tell me what your favorite books are.

Maddox: The Ellis books.

Interviewer: The Ellis books? I don't know what those are about. Can you tell me what those are about?

Maddox: About my friend Ellis in my class.

Interviewer: Oh, they're about your friend Ellis! Are these books that you write? Or are these books that someone else wrote?

Maddox: Someone else wrote. Ellis.

These stories were often written by hand by the students and then typed and printed by the staff, as mentioned earlier by Ms. Wezner. This is another example of the functional uses of digital technologies at FVA, and writing as a relational and social endeavor, that supports student voice and classroom connection. As such, writing, and its formalized presentation in the library, becomes a way for students to amplify their voice as authors (e.g., Ellis) for their classmates (e.g., Maddox) as audience. Maddox also discussed his own writing practices, primarily produced using paper and pencil:

Interviewer: Do you like to write? What kinds of things do you write?

Maddox: I like to write a draft.

Interviewer: What do you write about?

Maddox: I write about elephants.

Interviewer: So, you like to write about elephants. What do you like about elephants?

Maddox: It's because they can drink the water.

Interviewer: Right! Through their long trunks. That's right.

Maddox's discussion of his writing practices at school indicates an understanding of writing as a process, including the need for drafts. His discussion of elephants also places animals as a central topic of interest—common for children in lower elementary grades. Maddox did not indicate using his Chromebook for writing, which was corroborated by the lower elementary teachers.

Younger students' preference for reading physical books and writing with paper and pencil rather than digitally with their school-issued Chromebooks and iPads was reiterated by Marco, a second grader in Ms. Wezner's classroom:

Interviewer: Thinking about reading on paper or on a computer, which do you like better?

Marco: Paper because it is almost the same thing as reading on a computer but without a screen.

Interviewer: What do you like about reading with paper better?

Marco: It's much easier for me to read on paper because sometimes when I read a lot, like looking at a screen too long, my eyeballs a little bit hurt.

As we found in our prior reading intervention research, eye strain was a common reason given by students who preferred to read on paper compared to digitally.[10] Marco's preference for reading on paper is unsurprising, given these sensory barriers.

LLT practices in upper grades: Maya In the upper grades, reading was done either using physical books or digitally with Epic, educational technology software installed on school-issued Chromebook laptops (see appendix B). Maya describes LLT practices common in her fourth-grade classroom with Ms. Gomez:

Maya: I read on paper, like the "Steps into Reading." I usually just start at the beginning and then work my way to the end.

Interviewer: And do you read on computers in the classroom, or is it mostly paper?

Maya: Mostly just paper. Sometimes computer.

Interviewer: When you sometimes do it on the computer, is it a specific program?

Maya: It's "Get Epic," I think.

Interviewer: Can you tell me a little about what that is?

Maya: It's technically a website that has almost all the books, and I usually just read on there if I don't have the [paper] book.

Interviewer: Is that usually independent reading, like during centers and things like that?

Maya: Usually. We don't really do it often.

In this example, Maya mentions the infrequent use of digital technologies in the classroom for reading that we observed at FVA. Moreover, Maya reiterates the functional and secondary nature of students' digital technology use by discussing her use of Epic as a last resort should the physical paper version of the book not be available. In the following passage, Maya provides her reasons for preferring to read physical books rather than digitally:

Maya: I like reading with paper.

Interviewer: Can you tell me why?

Maya: Yeah. Because I can just turn a page and then I can just read.

Interviewer: So, you like being able to turn the pages?

Maya: Yeah. I also like looking down [the page] instead of looking forward [at a screen].

Interviewer: Looking down instead of looking forward? Why?

Maya: Because it's just calming.

Here, Maya is adamant about her preference for reading physical books over reading digitally on her Chromebook. She indicates feeling more comfort (looking down rather than forward), enjoying the tangible "feel" of holding a physical book while reading, as well as the physiological calm that Maya gets from manually turning pages in a paper book. From Maya's perspective, the benefits of reading physical books let her know where she stands as a reader in the course of moving through a book or passage. These sentiments were also expressed by students who preferred reading with physical books, particularly those who identified as being confident and proficient readers, as Maya did, in our study of the affordances of a digital reading intervention on students' reading practices.[11]

Digital technology use for writing in the upper grades included a more active integration of Google Workspace word-processing software (see appendix B) installed on students' Chromebooks, particularly for the final editing and revision phases of writing. As a result, we observed more positive responses to using Google Workspace word-processing software for writing in the upper grades, in contrast to the less positive responses for reading digitally, as described here by Maya:

Interviewer: Can you tell me a little bit about what writing looks like in your classroom?

Maya: Okay. First, we just write in our journals. If we're writing, we're usually doing a project. Then, we would put the first draft, and then the next draft, and then the final draft. I did a writing in January last month about how to make French toast.

Interviewer: When you do the writing, are you writing by hand or on the computer?

Maya: First, we start writing with pencil, and then, for our final draft, we do the computer.

Interviewer: Okay. Do you like writing by hand better or with the computer better?

Maya: Computer.

Interviewer: Can you tell me why?

Maya: Because I can memorize the keys with only a push of one button.

Maya's description of the affordances of writing digitally was typical of what our upper elementary student interviewees reported. Moreover, an increase in students' use of digital technologies to support the writing process, particularly as it relates to the revision process, was reported in the upper elementary grades. Increased usage also corresponded with an increased preference for writing with digital technologies in the upper grades. For Maya specifically, her preference for writing with digital word-processing software installed on her Chromebook laptop centered on ease and convenience, in this case the ability to produce a digital script with "only a push of one button," an affordance commonly given by students who prefer digital writing.[12]

Interestingly, student preference for reading and writing with digital technologies was sometimes at odds with teacher and parent preferences. We saw this with the teacher responses above, and we will see it again below in parents' descriptions of students' LLT practices at home. The mismatch observed at FVA between teacher, parent, and student interests and preferences for using digital technologies to support reading and writing practice is not uncommon and indicates a need for professional development, technical assistance, and support for school communities to institutionalize integrated approaches for using digital technologies to support students' LLT practices more fully.[13]

Supporting LLT Practices at Home

In this subsection, we shift to discuss LLT practices in the home. We analyzed parent and student interviews to identify the ways that parents reported cultivating LLT practices at home to support their children's schooling. This exploration included family home LLT practices broadly, with a focus on parents' LLT practices to support their children both with and without disabilities.

Concerted Cultivation of LLT practices: Mira and Hilda

Family interviewees—the majority of whom were middle- and working-class families of color—were very intentional in their cultivation of LLT practices and routines at home to support their children's growth and learning. This was partly due to our purposive participant sampling (see appendix A) as well as FVA's strong school culture, which required parents to commit to supporting their children's learning actively in and out of school (see chapter 4).

Commonly reported LLT practices included utilizing resources found in community spaces, such as public libraries, to support their children's literacy development as detailed by Mira, mother to neurotypical Maya, Marco, and Maddox, at FVA:

> We try to go to the library at least once or twice a week and I have them do their homework and pick out some books. And sometimes, we bring them home and read them. They love to read books . . . Maya, she reads on her own, and I try to encourage her to read before bedtime. It kind of makes her calm and fall asleep easier. So, she always reads on her own, and it's not like a daily thing a couple of times a week. I'll try to push it every day. I'll say, "Did you read?" And then, Marco likes to read on his own. He actually just started wanting to read independently. Before, it would be like, "Will you read this to me?" And I still do. I'll still read him books. Like Maddox, I read to him all the sight words in the book. I point them out, and he'll try to sound the sight words. If I see a sight word, I just stop and I say, "What's this word?"

We noticed a focus on reading not just for academic advancement but also for pleasure among the upper- and middle-class families of color we interviewed. We also noticed an explicit focus on structured routines—for example, the incorporation of independent and joint reading in bedtime rituals. Routines and practices in upper- and middle-income families also included the integration of intentional reading strategies (i.e., sight word memorization, letter-sound correspondence) indicative of the funds of knowledge around literacy best practices that this subset of our family interviewees had developed. Families' intentional cultivation of their children's learning experiences at home reflected FVA's school culture and messaging focused on literacy practices being formative and engaging experiences.

Reading for academic advancement as home literacy practice was also frequently reported among the working-class immigrant families we interviewed. The focus of reading was not as much for pleasure as it was to reinforce academic subjects learned in school as well as to supplement the perceived lack of homework, which was deemed extremely important by the immigrant families we interviewed. In the following excerpt, Hilda describes her supplementation in relation to what she perceives as a lack of sufficient homework for her two boys, one with and one without disabilities. Hilda said she was quite perplexed initially by the lack of homework, as homework was the norm at the boys' prior school and a very common form of academic supplementation in Mexico:

> ¡No hay tarea! Los pongo hacer otras cosas como leer un libro. ¡Necesito que estén haciendo algo! No solo viendo la tele.

> They don't assign homework! So, I give them additional things to do like reading a book. I need them to be engaged! Not just watching TV.

Hilda iterates a strong push, grounded in Mexican culture, always to be working—work being morally rooted as signaling a disciplined commitment to serving the higher purpose of taking care of one's family and, by extension, one's community.[14] Promoting a good work ethic is central to Mexican sociocultural norms and is an important component of the moral support for schooling that parents offer their children from an early age.[15]

Moreover, Hilda shared that she despised the idea of her children being unproductive. She wanted to use academics, specifically reading books, both to advance her children's learning and to keep them busy and productive at home and "no solo viendo la tele." Hilda's perspectives on the value of productivity in relation to academic success were reiterated by another Mexican mother, Sara, whose story we discuss in greater detail in chapter 6.

Families' intentional literacy supplementation at home was evident in all our interviews, regardless of socioeconomic status. However, the incorporation of technology toward this endeavor was reported more frequently in the upper- and middle-class families. This digital equity gap was largely due to issues of both access and knowledge, indicative in Hilda's brief response to our questions regarding the role technology played in supporting literacy at home:

> Disculpa, pero no hay computadora en la casa y no se como usarla. ¿Es necesario tener computadora para la escuela?

> I'm sorry, but we don't have a computer at home, and I don't know how to use one. Is it necessary to have a computer for school?

Hilda apologized for her lack of computer knowledge and not being able to answer our questions about digital technologies. Hilda experienced issues of access related to both a lack of connectivity and devices and limited knowledge in how to navigate digital applications, devices, and tools. Unfortunately, a lack of support in gaining access to digital technologies for

Amplifying Student Voice

academic and social purposes can preclude historically marginalized families and communities from securing the resources they need to meet the twenty-first-century demands of living in the United States.[16]

Hilda also confided that the family did not have money to buy a computer and was worried that the lack of digital resources at home could negatively impact her children's schooling. In response to her question regarding the need for a computer at home to support schooling, I explained in Spanish that as children progress into the upper elementary grades, they are increasingly asked to use computers with access to the Internet to write papers and conduct research for projects. Upon hearing this, Hilda stated that she would start "ahorrando poco a poco" (saving [money] little by little) to buy a computer for her children eventually.

However, despite having limited financial and technological resources, Hilda was incredibly resourceful in using her linguistic funds of knowledge, as well as local community resources, to support her children's literacy practices at home, as she describes here:

> Los niños tienen colecciones completas: *Cat in the Hat*, *Dog Man*. Les digo, "te lo compro si lo vas a leer." Y vamos a la biblioteca para los que no puedo [comprar]. Al chiquito, le invento porque no leo en inglés. ¡Ahora me corrige! Con el grande, también leo. El me lo lee. Al chiquito, le gusta "books on tape" y "CDs."

> The boys have complete collections: *Cat in the Hat*, *Dog Man*. I tell them, "I'll buy it for you if you'll read it." And for books I can't afford, we go to the library. With the little one, I invent stories because I don't read in English. And now he corrects me! I also read with the older one. He reads to me. The little one likes books on tape and CDs.

Hilda used free resources from the library to expand her children's literacy activities and to cultivate her family's engagement with reading, using the gifting of books as rewards for consistent reading routines. And while Hilda confessed to not having a computer at home, she used other low-cost technologies, such as CD and cassette-tape players, to listen to audiobooks and CDs borrowed from the library.

Hilda leveraged her children's linguistic funds of knowledge as bilingual Spanish-English speakers to engage in joint reading of English language books. She also used her own linguistic resources as a Spanish speaker to engage in imaginative storytelling, using illustrations in English language books as guides with the youngest boy, who was still an emerging reader in both languages. Hilda's use of community resources to access books, as well as her use of linguistic sources of knowledge, are indicative of the ways that many working-class multilingual families engage in the concerted cultivation of their children's education.[17]

Using Digital Technologies to Support LLT Practices

For upper- and middle-class families at FVA, educational technologies to support literacy skills development, including the use of educational websites and applications on mobile or laptop devices, were very common. Here, Mira describes her use of Lexia and Prodigy (see appendix B) to support her children's literacy skills at home: "I did get the Lexia program for home for all three of them because I know what they're doing [at FVA] is great, and they're getting a lot. But I just wanna supplement, right? I got that program and I try to push them to do it at least a couple hours a week. Just to try to get them off from the other games to do more educational stuff." Mira's focus in using educational applications was to reinforce the literacy skills being developed at FVA. As such, the majority of our upper- and middle-class families used multiple devices in the home, including mobile phones, tablets, and laptop computers, to access educational applications, websites, and videos to supplement their children's schooling.

The parents often indicated a belief that it was their responsibility to provide additional support outside of school and to continue the process of learning at home, as Mira describes here: "[Lexia] has to be done on the laptop, and I have a sticker chart for them. So, every time that they spend thirty minutes on it, they get to put a sticker on their sticker chart. I try to encourage them too. Maya doesn't like doing all the reading. Marco is totally into it. Loves it. Maddox as well. He likes it." In upper- and middle-class homes like Mira's, LLT practices and routines incorporated independent usage of digital educational applications, such as Lexia, to supplement FVA's school curriculum. Digital technology use was intentionally promoted in tandem with developing good study habits (i.e., using sticker chart/rewards system) to keep track of, and reward, children's' LLT activities at home.

Additionally, the majority of middle- and upper-class families interviewed made it a point to distinguish between the different forms of technology they used in their home routines, including Dina, mother to third grader James and kindergartener Daniel: "So, we're constantly getting information through our phone. We also have a home computer that James uses to do Smarty Ants on or just learning activities. When he feels like he has to

Amplifying Student Voice

do something on his iPad, we encourage that he does Smarty Ants first, and then he can have fun time on his iPad. iPad for him usually means video games [laughs], but in regard to supporting learning, I would say the home computer is more for that." In this example, Dina intentionally divides the uses of technology in her household, with the desktop computer being used for academic (i.e., Smarty Ants; see appendix B) and research purposes. Mobile and tablet technologies, such as the iPad, were more likely to be positioned as a source of fun and relaxation, including activities for information seeking (news) and fun (video games). Also significant was Dina's prioritizing her children's digital device use for academic purposes before recreation—a prioritization that was reported by parents across most of our family interviews. Families' differentiated technology use across contexts is consistent with findings of differentiated technology use among families.[18]

In our interviews with students, the most popular devices for accessing digital content were mobile devices and tablets. Video gaming, particularly dance/movement, educational, and fantasy-based games, were the most popular, as described by James, Dina's third-grade son:

Interviewer: Do you use things such as iPads or phones, and how do you use those?

James: I have an iPad, and I go on it mostly. But not for learning.

Interviewer: That's okay. Can you tell me what you use it for?

James: I use it for playing. I play some of my games, and I played this song game.

Interviewer: Oh, what's the song game?

James: You tap on the screen toward the jump, and then the more you go further into the level, the more harder it's gonna get.

Interviewer: Do you remember what it's called so that I can look it up?

James: Geometry Dash Meltdown

James's recreational use of the family iPad was an example of how technologies were used differentially, with tablets and mobile devices used primarily for recreational engagement and desktop and laptop computers for academic purposes, such as homework completion and writing tasks. Marco, Mira's second-grade son, elaborates on his reasoning for differentiating his use of digital technologies for different purposes: "I like to use my phone. But I also like to use a computer because when I use a phone to use a website, it's not really that easy. If I use a computer or a laptop, it's much easier to use a website because it's really hard to see it [on a phone]. It's a smaller screen. I like to watch videos and play games on my phone. But on the computer, I like to use websites." Marco's explanation of his differentiated technology use illustrates how accessibility and convenience play a significant role in users' decisions of how and when to use technologies for various purposes.[19] Accessibility features as a determinant of technology use—in this case, smaller screens in mobile technologies making research and academic activities via the Internet more difficult—is a common finding in research examining uses of technology. As such, feasibility and ease of use are determining factors in how families use digital technologies.[20]

Supporting Disabled Children's LLT Practices at Home: Dina, Noah, and Madeline

An important aspect of our ethnographic work at FVA was documenting the LLT practices that families from diverse backgrounds engaged in to support children with disabilities identified as having moderate-to-substantial support needs on their IEPs. Toward this endeavor, we discuss interview findings from two representative family interviews: the first with Dina and Noah, a working-middle-class couple of Mexican and Pacific Islander descent with two sons at FVA, and the second with Madeline, an upper-middle-class mother of Filipina descent with one daughter at FVA. Dina and Noah's sons are James, a neurotypical third grader without an IEP in Ms. Wezner's classroom, and Daniel, a kindergartener with Down syndrome and an IEP outlining substantive accommodations in Ms. Macias's classroom. Madeline's daughter, Star, is a second grader with Down syndrome with an IEP outlining moderate accommodations in Ms. Ohlin's classroom.

Dina and Noah's family, like all the households we interviewed, demonstrate many of the LLT practices often reported by upper- and middle-class families with neurotypical children. These include parents intentionally having, and making visible, their own reading routines to their children, as well as having a variety of books available at home, as Dina shared with us:

> As far as what we do at home, books are accessible. I've always made it a point to have a bookshelf that's loaded—just something that they can grab . . . Like if we go to the swap meet, I love going to the one that has the books because I could

Amplifying Student Voice

literally spend probably two hours picking out good books that I like. I love going to bookstores. I'm inspired by story. So, I plan to grow our library with time. Reading is just really strong within myself. And I know my husband enjoys reading too. I want for my kids and my grandkids, and any kid who comes to my house, to know that we love books.

Madeline also reiterated literacy practices at home that were similar to what Dina and other parents reported. These included promoting a joy of reading, engaging in extracurricular reading and writing activities, and utilizing outside resources, such as a community tutor who we will refer to as Ms. Jones:

> She loves reading. So, we have a lot of books. Star loves homework. So, I have those Ms. Jones [workbooks]. Have you heard of Ms. Jones? She has a system for teaching kids with Down syndrome. At Costco, they sell the kindergarten and first-grade [workbooks], and we just go through those. She could literally do homework twenty-four hours a day. I have to tell her "no" sometimes [laughs]. But yeah, a lot of reading and writing at home. Sometimes [for homework], I'll write a sentence. I'll ask her questions. She gives me an answer. I write out her words, or the sentence, and she copies it.

Engaging in writing practices at home, including the use of sentence frames to support Star's writing and homework completion, as well as accessing reading and writing materials designed for children with Down syndrome, were strategies Madeline used to support Star's literacy development. Incidentally, Dina also mentioned in her interview that she too used Ms. Jones' materials, and both Madeline and Dina indicated that their participation in resource communities for families of children with Down syndrome was quite strong.

In our interviews with upper-, middle-, and lower-income families of color, we found the intentional cultivation of literacy practices to be commonly reported across socioeconomic status. This is in line with prior research examining the concerted cultivation practices of diverse families.[21] Family literacy habits and traditions, such as engaging in and cultivating a love of reading, extend to include children's diverse families of varying socioeconomic backgrounds with and without disability.

Like Mira's family reported above, Dina and Madeline prioritized and monitored their children's technology use to promote learning, not uncommon in middle-class households with multiple digital devices.[22] Dina and Madeline's prioritization of device use for learning was a prerequisite for their children to have access to devices for recreation—a reported practice among the majority of families we interviewed. Here, Madeline discusses how she monitors Star's and her older brother's access to the family's iPad devices: "She's learned a lot from it, but we have no iPads during the week, only on the weekends . . . I think for her, it's more innocent. Whereas my son, it's YouTube. We have to watch him now . . . But for her, it's all innocent: nursery rhymes and Baby Shark." Monitoring of devices and worries about children's use, particularly for older children and children with disabilities, is a common parent concern.[23] With that said, for the majority of parents interviewed, these concerns were coupled with a positive belief in the potential for using digital technologies, particularly educational technology applications, to support children's LLT practices.

Presuming Competence in Supporting Disabled Children's LLT Practices

During our interviews with Dina, Noah, and Madeline, we also discovered a need to discuss misconceptions, particularly those related to academic outcomes, held about their children. Children with Down syndrome, a genetic condition in which a person is born with three copies of chromosome 21 instead of two, often have physical and intellectual differences across a wide range of abilities.[24] By law, children with Down syndrome are protected under the IDEA and are entitled to supports and accommodations as typically outlined in an IEP (see chapters 1 and 2).

Misconceptions about the literacy practices of children with Down syndrome and their caregivers abound, including the perception that children with Down syndrome cannot read and write.[25] Tied to these misconceptions is the idea that children with Down syndrome are less interested or able to engage in practices that support their literacy development.[26] Dina sought to dispel this myth in her discussion of Daniel's love of reading:

> For Daniel, he loves to pick up a book and say, "I'm going to read you a story." And even though we're not articulating the words on the page, he's able to point to the illustration and tell me a little bit about it. And he knows how to start the book. He'll read it, and then he'll close it and say, "The end" [laughs] . . . For me, it's having fun with it, you know? It's not necessarily making it a heavy chore. We do need to read twenty minutes a day, but if he's more happy about doing it, then I'll [read with him] as long as he's excited.

Dina not only shares Daniel's enjoyment of reading but also points out how his knowledge of narratives and storytelling conventions—crucial early literacy skills—make his participation in joint reading practices possible. Dina

Amplifying Student Voice 101

and Daniel's attitudes and approaches toward joint reading and reading for pleasure align with literacy practices we know to be effective in supporting children's reading development and engagement.[27]

Dina and Noah explained that Daniel's enthusiasm for reading extended to his desire to complete his homework. They described how Daniel viewed his brother James as a role model, an effective motivator that Daniel's family used to support meeting his homework goals:

Dina: Daniel is very eager. He's very excited when he gets homework. He mimics everything his brother does. He sees us consistently with James [and] his homework. He wants to be a part of that too. I don't have to talk him into checking his backpack and showing me what's there. He gets very excited, "I have homework!" and we'll sit down.

Noah: Dina will sit with him, and he'll actually do it. He'll stay engaged the whole time. And he'll answer questions. If she says something, he'll listen and respond back to her. He'll finish it [laughs].

Peer modeling is useful for all children, particularly those with developmental and cognitive disabilities, in supporting the noticing, developing, and practicing of academic and social routines and behaviors.[28] As discussed in chapter 4, peer modeling as an inclusive support strategy was widely used within FVA's classrooms, with many students carrying the practice home. The ability to ask and answer questions about one's own work, as Noah reported Daniel doing with Dina, is an effective strategy for engaging with academic content.[29]

Dispelling myths about what their son Daniel could and could not do was very important to Noah and Dina—something they indicated having to do constantly with family and friends. This came through in the examples that Noah and Dina gave of Daniel's and their family's practices, as well as in the language they used to describe Daniel's accomplishments—for example, when Noah said "and he'll actually do it"—as if beseeching us, the researchers, to suspend misconceptions we might have of Daniel's abilities or competence.

Similar to Dina and Noah, Madeline was also eager to dispel myths about her daughter Star's literacy abilities: "I know she'll always be not at the same 'level,' but what she has just learned in this year and a half is amazing. I mean, I'm shocked at times because she's reading. She's picking up a book, and she's sounding out the words. If she doesn't know it, she'll ask me. I would say 95% of her sight words, she knows. We're working on math with her, and her art is amazing. Her dancing, it's amazing." Madeline, Dina, and Noah's belief in their children's abilities and competencies echoed Ms. Wezner and Ms. Gomez's sentiments about presuming competence, believing all students can succeed when given opportunities to do so (see chapter 4). Madeline shared her experiences with the lack of presumed competence as informing her decision to move Star to FVA:

> I was in the back of my mind thinking about sending, or actually advocating, at her school. Back then, she was going to Warner Elementary, which is a public school. And I was thinking about asking them to change her education goals because I noticed she was very bright . . . This girl sitting next to me at [a Down syndrome conference] told me about FVA, and she said, "You know it's open. You just have to sign up and win the lotto." And we did, and we got in! This is her second year here, and she's doing great. I mean, socially, she's always got along with everyone, but educationally, she's reading!

Madeline echoes Ms. Wezner's observations from chapter 4, reflecting on presumptions schools make that children with moderate-to-substantive support needs are incapable of learning in general education classroom settings and are best served in segregated classroom environments. This belief, as explained by Ms. Wezner, is prevalent among teachers and schools.[30] Both Madeline's and Dina's commentaries reflect the view that supporting their children's growth and engagement centers on presuming competence.

Parents' active cultivation of their children's LLT practices supported a necessary relationship between presumed competence and opportunity and was integral to extending FVA's vision of inclusion to families. Parent commentary also pointed to the leap of faith that families at FVA take in advocating for the full inclusion of their children. As demonstrated by Dina, Noah, and Madeline, this leap of faith included believing in their children's abilities to achieve levels of success that extending beyond preprescribed notions of what disabled students can and cannot do.

Supporting Disabled Children as Creators and Writers: Star and Finn

In addition to discussing observed and reported LLT practices at school and home, we were also interested in exploring how the integration of physical and digital technologies might empower disabled students' agency and

Amplifying Student Voice

voice. Moreover, we were interested in understanding disabled students' own perceptions of themselves as creators and writers, as well as staff perceptions of the affordances of technology to support students' writing in the classroom. In this section, we focus on the stories of Star and her classmate Finn, an autistic second grader of European descent.

Using Multimodality to Support Expression: Star

Multimodality refers to interactions between multiple modes of expression (i.e., artistic, literary, and written) across diverse media.[31] Multimodality mediates how we communicate and express ourselves as creators.[32] In *Giving Voice*, Alper argues that children's creation and consumption of diverse media afford alternative avenues for communication and expression. For children with disabilities, access to multiple modes of content representation afford diversified opportunities for fuller expression as creators.[33] This became evident when we interviewed Star, as she was very eager to share her interests, including how she used her writing and drawing abilities to express herself. In prefacing my interview with Star, her mother Madeline indicated that Star was performing near grade level. I corroborated with Star's teacher, Ms. Ohlin, that she was doing well in the general education setting and was a very engaged member of her class.

Prior to the interview, Madeline offered to help facilitate, stating that people new to Star sometimes had difficulty understanding her articulation. As a result, Madeline's facilitation is reflected in the conversations below. The first thing Star did during our interview was show me a birthday card that she had drawn, depicting herself with her father (figure 5.1), which we discussed at great length:

Interviewer: Thank you so much for talking with me, Star. Can you tell me about the picture that you drew?

Star: Yeah. I draw my daddy. I love my daddy.

Interviewer: Your house?

Star: Yeah. I went swimming with my dad.

Interviewer: Is this a birthday?

Madeline: What is this honey?

Star: Birthday.

Figure 5.1
Star's hand-drawn picture for her daddy.

Madeline: Who is this for?

Star: Daddy.

Madeline: Oh, it's for daddy? Is this his birthday card?

Star: Yeah.

Interviewer [Reading the card out loud]: "'I love you daddy' by Star." This is beautiful!

It was clear that Star viewed herself as a creator and enjoyed using her art and writing as visual forms of personal expression. Star used her art to express her love for her dad and for her preferred activities (i.e., swimming with dad). Star's birthday card to her father was on par with the forms of visual and written self-expression that younger elementary-aged children in the early stages of literacy tend to engage in.[34]

Star's use of writing to express her emotional world and share her connection with others was also evident when asked what she liked best about school:

Star: I like writing.

Interviewer: You like writing? Why?

Star: I write about my daddy and my mommy.

Interviewer: Lovely! . . . So, you like that you get to write?

Star: Yeah.

Interviewer: How do you feel when you write?

Star: Happy.

In Star's response, we see that she views herself as a writer, and she sees writing as a source of personal joy—giving writing the power to amplify our identities as creators.[35] Star's intentional choice to write about her mother and father, the two most important people in her world, is a nuanced and thoughtful move to create connection and express love for others that dispels myths about the emotional worlds of children with disabilities.

Using Digital Tools to Expand Writing: Finn

Initial observations of how Finn, a minimally speaking autistic second grader, used digital tools to support his writing led to exploring assistive uses of mainstream digital technologies in the classroom. Observed assistive uses of digital technologies for writing at FVA included the use of speech-to-text and spell-check functions in word-processing applications such as Google Docs (see chapter 3 and appendix B). General and special education teachers, with paraprofessionals' support, managed assistive uses of these applications on students' Chromebook and iPad tablet devices.

Following classroom observations, we reached out to Finn's mother, Blake, an English-speaking upper-middle-class woman of European descent, for an interview. However, when we attempted to interview Finn, he was apprehensive about speaking with us, which led to Blake offering to facilitate the interview. Blake's facilitation is reflected in the excerpt below. Congruent with classroom observations, Finn's preference for engaging in literacy activities using both mainstream and educational technology tools and applications was reflected in his interview:

Blake: What kinds of things do you like to read or write about? Do you have a favorite story or book?

Finn: I like to read the book *Up*, and I like writing about movies.

Blake: Do you use computers for reading and writing? What is your favorite thing to do on the computer?

Finn: Read on Epic.

Blake: How do you feel about reading and writing? Do you like reading and writing with paper or with computers better?

Blake: Happy. I like computers better.

Finn indicates that reading with Epic, an interactive digital reader app that affords both "read to me" and the independent reading options of high-interest-leveled readers (see appendix B), was his favorite thing to do on the computer. When asked about writing, Finn also indicated a preference for using his computer to read and write, using "happy" to describe his positive feelings toward engaging in literacy practices with his computer.

How Finn felt about using technology for his reading and writing was corroborated in both classroom observations and staff reflections, and revealed how Finn, and students with similar support needs, responded to integrating digital technologies into their writing practice. For Finn and for students with similar support needs, the sensory act of writing with pencil and paper can prove to be difficult (see chapter 3). Transitioning to writing using his Chromebook device, with the allowance of the Google Docs speech to text and other accessibility functions, allowed Finn to improve both the quality and content of his writing. Finn's use of mainstream digital technologies afforded him an opportunity to mediate his writing experience positively, freeing him to focus on content generation and expression of voice rather than the mechanics of writing.[36]

In Ms. Carina's view, the affordances created by incorporating assistive uses of mainstream digital features and tools, such as speech to text, into students' writing practices were instrumental to creating a motivating learning environment for students to engage in writing:

> One of the ways that it really helped a lot of the students was [with speech to text]. We had a student in particular who just, he would get really overwhelmed when it came to writing. He couldn't form the words together. He would get frustrated really easily. So, the way that we helped him with technology is we introduced him to speech to text. And so, he was able to calmly share a story, tell us what he wanted to say, and then we would go through it together and edit it. We'd sit there and comfort him. Like, "Oh, you're doing great. Should that be capitalized?" So, he would [revise] after that because he saw it written out. It was like, "Okay, I'm halfway there." So, he was able to keep going.

Ms. Carina saw the use of technology to support writing as empowering for students. This was particularly true for students with developmental disabilities like Finn, who benefit from additional support in the writing and revision process. For these students, the use of digital tools supported participation. Ms. Carina's view was shared by other paraprofessionals, including Ms. Sandy and Mr. Gabriel, with whom Ms. Carina constantly communicated regarding students' progress. Next steps for the paraprofessionals included sharing observations and intentionally incorporating digital tools into other students' writing practices:

> After we saw that it was successful, we noticed a kid in Ms. Gomez's class. He was also having trouble and started using speech to text. And that helped him a lot too . . . He was able to write more than he typically would. I mean, the detail, he was able to include more details. So, the quality of his writing was better as well. And then just overall him feeling successful too. He didn't completely hate writing. He wasn't crumpling his papers and throwing them away. He was like, "All right, let's get to it."

The ability to write more, with greater quality and detail, using digital technologies, as observed by Ms. Carina, has been established in the literature (see chapter 3).[37] In this case, emerging writers were able to use the word-processing features in Google Docs to support and facilitate the editing and revision process, alleviating cognitive and physical strain.[38]

Studying the supports provided by paraprofessionals such as Ms. Carina, in tandem with disabled students' own perspectives and practices, affords insight into how to support disabled students in sharing a fuller picture of themselves as readers and writers. This includes supporting the use of assistive features in digital technologies to afford alternative means of textual expression and to facilitate students' agency, engagement, and inclusion in the classroom.

Supporting Linguistic Expression Using Assistive Technologies

In this section, we analyze how minimally speaking students at FVA used assistive technologies and tools to express themselves and connect with their school community. Assistive technologies and tools for communication are technologies that support students' linguistic expression to share thoughts and feelings, make requests, and solicit or give information (see chapter 3 and appendix B).[39] At FVA, assistive technologies ranged from low tech to high tech.[40] At FVA, low tech included the use of behavior charts and visual calendars to support and reinforce classroom behavior. High-tech tools at FVA included the use of LAMP and Proloquo2GO AAC applications downloaded onto iPad tablets assigned to minimally speaking students. PECS was also a common low- to mid-tech assistive technology used at FVA.

Ms. Davis managed these AAC interventions with the support of Ms. Alexa and Ms. Blaire, a graduate student completing her practicum for the SLPA designation at FVA. Providers were also supported by the special education teachers Ms. Severin and Ms. Haberly, an English-speaking teacher of European descent in her second year of teaching, as well as paraprofessionals. Below, we discuss how staff supported students in their use of assistive technologies at FVA, specifically those utilizing AAC to support linguistic expression.

First, we discuss how Conrad, a minimally speaking second grader with Down syndrome in Ms. Ohlin's classroom, uses LAMP to negotiate interactions with his classmates. Then, we discuss how Santiago, a minimally speaking first grader with Down syndrome in Ms. Macias's classroom, uses PECS to collaborate with peers during literacy centers. Finally, we discuss how Tammy, a nonspeaking fourth grader with Down syndrome in Ms. Gomez's classroom, uses Proloquo2Go to make her participation visible in classroom discussions. We also use Tammy's case to explore how students' assistive technology use impacted teachers' understanding of student competency and voice, as well as efforts to presume competence.

Negotiating Embodiment of Voice with LAMP: Conrad

Observations of Conrad's use of LAMP for iPad with his peers revealed the kinds of interactions minimally speaking students navigate in their use of high-tech AAC devices in the classroom. For Conrad, negotiating the use of LAMP on his iPad was complicated by the social allure that iPads hold, which can sometimes detract from their use as communication devices.[41] This resulted in issues of boundaries around use, as seen in the following observation of a guided reading lesson facilitated by Ms. Severin:

> Ms. Severin's guided reading group includes both Star and Conrad. Star decodes her book as Ms. Severin uses her pen to help her track her eyes. Ms. Severin then moves to Conrad and begins a picture walk of the drawings that Conrad made for his book. Star moves next to Conrad and grabs his iPad. Ms. Severin immediately

responds, "You need to ask Conrad if you can use his voice. Conrad, can Star touch it?" Conrad shakes his head [no], and Star gives the iPad back to him.

Negotiating boundaries in the use of Conrad's AAC device (i.e., his iPad) centered on two elements: first, defining Conrad's "voice" as embodied by his AAC device, and second, deciding whether others were allowed to partake in the embodiment of Conrad's voice—in other words, use his device. Debate continues as to whether others should be allowed to use AAC devices dedicated to specific users—particularly if these devices are being situated as that person's voice.[42] Variations in whether voice should be limited to one or multiple bodies evidenced itself as boundary shifts in how voice was both interpreted and embodied among Conrad and his classmates. These tensions revealed themselves as students negotiated their engagement with Conrad and his iPad during the remainder of the lesson:

> Conrad types "Finish banana best" into his iPad. Star leans over and adds "little" to form "Finish banana best little." Star takes Conrad's iPad again, and Isabelle, another classmate, exclaims, "Star touched his iPad!" Ms. Severin responds, "Star needs to ask Conrad . . . We are going to get a second iPad for us to touch so Conrad will have his and we will have ours . . . For now, let's leave it for Conrad." Ms. Severin hands the iPad back to Conrad, who continues typing, while Isabelle sits between him and Star. Star returns to her own work.

Negotiations and tensions in the use of Conrad's iPad between students reveals his device to be a site where "identity and personhood are negotiated."[43] Whereas Star's interest may be situated in both the utility and novelty of the device—not necessarily viewing it as an embodiment of Conrad's voice—Isabelle appeared to view Star's use of Conrad's device as a violation of his personhood. This belief is reinforced by Ms. Severin's affirmation that, yes, Conrad's iPad is his voice: if the class wants to communicate via a device, they need to get an additional iPad to do so. From Isabelle's and Ms. Severin's viewpoints, voice embodies individual personhood and needs to be bounded as one person, one voice, one device.[44]

Differences among Conrad's classmates about whether and how to engage with him via his iPad device were also evident in the FVA staff's approaches to integrating AAC devices into classroom interactions. In the following excerpt, Ms. Alexa adopts a more fluid approach to engaging with Conrad's iPad compared to Ms. Severin during a different literacy center rotation:

> Ms. Alexa shows Conrad a book of foods and prompts: "Can you tell our friends, 'I want . . .'?" This prompt is directed toward Conrad, who uses his iPad to say, "I want French fries." Ms. Alexa asks each of the students in Conrad's group what they prefer. As the group grows more boisterous with conversation, Ms. Alexa asks for quiet: "I want to hear Conrad." Conrad uses his iPad to say, "I want yogurt." Ms. Alexa takes the iPad from Conrad to show it to his classmates and says, "Conrad chooses yogurt."

In these examples, distinctions about how, and to what extent, others should use students' AAC devices to support classroom engagement and communication are not always clear. As Alper noted in *Giving Voice*, for adults who intensively engage with disabled children, such as caregivers who speak on behalf of and as intermediaries for their children, an integral aspect of advocacy can include embracing the fluidity between bodies and device, entering what she describes as "a liminal state in terms of where one person's body or voice ended, and another's began."[45] For Ms. Alexa, modeling and scaffolding Conrad's communication was of utmost importance and what she was charged to do in Conrad's IEP as his SLPA. This presented as Ms. Alexa adopting a hand-over-hand approach in negotiating the use of Conrad's device by, and with, him.

Supporting Collaborative Peer Communication with PECS: Santiago

Staff were also observed intentionally negotiating the use of assistive technologies to encourage collaboration and communication among students. In the following interaction, Ms. Blaire demonstrates a hand-over-hand approach, similar to Ms. Alexa's, in negotiating the use of Santiago's PECS board between Santiago and his classmates as they selected books for their literacy center:

> Ms. Blaire is helping Santiago, along with six classmates, select books for silent reading. Ms. Blaire shows the students how to use Santiago's PECS board to make requests and has both Santiago and his classmates use the board to discuss the books they are going to read silently. Afterwards, Ella, a classmate, helps Santiago select a book, while another student flips through Santiago's PECS board.

This observation demonstrated how service providers might structure students' use of assistive technologies to leverage peer-to-peer modeling while encouraging communication. Ms. Blaire's intervention supported Santiago's classmates' interest in learning how to use his PECS board to communicate with him. This observation was notable to us, having observed provider interactions in other, often less integrated, classroom settings where PECS and

Amplifying Student Voice

other assistive technologies were used exclusively by disabled students and their designated service providers—a dynamic that can result in disabled students remaining communicatively segregated from their peers.[46]

Inclusive collaboration among Santiago and his classmates in using the PECS board together supports FVA's messaging that *all* forms of communication be equally valued and given space. This also supports the notion that voice transcends the parameters of speech. Moreover, communal use of Santiago's PECS board situates the concept of voice across Alper's fluid "liminal space" of multiple bodies in contrast to the positioning of Conrad's device as singularly his voice.[47]

Making Agency and Participation Visible with Proloquo2Go: Tammy

In the following excerpts, we use Tammy's case to explore how students use their AAC devices to exert agency and make participation visible. Technologies that aid communication hold a charged, non-neutral presence in the classroom because they make visible otherwise marginalized thoughts, feelings, and actions. In other words, technology politicizes voice.[48]

I first met Tammy during the winter of 2020 in FVA's front office prior to the start of that day's classroom observations. Tammy was seated near the front entrance, exploring Proloquo2Go on her iPad. She looked up as I walked into the office and, using Proloquo2Go, introduced herself with a big smile: "Hi, my name is Tammy. I am nine years old." In this brief encounter, Tammy asserted her presence in the office and made visible her personality and energy, using Proloquo2Go to give voice to her thoughts and engage with me.

Later that morning, I got to see how Tammy used Proloquo2Go to support her classroom participation. Ms. Blaire, under Ms. Davis's supervision, was facilitating a whole-group social skills lesson about empathy in Ms. Gomez's classroom. Ms. Blaire began the lesson by providing a definition of empathy on the whiteboard: "Empathy: to imagine how someone might feel, to put yourself in their shoes." This was followed by a social skills video about empathy from Everyday Speech (figure 5.2, appendix B), prior to initiating the following interaction:

Ms. Blaire: Okay, now we are going to do a few scenarios and try to think about how they might feel. If Jose is a new student and doesn't know anyone, how might he feel?

Tammy [using Proloquo2Go]: Nervous.

Ms. Blaire: What do the rest of you think?

Multiple students: Sad, anxious, shy . . .

Ms. Blaire: So, what can we say to him to make him feel better, make him feel included?

Iggy: We can help him meet new people?

Ms. Blaire: What if Ari is having a birthday party and nobody went, how would she feel?

Tammy [using Proloquo2Go]: Sad.

In this classroom discussion, Tammy uses Proloquo2Go to give voice to her thoughts and to share a fuller picture of her emotional world with her teachers and classmates. This interaction makes clear the potential affordances of students' uses of AAC technologies, such as Proloquo2Go, to participate in the classroom.[49] In this example, Tammy uses Proloquo2Go to exert herself as a participant and make visible her opinions and thoughts,

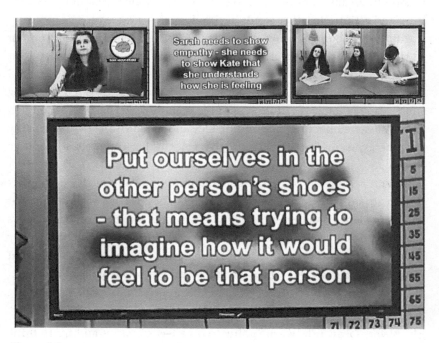

Figure 5.2
Everyday Speech digital social communication and socio-emotional skills video lesson at FVA.

Amplifying Student Voice

113

countering her own marginalization. We see this again in the following lesson in which Ms. Davis supports Tammy in her use of Proloquo2Go to participate in Ms. Blaire's lesson on idioms:

Ms. Blaire: Have you ever heard the term "snug as a bug"?

Tammy [using Proloquo2Go]: No.

Ms. Blaire: "Snug as a bug" means feeling very comfortable, for example under the covers when you go to bed. Last one! "Dead of winter . . ."

Ms. Davis: Tammy, would you like to pick the next speaker?

Tammy [using Proloquo2Go]: I choose Carissa.

Tammy uses Proloquo2Go to make several things known. First, Tammy makes known which content she is and is not familiar with in the lesson. This is important because it allows staff to tailor their instruction better to Tammy's needs. Second, Tammy actively influences the direction of classroom discussion by selecting Carissa, another minimally speaking fourth grader with Down syndrome, as the next speaker. Amplifying students' use of assistive technologies to engage in class discussions, as Tammy does using Proloquo2Go, centers disabled students as agentive participants in their classroom communities as opposed to more commonly positioning disabled people as passive and acted upon.[50]

Empowering Student Voice and Competency: Assistive Technologies as Assets

While I didn't interact with Tammy directly until the winter of 2020, I had heard about her and the progress she was making using Proloquo2Go from staff in the fall of 2019 upon commencing field studies at FVA. Our first observed conversation regarding Tammy's use of Proloquo2Go occurred during a team collaboration meeting. FVA's collaboration meetings, as discussed in chapter 4, are opportunities for community building among staff. Each staff member participates by sharing a success, a challenge, and an action round-robin style.

That day's discussion featured Tammy's introduction to Proloquo2Go. According to staff, Tammy had been excitedly learning to use Proloquo2Go, even taking her iPad home on weekends. The following story, as told by Ms. Sandy and Ms. Gomez, of Tammy creating a sugar skull for Día de los

Muertos illustrates the potential for students' use of assistive technologies to embody and empower student voice:

Ms. Sandy: This skull was filled with beautiful colors, and Tammy found the description tab on her iPad and typed "Pretty."

Ms. Gomez: I said, "Why yes! It is pretty!" to which Tammy typed "Proud."

Ms. Sandy: It just made me realize how much we didn't know about Tammy.

Tammy's experiences using Proloquo2Go to communicate had a profound mediating impact on how staff came to understand her competencies. For Ms. Sandy, this incident afforded a valuable lesson in presuming competence (see chapter 4). Tammy's story presents a compelling example of how, through her use of Proloquo2Go, she was able to give voice to her feelings and thoughts, sharing a fuller picture of herself as a creator with classmates and teachers alike. Tammy's use of Proloquo2Go afforded her alternative means of linguistic expression, allowing her to facilitate her own agency, engagement, and inclusion in the classroom.

As Alper describes, incorporating digital technologies into discourse expands communicative possibilities, affording students additional opportunities to share views of themselves that might otherwise remain invisible within school communities: "In sum, recreational media and technology use can help nonspeaking children reveal a side of themselves that the scientific, medical, and educational communities either do not or choose not to acknowledge . . . This view enables us to imagine a world with greater collective communicative power, for it extends recognition or competence that is often not presumed among children and individuals with communication disabilities."[51] As the examples in this chapter have sought to demonstrate, technologies can be used by students to negotiate the presentation of their ideas and thoughts, reveal their identities and personality, and exert agency and engagement across home and school contexts. Just as important, students can use technologies to demonstrate competence, illuminating funds of knowledge, understanding, and insight to reveal inner worlds that might otherwise remain unobserved. Finally, students can use technologies and tools for figurative and textual expression to engage in multiple forms of expression and share their identities as creators with the world around them. It is with this theme of using technology to cultivate sharing and connection that we now turn to chapter 6.

6 Technology as Connection

Originally, this was going to be a yearlong study focused on classroom observations of in-person instruction, interviews with families and staff, and collection of physical and digital artifacts during the 2019–2020 school year. However, the closure of schools, including FVA, in the spring of 2020 due to the pandemic precipitated changes in our field study. We shifted to remote fieldwork in spring 2020 (see appendix A). At this time, we proceeded with remote communications and interviews via email and Zoom, and we observed asynchronous classroom practice via Google Classroom.

Moving into the 2020–2021 school year, we decided to extend the focus of our research-practice partnership to supporting the immediate emergency remote learning needs of the school. Our assistance included placement of university undergraduate students in three of FVA's four combo-grade classrooms to offer remote learning support. Additionally, we continued chronicling FVA's practices during the 2020–2021 school year through monthly check-ins via Zoom with Dr. Tully, as well as follow-up interviews and member checks with families and staff in the spring of 2021. This formed the basis for the case-study findings we report in this chapter. As a result, this chapter combines analysis of remote interviews and classroom observations collected during the pandemic to examine how FVA used digital technologies to maintain connection throughout the transition to remote and hybrid learning.

Connection at FVA

As we've documented in chapters 4 and 5, FVA maintained a connected, caring school community through the provision of regular, diverse, in-person opportunities to engage students and their families in a prosocial way throughout the fall and winter months of the 2019–2020 school year. However, FVA's high-touch approach to engaging and learning was put in danger during spring 2020 when physical school sites across the country closed due to COVID-19. This chapter discusses the history and context of schooling during the pandemic that resulted in the shift to online remote and hybrid learning that occurred across schools, including FVA, at the end of year 1 (spring 2020) and through year 2 (fall 2020–spring 2021).

In this chapter, we specifically focus on how connection was maintained at FVA during the pandemic and how the transition to emergency remote learning precipitated a shift in how FVA used digital technologies to maintain strong networks within the school. This chapter examines technology as a vehicle for cultivating connection during the period of remote learning brought on by the pandemic, including how technologies were specifically used at FVA to mediate and conserve interdependent connection.

Moreover, this chapter illustrates how motivations for technology use during the pandemic centered on maintaining family support, connection, and inclusion. We also discuss how schools might use digital technologies to mediate connection. This includes exploration of the use of synchronous platforms such as FaceTime, Zoom, and instant messaging, as well as asynchronous uses of platforms such as Google Classroom and YouTube content, to offer support and mitigate isolation as experienced by school communities during the move to emergency remote learning.

Schooling during the COVID-19 Pandemic

In this chapter, we document a history of schooling during the pandemic period spanning from 2020 through 2022. We examine the challenges and affordances of using digital technologies to facilitate schooling across complex remote and hybrid learning environments and lay a foundation for examining how we can address future emergency disruptions in schooling.

Due to the pandemic, social, economic, and academic support usually offered by schools became unavailable to students. For example, in Los Angeles, California, more than 64,000 culturally and linguistically diverse students with disabilities—13 percent of the student population—normally benefit from services exclusively provided by public schools.[1] Tragically, the

Technology as Connection

nation's shift to remote learning resulted in these students being disproportionately impacted by the removal of school supports.[2]

As states across the US responded to the pandemic, the transition of schools to remote learning occurred with little time to plan or implement research-based strategy.[3] This resulted in just-in-time emergency measures aimed at keeping students enrolled and accessing some level of academic content by whatever means schools had at their disposal. For many schools, this initially meant extended breaks with communication between teachers and their students via email and phone. Eventually, this meant distributing one-to-one Chromebooks for families to pick up from school sites so that they could connect with their child's classroom via co-opted video communications platforms, such as Zoom.[4]

As a result of these rapid and improvised shifts, the need to design for learning facilitated by digital technologies in real time during the pandemic created a context entirely distinct from what had come before. Alongside the difficult challenges emerging from school closures, this crisis presented the opportunity to re-envision the role digital technologies could play in inclusive education. Of particular concern in this context are those students most likely to face significant barriers to engaging in meaningful learning through digital formats: young students, students with disabilities, students who are multilingual, and students living in poverty. Addressing the needs of students most likely to face access barriers to meaningful learning through digital formats, as previously discussed, is also of particular concern in this context, while supporting educators and policymakers in the pursuit of maximizing the inclusion of *all* students, has become even more important than ever.

The pandemic also resulted in a reimagined shift in boundaries and roles between parents, teachers, and community members. This included shifts in the rules of engaging in and enacting schooling, as well as shifts across home, school, and community environments as acceptable places of learning. This was made particularly evident with the introduction of remote learning into homes and the cultivation of alternative learning configurations across school communities.[5] Shifts in boundaries and roles in the spring of 2020 benefitted from efforts to scale the use of digital technologies to support alternative schooling modalities for students impacted by the pandemic. For example, community and recreational centers, along with libraries, worked to provide learning hubs and extended childcare support. Tutoring

118   Chapter 6

and enrichment programs also expanded their scope and reach to address the learning gaps resulting from school closures.[6]

In addition to districts partnering at the county, state, and federal level to bring alternative learning solutions integrating digital technologies to scale, individual schools also partnered locally with their Parent–Teacher Associations, community resource centers, and universities to bring customized support to their immediate school communities during the pandemic.[7] One such effort was the Community Education Fellows initiative, which investigated how universities and community partners could equitably take innovative educational efforts, such as learning pods, and partner with schools to make them accessible to a broad range of families.[8]

Emergency Remote Learning at FVA

The shift to emergency remote learning at FVA was disruptive in several ways. First, remote learning placed increased demands on families and staff to manage, support, and cultivate student learning in the absence of direct in-person instruction and support—a daunting challenge amplified by widespread illness, economic instability, work obligations, wide-ranging student needs, and limited access to technology and technical assistance.[9] Second, the sudden nature of the shift did not afford FVA the opportunity to prepare families and staff physically or mentally for the sudden rupture, as Ms. Gomez described to us: "I feel like things are kind of just ripped apart. Like, we were there on Friday, 'See you guys on Monday,' and then the notice after school: 'Hey, there is no school on Monday, it's going to be through the computer.' I feel like that is almost traumatic, you know?" Ms. Gomez used "traumatic" to describe the feelings that she, as well as most staff and families whom we spoke with, felt about the abrupt shift to remote learning. This trauma included, as Ms. Gomez alludes to here, students being separated from each other and from the greater school community.

As we will discuss in this chapter, the physical separation of students from their classmates and teachers significantly impacted their socioemotional states during the pandemic. Trauma was also attributed to the sudden shift to the remote teaching modality, which none of the families or staff had previously encountered. What was also noticed at FVA, and more broadly across schools in the United States, was that the disruption caused by the abrupt move to remote learning also amplified already existing issues of digital equity for families and staff.

These shifts, which occurred throughout the pandemic to varying degrees across US schools, also served to drive what Dr. Tully referred to as an existential crisis. In her view, as she describes below, this existential crisis was a catalyst for many of the changes in both staffing and families at FVA and beyond: "The world is undergoing an existential crisis, it feels like. So, people are making very big changes. Families are moving . . . Staff, are like, 'I'm leaving the field now.' The shifts that I've seen that have been really striking to me are the unpredictability, or the new predictability, of how people will react and behave." As Dr. Tully references, the circumstances of the historical moment school communities found themselves in created a forced reevaluation and prioritization.[10] At FVA, this culminated in shifting boundaries, expectations, and roles, as well as actual economic, geographical, personal, and professional changes in how people reconstructed their lives in the face of uncertainty. FVA, in many ways, reflected the existential changes school communities were undergoing across the United States.[11]

Finally, the move to remote learning also precipitated a shift in teachers reprioritizing essential learning goals for students. Prioritizing essential learning goals in remote learning environments required closely monitoring students to identify core needs and reconsidering traditional content standards. This included encouraging teachers to prioritize manageable curricular areas, content, and skills essential to success in the next grade.[12] Inclusive practice during this period of emergency remote learning also included documenting student progress through formative rather than summative assessment and opting out of a formal grading process—approaches that were considered controversial then and now but have since gained attention and momentum from the "humanizing education" and "ungrading" movements fostered by the pandemic.[13]

Using Digital Technologies to Support Remote Learning

FVA's motivations for technology use during COVID-19 centered on maintaining community support and connection. Mediating connection through digital technologies included innovating new uses of synchronous platforms, such as FaceTime and Zoom (figure 6.1), to meet remote learning

Figure 6.1
A student uses the Zoom platform to participate in remote learning during the pandemic.

needs, professional development, and planning in ways not seen prior to the pandemic.[14]

Supporting Inclusion with Synchronous and Asynchronous Technologies
Synchronous and asynchronous technologies, particularly digital communications media including email, instant messaging, and video, were used to inform families of the different phases of remote learning at FVA. These included phase 1 (100 percent distance learning) in spring 2020, phase 2 (hybrid learning) for particularly high-need students commencing winter 2021, and phase 3 (in-person learning) for everyone starting again in spring 2021.

Technology as Connection

Synchronous and asynchronous digital communications were also used to address barriers to accessing synchronous instruction through Zoom due to unstable wi-fi/technical access gaps, particularly in lower-income households; supporting families in understanding and adjusting to the increased demands of remote schooling as outlined in the Family Distance Learning agreement; and challenges related to childcare and caregiving responsibilities for families who were dependent on in-person schooling and after-school programming as sources of education, enrichment, and supervision for their children.

At FVA, the full inclusion model was adapted to a remote environment by virtually "pushing in" the special education teacher and paraprofessionals into both the general and breakout rooms afforded by the Zoom platform (see appendix B). However, delivering speech and OT services as push-in supports was difficult to do virtually without resorting to stand-alone sessions between providers and students. Inclusion was not violated in the sense that students were not removed from their general education instruction in order to receive their services. However, the approach wasn't fully inclusive by FVA's standards in that students were segregated from each other in the provision of services via the use of stand-alone or breakout rooms.

These digital limitations were not lost on Dr. Tully who, while grateful that synchronous multimedia technologies such as Zoom existed to afford connection while schools were forced to quarantine, also felt that the limitations of technologies impacted the most vulnerable students and offended FVA's instructional philosophy:

> FVA's student population is almost entirely comprised of people who are noted as those that would have the most difficulty and barriers to access learning in a remote format. So, that's young children, people TK through second grade, people with identified disabilities, English language students, lower-income students who don't have secure Wi-Fi or facility with technology. That's basically everybody at our school with few exceptions . . . I think the features that have made it particularly challenging for this school is that our prior instructional format was very intentionally hands-on. Very physically engaged. A lot of close contact among kids. A lot of close talking, partnering, and sharing of materials. So, it really offended our entire instructional philosophy and approach to transition.

Reflecting on the impact of the pandemic on schools, including the burgeoning use of digital technologies to provide instruction, Dr. Tully provides a clear synopsis of why remote learning was particularly difficult for FVA's school population, as well as for schools with similar demographics. As has been retrospectively born out in subsequent media and research reports, the impacts of remote learning have been compounded for marginalized school populations.[15]

With that said, for schools that did not originally use a full inclusion model of instruction, the virtual format created affordances for students who were able to receive services without it impacting their participation in the general education setting, essentially creating inclusion for those students where there was none before by allowing them to participate fully in their regular sessions without the need for service pullouts. In some instances, it also afforded opportunities for services to be pushed in—for example, as Zoom breakout room sessions. These opportunities to support the inclusion of students by avoiding removal from the general education setting via asynchronous uses of digital technologies would not have been conceived in public schools were it not for the shift to remote learning precipitated by the pandemic.

And while the majority of emerging stories to date rightly focus on the challenges inherent in remote learning, a significant number of stories of families who have benefited from remote learning have also begun to surface.[16] These include reports of increased access to services, resources, and events for immunocompromised, lower-income, and homebound individuals who otherwise would have been shut out from participating.[17] While not the focus of this chapter per se, these stories, and the lessons gleaned from them, deserve attention.

Just-in-Time Messaging for Collaboration

Another example of new uses of digital technologies during the pandemic included the synchronous use of FaceTime, instant messaging, and texting as accepted forms of professional communication between staff. This included using these technologies to engage in the day-to-day coordination of classroom instruction and lesson planning. So, while these technologies were originally designed for on-demand informal entertainment and communication purposes, the in-person restrictions precipitated by the pandemic stretched their affordances, particularly in the areas of professional development and family outreach. Due to these shifts, communication at FVA, as was the case in many US schools, became more fluid, just-in-time, and informal (i.e., instant messaging and texting) and less constructed, premeditated, and formal (i.e., scheduled in-person meetings, email correspondence). Ms.

Wezner describes the affordances of messaging and texting for just-in-time communication as a supplement to regular teacher collaboration meetings:

> We're sharing all of our resources. We help each other out with so much that I feel like this has brought the teachers a lot closer. Even though we teach different grades, I think this is helping us learn what we can all use or do, which has been really cool. I think just being able to check in with each other all the time has been helpful . . . We have a teacher meeting a couple of times a week where we are on Zoom. Then, me, [Ms. Ohlin], and [Ms. Gomez] have created our grade-level team where we're constantly texting each other: "Hey, I just found this. I found that. Do you want to do this together?"

Using Cellular Technologies to Address Engagement Barriers

Shifts in technology use also precipitated boundary changes across time and space of when, and how, professional communication was accepted. It also opened new avenues for the cultivation of relationships between staff and families, as illustrated in Ms. Carina's experience using FaceTime to assist families with their home Internet connectivity:

> I have been on FaceTime calls with parents and their kids saying, "Alright, show me your screens. Let's do this together" And that's been difficult for the ones that don't have an iPhone . . . having to visualize what's going on with their computer . . . I feel like I've done a lot more work online than in person. The amount of time I'm spending with stuff being planned and communicating with the parents. It's a LOT of communication with the parents. A lot. A lot.

As described by Ms. Carina, FVA used digital technologies, such as FaceTime, to mediate and conserve connection in ways that transcended previously held boundaries between home and school. This included synchronous "virtual check-ins" with families focused on learning how to use the technology and addressing needs and accommodations, as Ms. Carina describes here:

> I never used Google Classroom. Didn't even know what Zoom was. Just having to walk parents through that in a way that makes sense. I'm not your techiest person, so what am I doing? I don't know, "Let's figure it out together." So, that's been challenging. But thankfully, the parents have been very cool like, "Okay, we'll figure it out. We got this. We're going through this together." Between the emails, calls and text messages, I communicated with about five parents today.

As Ms. Carina describes, using cellular technologies to engage collaboratively via texting, messaging, and calling supported engagement during remote learning and facilitated connection.

Eye of the Camera: Making Visible Affordances and Challenges

There are both affordances and challenges to having the camera in teachers' classrooms and families' homes. The affordances include opportunities for parents and teachers to collaborate more deeply than was previously possible. The just-in-time and on-demand nature of video-facilitated engagement enabled parents and teachers to work together to support students' schooling and well-being—for example, through easier scheduling of IEP team meetings. On the other hand, the challenges of violating the social boundaries between home and school included families and teachers feeling a sense of intrusion, discomfort, or even shame at the increased level of visibility into previously undisclosed aspects of their lives, which we describe below.

Increased Visibility of Teacher Practice

Shifting to the use of Zoom for virtual classroom instruction precipitated shifts in boundaries of time and place, with teachers entering students' homes and parents becoming privy to teachers' instruction. The pandemic upended the social contract between home and school and between teacher and parent that essentially states that children fall under the direct responsibility and purview of teachers the moment they step onto school grounds.[18] This includes the expectation that parents afford teachers and schools a generous degree of latitude in what they do with their children during school hours. The advent of parents being privy to internal classroom happenings turned all that upside down. As Ms. Wezner shared, the advent of parents:

> At first, I was like, "I don't know if parents are gonna see their kid in a breakout room alone with another kid and be like, 'Why are they doing this? That's not appropriate.'" Or what if bullying is happening that you're not seeing? But then I had a couple of parents be like, "No, they love it! 'Cause they want to talk about what you taught them. And they want to hang out with their friends." And we rationalized it. If we were in school, and they're playing on the playground or they're in a group without a teacher, they're talking to each other, without me hearing every word they say.

In reflecting on remote learning in her classroom, and parent perceptions of it, Ms. Wezner came to view being in the eye of the camera as increasing the visibility of her teaching practice. The dynamics that developed around the use of breakout rooms to "see" and "be seen" by peers, as Ms. Wezner alludes to, affords a glimpse into how digital technologies could be

Technology as Connection

used to mirror in-person school practices virtually, such as recess and peer-to-peer class discussion, as a tool for building school culture and creating connection.

The viewing of teaching and home life through the camera also created the necessity to renegotiate relationships between teachers and parents. Teaching children remotely in their homes via Zoom presented a different dynamic to what had come before with in-person instruction—in a sense breaking a "third wall" that separated school and home life, including the roles and expectations that come with each. For many staff, including Ms. Wezner, the camera merging home and school life created tensions between these two audiences:

> I had the [fear of] parents listening a lot in the beginning where I would hear parents in the background, telling their kids to ask me something. And they wouldn't stand in the camera. It was like, "You could just ask me." It, like, feels really awkward when I know they're asking their kid to ask me something because they're not comfortable talking to me. That I think makes it more nerve-racking rather than less.

Ms. Wezner's comments point to assumed burdens that remote learning placed on teachers and parents to manage new domains of engagement and obligation. Moreover, having the eye of the camera disrupted notions of privacy, including the unspoken promise of in-person schooling that the classroom and home are teacher and parent domains, respectively—with the expectation of minimal intrusion between the two.[19] Bringing the camera into teacher practice upended that.

Increased Visibility of Students' Lives

Remote learning also created a window into students' lives and homes, particularly for teachers who had been shielded from the realities of their students' lives. According to Dr. Tully, this afforded teachers an expanded awareness of their students' personal circumstances and barriers to access:

> One thing that the pandemic and the school closures did that I want to take forward—especially for teachers who are culturally misaligned with their students—is it unveiled a lot of the barriers that kids face in ways that I don't think they ever knew . . . Like the impact of a parent who doesn't speak English and isn't familiar with how to use technology, not being able to help their child learn at home and what that looks like. It gave teachers more insight into the children's lives and the specific barriers for their progress that I want to build on next year.

Dr. Tully's observations echo the tensions expressed by Ms. Wezner in navigating the relationship between primarily white upper- and middle-class teachers and primarily middle- and working-class multilingual and multicultural families—a dynamic present in many US schools, including FVA, serving diverse students.[20] The use of cameras to connect teachers and families served as a window—a third eye—into the previously unknown worlds of working- and middle-class families of color that revealed already existing inequities amplified by the pandemic.

Being in the eye of the camera also raises critical points of discussion for understanding the role that intersectionality and interdependence play in informing culturally responsive practices to support diverse multilingual students with and without disabilities. How can we use and understand pre-planned and just-in-time remote learning experiences to develop connection and critical understanding of students' lives? This gets to the heart of the "mismatch" between the teaching population (largely white, English-monolingual) and diverse student populations (multicultural, multilingual, disabled) in US public schools.

Discomfort with Teachers Entering Homes

For many families, having the eye of the camera document their home-lives proved to be problematic.[21] Particularly for families living in poverty, the presence of the camera created the potential for shaming and feeling shame about their personal circumstances—once previously private and confined to home but now publicly shared with their school community.[22] This is an example of how digital technology use brought on by the pandemic violated the social boundaries between homes and schools as separate spaces. With that, a problematic context was created in relation to the treatment of students' homes as classrooms where families no longer felt the safety of privacy, as Dr. Tully explained: "There were issues for a while. Kids wouldn't turn their cameras on. No cameras. So, we're telling them they have to. They don't. Well, we investigate a bit. Work with a family. That child is taking care of a baby during class. And that's embarrassing and difficult. That child is cooking breakfast for a younger sibling during class. That's a barrier to learning. Now, put yourself in the place of that fifth grader who you're like, 'Why didn't you get this done?' It really changes what your mindset is." As Dr. Tully illustrates, being in the eye of the camera creates an invasion into the often-unspoken and hidden lives of what it means to be poor in the United States. Moreover, having a camera in the home redefines schools' scope of access into families' private lives. Circumstances, which when revealed, compound the potential shame of being "discovered" and also shed light on the barriers to learning that living in poverty places on families.[23]

Tied to issues of privacy are the ethics of balancing the monitoring of student participation with students' level of comfort with being on camera. Ms. Yadira, echoing Dr. Tully's sentiments, expressed her view of the tensions created by having cameras in the classroom: "There were a lot of missed opportunities for teachers to support them because we weren't even sure if they were behind the screen or not. For some of them, it's a cultural thing. Certain students felt embarrassed by the way that they live either because they live with somebody else or there is family around. So that's why they didn't turn on their camera." As Ms. Yadira suggests, turning cameras on and off potentially came to signify to students a way they could control and preserve boundaries that felt acceptable to them. This was evidenced by the contexts, as elaborated by Dr. Tully and Ms. Yadira, in which students chose to turn off the camera—for example, in moments of familial privacy (i.e., older sibling caring for new baby in background), moments of embarrassment (i.e., adults intruding into the students' "bubble"), and commentary or behavior deemed not suitable for teachers' ears. In these ways, the challenges of camera use in remote learning blurred the boundaries between school and home, creating the potential for discomfort for families and staff alike.

Shifting Expectations: Challenges and Surprises in Remote Learning

The move to remote learning during the pandemic resulted in schools needing to shift their expectations to meet students' changing needs. These shifts included redefining what it means to be in school, what it means to provide inclusive instructional practices and services online, and shifting attitudes toward using digital technologies in new and revised ways to support remote instruction.

Shifting What It Means to Be in School

The shift to remote learning precipitated a redefining of what it means to be in school when students and teachers are not actually in physical classrooms. Coupled with this was the need to establish expectations that online schooling was in fact "real school." For staff, this became an exercise in balancing families' socio-emotional needs in light of the disruption the pandemic caused with the school community's need to establish routines and practices that promoted learning.

For school staff, this meant that remote classroom expectations and rules needed to be explicitly redefined for students and families to accept the transition to remote learning as legitimate. This was doubly difficult for a high-touch school such as FVA whose instructional philosophy, as Dr. Tully expressed earlier, was grounded in the in-person interactions that came to characterize its full inclusion model. Ms. Petersen, a newly arrived experienced English-speaking special education teacher of European descent for grades TK/Kinder, 1/2, and 2/3, explained this tension in the classrooms she supported:

> It [remote learning from home] is a whole different dynamic. They might literally be laying down on a pillow. They're eating! You'd never see this in a classroom. It's just that boundary . . . I've seen family members come by, and they're talking to them when we're in class. There has to be people, family members, seeing this, but it's just like, "Distance learning, oh well." It's not given the same priority as going to [in-person] school and being in class because they're at home and they're in a comfortable environment. Not that school is not comfortable, but it's different when you're expected to sit up in a chair.

As Ms. Petersen discusses here, staff at FVA had to contend with negotiating differing expectations and norms for remote versus in-person learning. This included challenging the lower status, and in some cases priority, that both families and staff sometimes assigned to remote learning. This renegotiation of what it means to be in school included redefining the range of acceptable remote school behaviors, particularly in the younger grades.

In addition to redefining what it means to be "in school," teachers mentioned that the shift to remote learning also increased parents understanding of the day-to-day instructional challenges, tensions between adherence to standardized curricula and teaching children with diverse academic needs, and differences in behavior between school and home environments that teachers often contend with, as Ms. Severin shared with us:

> Parents are getting a clearer picture of where their kids are academically. I've read with our kids and then the kid reads a book with the parents as well, and "What happened? I don't know what's wrong with my kid." They're finally getting it:

Technology as Connection

"Yes, your kid has attention problems." Or finally they're seeing the insanity of Common Core math . . . So, that is kind of a little bit of a silver lining. Right? We're not going to get quite as much, "Oh, my kid never does that at home" or "I don't know what you're talking about."

These shifts in expectations and understanding within school communities—coupled with increased surveillance via the use of cameras—led to new understandings of teacher instruction.

Shifting What It Means to Be Inclusive

The shift to remote learning also spurred the need to redefine being inclusive to include quickly pivoting instructional practices and roles to support the emerging and changing needs precipitated by emergency remote learning. Dr. Tully described this shift as contingent on the need to make the remote learning environment accessible to all—illustrated here in the context of paraprofessionals pivoting to meet school community needs at FVA:

> Their [paraprofessional] job description is direct support for individuals. So, now, why are they making Spanish lessons? Well, that is the result of thinking through a redefinition of their job. Why are they calling parents and doing food distribution? Because that's a redefinition of their job. If their job, as a person, is to make an inclusive environment accessible to all, what the nature of that work looks like has shifted in the pandemic. So, they can't keep sitting on a Zoom call and reminding a particular kid on their caseload. No. It looks like distributing food to that family because that's inclusive right now.

Dr. Tully's example of pivoting to meet need is in direct tension with the often-bureaucratic norms that typically govern provision of services to students with IEPs.[24] However, the dynamics of FVA being its own county charter specifically charged with maintaining a full inclusion model afforded greater latitude than might typically be afforded in other school contexts.

Shifting What It Means to Provide Services

Redefining what inclusion looks like in the context of emergency remote learning was also tied to shifts in the delivery and implementation of services for students with IEPs. At FVA, shifts in the provision of services included, in Dr. Tully's words, "doing their best to approximate what they did when we were brick and mortar"—for example, via the use of synchronous and asynchronous instructional videos. This included the SLPs and the occupational therapist recording themselves weekly either reading stories, as they would normally do in the classroom, or leading station or social skills activities. These synchronous and asynchronous videos were built around IEP goals for students on their caseloads but made available to all students.

Dr. Tully and the special education teachers also had weekly meetings via Zoom with families of students with IEPs. These meetings centered on identifying and prioritizing IEP goals that families felt they could support at home. Provision of remote services also included inviting speech therapy and occupational therapy providers, as needed, to join these weekly calls to support accessibility to the remote learning curriculum and provide additional materials.

In Dr. Tully's mind, providing services in this manner was acceptable: "On paper, and in practice, I actually think that's excellent. And if you talk to the parents, they're happy." However, in discussing the provision of services with the providers themselves, tensions arose regarding the feasibility of meeting students' goals remotely as outlined in their IEPS, the reporting of which was still a prerequisite at the district level, even during the pandemic. As Dr. Tully acknowledged, this created tensions in the adaptation of FVA's push-in model of service delivery to the remote learning environment:

> With the exception of our OT—who works for us and had no experience prior to working for us—the PT and the SLP wanted to transition to an individualized teletherapy format. All students separately and discreet individualized sessions. And I was like, "No, because then we're introducing a different format of service delivery that I'm going to have to undo with the same families on the backend." Why would we choose this time to introduce individualized therapies when that's not how our school works?

The tensions between FVA's school administration and service providers are indicative of the challenges that many schools faced in deciding how to deliver services in remote settings.[25] For Dr. Tully, this meant providing widely accessible content via video for all students to access so as not to pull specific students away from the general education setting. However, for service providers at FVA, as well as the majority of service providers we spoke with across other districts and schools, provision of services consisted of virtual one-to-one sessions with individual students and small groups. Typically, these service hours would be in addition to time spent in remote general education settings.

Technology as Connection 131

These very real frustrations about how best to use digital technologies to support inclusive services were compounded by the fact that providers received little support from districts or state or federal agencies, who themselves were at a loss regarding how best to support remote provision of services for students with IEPs. These frustrations were also felt by the extended FVA staff, particularly the special education teachers. Ms. Severin explained to us how the shift in her role—from providing services specifically focused on students' IEP goals to providing services aligned with families' broader socio-emotional needs—challenged her ability to meet district and state reporting requirements for children with IEPs:

> There's no service. What I'm doing is saying, "Here are some options. If you need help accessing the option, like your Internet doesn't work, I'll help you access it." But that's it. I'm at work today because I'm printing out packets for kids. Social stories about "What is COVID?" and "Why am I home?" I write a little note to the kids, and I think it makes a difference, but they can just throw it in the trash. It's a very weird gray area where IDEA is in place, but school is closed. So, nobody's really quite sure what to make of that.

Ms. Severin's commentary on the lack of an accountability framework for services rendered remotely was a common concern for many schools and districts throughout the pandemic.[26] A significant source of this conflict was a lack of directive at the county, state, and federal levels for service providers and staff about what counts as data, the end result being that what was counted as data in the world of remote learning was quite loose.[27] This lack of guidance for the provision of services to students with IEPs left the world of special and inclusive education, of which FVA was no exception, in the dark.[28]

Shifting Attitudes toward Technology

Shifting to a remote learning format also precipitated changes in staff's attitudes toward technology. For example, Ms. Gomez reconsidered her views on the affordances of digital technologies, which she had previously eschewed when her instruction was in person (see chapter 5). In our follow-up interview with her, Ms. Gomez described her expanded use of several digital platforms (i.e., Google Classroom, Seesaw, Flipgrid) and expressed a newly discovered interest in using educational technologies to support her classroom instruction: "With Seesaw, you could definitely put in your voice. Either it's reading or responding to something with Google Classroom that we're doing now, depending on what the assignment is. You can have audio recording as well, especially using something called Flipgrid, which I just became new to. Oh my gosh. I wish I would've known about this prior to COVID happening because I think I would have utilized it in our classroom." In describing her new attitudes, and uses, of educational technologies, Ms. Gomez reveals a shift in her understanding for how digital platforms and tools could be used to support students' creative expression and voice (see chapter 5).[29]

Mr. Gabriel, who prior to the pandemic was already interested in using digital technologies to support learning, found new opportunities to utilize and expand his digital tech skills to support FVA's shift to remote learning. Mr. Gabriel discussed with us how he finally found a good outlet for his skills in digital storytelling—defined as multimodal uses of digital tools to tell stories—learned the prior year during a digital storytelling workshop we had presented on using WeVideo to create digital stories (see appendix B).[30] While Mr. Gabriel found the workshop engaging (see chapter 9), the priority had been on supporting other aspects of in-person instruction. The shift to remote learning, however, created an opening for Mr. Gabriel to use his digital storytelling skills to create remote learning video content for teachers and students: "I've used [WeVideo] for all the YouTube videos that I've shot. I've been screening video so that we can put the lessons up on YouTube. I'm still editing for our winter program, which I'm trying to get done as soon as possible. Prior to this, we hadn't really used it much. Now I've used it a lot." It was interesting to see how the affordances of integrating digital storytelling into instruction at FVA, which we had hoped would occur the prior year at the time of the workshop, became more feasible and attractive to staff as a tool for creating asynchronous instructional content. This presented a shift in the original intent of digital storytelling—which was to develop students' narrative storytelling skills—to being used by staff as a tool for creating instructional content. This represented yet another change in the intended uses of digital technologies that were coupled with shifts in attitudes toward using tech to support classroom instruction.

Shifting Future Technology Use to Create Connection

Staff attitude shifts also included considering how digital technologies could be used to support classroom connection in a post-pandemic future.

Technology as Connection

This included thinking about integrating new routines, developed during the pandemic, into future instruction, as Ms. Wezner describes: "We've started some really good routines that would never have started without the pandemic. On Fridays, our schedule is independent work for them, but they have fifteen-minute check-ins with me where we have a one-on-one Zoom, and we can either do some work together or they can talk to me about anything and just chill. It's so fun to have them tell me what they're interested in or tell me what they did over the weekend." The expanded flexibility of the remote learning format afforded teachers opportunities to engage in alternative forms of relationship building with their students, as Ms. Wezner describes here. These opportunities for connection and relationship building were particularly critical to supporting students' socioemotional health during the pandemic, both at FVA as well as at schools across the United States.[31] One-to-one sessions also afforded students an opportunity to share alternative interests, skills, and talents cultivated during the pandemic. These included new and multimodal uses of digital tools using audiovisual content, text, and memes, such as Jamboard (see appendix B), which many students used during the pandemic to share extracurricular interests, as described by Ms. Wezner: "I had one kid today showing me Jamboards that he made on Google and all the pictures that he found, which is super fun. He likes to give me updates on all the sports going on in the world because he's into that. It's fun to hear what they're really interested in."

Ms. Wezner's one-to-one uses of Zoom meetings and students' extracurricular use of digital tools such as Jamboard to manifest hobbies and interests visually are good examples of new routines and uses of digital technologies brought on by the pandemic that school communities engaged with to create connection.[32]

Redefining Roles: Parents as Teachers in Remote Learning

When parents assumed primary responsibility for ensuring their children's day-to-day remote learning, they were inadvertently tasked with partnering with schools to co-facilitate their children's online instruction.[33] For many parents across US schools, including at FVA, this shift in responsibilities and roles was overwhelming, particularly for working families managing multiple school-aged children.[34] In documenting the shift to remote learning, we explored how parents managed the shift as co-facilitators of their children's instruction.

Negotiating New Norms and Routines

For several of the parents we interviewed, the shift to managing their children's remote learning relegated them to the role of teacher, aide, and parent. For working parents with multiple children, such as Mira, this meant toggling between managing the competing interests of professional work obligations and managing their children's behavior while attending school from home: "I like in-person because I can do my work! [In remote learning] they need that one on one. They need to be there in front because they're on a screen. They feel like they can walk away and be okay because the teacher doesn't say, 'Come back.' The teacher can't follow them and say, 'Where are you going?' So, they feel like there's more freedom." Mira felt that the shift to remote learning placed some of the responsibility for student discipline on the parent in the absence of a physically present teacher.

Mira's concerns about the processes and norms for classroom discipline were reiterated by other parent interviewees, and these were the top concerns more broadly for parents across the United States.[35] Sara further elaborated on shifts in norms and routines in her explanation of how she managed her children's remote learning:

> No es lo mismo. Atender a dos autoridades en ese momento—a la maestra y a la mamá. ¿A quién le hago caso primero? ¿Si mi mamá me dice, "necesito que termines de desayunar" cuando la maestra me dice, "necesito que termines otra cosa?" Pues había que dejarle la autoridad a la maestra, y yo quedar nada más como apoyo para no interferir.

> It's not the same. Paying attention to two authority figures at the same time—the teacher and the mother. Who do I follow first? If my mother says, "I need you to finish breakfast" when the teacher says, "I need you to finish something else?" Well, I had to give the teacher deference and be a support so as not to interfere.

This negotiation of when, and how, to support students in navigating their relationships with their parents and teachers was met with varying levels of deference from parents, as was the case for Sara. In other cases, such as Dina's family, who ended up leaving FVA for alternative schooling arrangements, the negotiations proved to be too much. This was particularly true for working parents of children with substantive support needs, such as Blake, for whom the shift to remote learning for Finn and his younger

Technology as Connection

brother Chandler, a kindergartener in Ms. Macias's class who was also diagnosed with autism, proved to be untenable: "My husband and I work full time. So, we had no help for three months, and they didn't go to school anymore. They didn't have any other therapies. We had no sitters. So, we kind of made school optional for the spring because we felt the health of our family and mental stability was more important. They weren't learning anyways. They weren't excited to go." For Blake's family, the cessation of in-person therapeutic services, coupled with inability to secure childcare due to the quarantine put in place by the state, proved to be too much.

Blake's case was unfortunately the norm for many families of children with disabilities facing a cessation of services due to the pandemic.[36] It wasn't until the eventual lifting of the quarantine and partial reopening of schools the following fall and winter that the situation for Blake's family began to improve, as she detailed to us in a follow-up interview:

> It was just a lot of trial and error. After two months [FVA] offered childcare where the kids could do distance learning at the school and have assistance. We started doing that because this is their home environment. As most kids, they couldn't separate school and home. It just didn't make sense to them. It was really challenging for them to see us as teachers and do school here, especially with their IEPs. We didn't want to damage or further fragment our relationship with our children.

Blake's choice to prioritize her children's mental health took precedence over attempts to engage in remote learning structures that simply did not work for her family. For many families, this negotiation between mental health and adherence to new remote schooling norms was devastating. For families of children with profound disabilities, particularly those requiring in-home therapeutic services, the shift to remote learning led to a catastrophic drop off, and in some cases disappearance, of students from participating in school.[37]

Developing New Perspectives

Parents' negotiation of relationships and roles between home and school also led to the development of new strategies and perspectives for navigating remote learning at home. For some parents, the increased responsibilities that came with the shift to remote learning afforded increased understanding and involvement in their children's schooling. As was the case with Mira and her family, the shift to remote learning also led to shifts in their evaluation of digital technologies for supporting connection:

> When they were in class, we weren't using our electronics as much at all. But when we went remote, I feel like the kids are always on it. And I am somewhat okay with it more than before because that's their social time. To me, they need that socialization. That's pretty much the only socialization they can get. I can't invite their friends over. Right? Definitely using Zoom for birthday parties. We did the whole Zoom thing all last year. We definitely are on all the electronics so much more than we ever used to be [laughs].

Reflecting on her family's experiences with remote learning in the spring of 2020, as well as their decision to remain in remote learning for the 2020–2021 school year, Mira was an example of a "reformed" parent who was initially ambivalent about the utility and value of technologies for supporting student's engagement, inclusion, and socialization. As she expresses to us, the shift to remote learning helped her see her children's technology use as having potential affordances to support their need for peer-to-peer socialization during the pandemic. Essentially, in Mira's view, technology transformed into a tool for socialization during a pandemic. Mira's new perspectives about engaging with digital technologies in novel ways were also tied to the empowering revelation that she could ably navigate her children's remote learning: "I surprised myself. I am capable. I did it. My husband's rarely home. He works all day long, and this is basically just me! Just being able to do that and work. I've learned that I can actually juggle having three kids at home virtually."

For Mira, doing what was previously inconceivable—managing both her professional work obligations with the remote learning needs of her three children—revealed new insights about what she was capable of undertaking. Mira's revelation, while in the minority of families' experiences navigating remote learning during the pandemic, was nevertheless indicative of the feasibility of remote learning for some families, including those with homebound or immunocompromised family members.[38] Even so, remote learning is an intensive endeavor that, even under optimal circumstances, requires significant sacrifices, as Mira described:

> But it definitely was hard because even though I'm at home, I still do work remotely. So, I had to juggle that. I had to sit down and come up with a schedule. Try to stay on a schedule so that I am present with the kids, making sure they're online, doing their work. And at the same time trying to get my work done. It was so hard. I couldn't even follow my schedule. I did it maybe for a month and then it just went away. But I was trying.

Mira notes how the responsibility for managing remote learning fell primarily on her shoulders—a common dynamic expressed by many mothers

Technology as Connection

across the United States.[39] These gaps in support for families were endemic of already existing gaps in the safety nets afforded to US mothers.[40]

Finding Resources for Remote Learning

In addition to changes in day-to-day schedules, routines, and perspectives, parents were also required to address the more practical logistical considerations associated with remote learning. Like many schools in the United States, FVA faced the challenge of supporting families with the provision of technology and school supplies necessary for remote learning. However, what was more difficult to mitigate was the circumstance of how to find physical space for remote learning itself in homes, particularly those with multiple family members living within the confines of small housing spaces such as apartments. These were challenges that families across the US, including at FVA, as explained by Sara, faced as they strove to find ways to cope with remote learning at home:

> Fue algo difícil por el hecho de que en casa no tenemos el suficiente espacio disponible para poder hacerle un lugar o un ambiente propicio para estar en la escuela. Se hizo lo mayor posible. Pues, no es el ideal. Obviamente, la retroalimentación que hay entre la maestra y ellos se perdió. Se diluyó por momento.

> It was difficult because of the fact that at home we don't have enough room available to create a space conducive to schooling. Well, it's not ideal. Obviously, the feedback between the teacher and [students] got lost. It got diluted for a while.

The lack of an ideal physical space for remote learning, in Sara's view, impacted the quality of the children's schooling. Sara explained that not having the right space for remote learning was a distraction that took away—or, in her words, "diluted"—the quality of classroom interactions. Sara admitted that the transition to remote learning wasn't that challenging for her family, given her and her husband's professions as computer graphics designers, however, challenges present themselves in other ways, including the creation of a proper learning environment at home.

Addressing Remote Learning Needs for Multilingual Students

Addressing the remote learning needs of multilingual families was a significant priority for FVA, given that 64.2 percent of the student population identified as being of Latino descent. The advent of remote learning

138   Chapter 6

made providing language supports to multilingual students all the more daunting.[41] For many schools, the shift to remote learning displaced many multilingual aides who would have normally assisted monolingual teachers in supporting multilingual students.[42] Situations in which there were disparities in linguistic knowledge and access between teachers and students exacerbated already existing equity gaps.[43]

Near the start of the pandemic, we reached out to both Hilda and Sara, two Spanish monolingual parents who had previously interviewed with us earlier in the year, to discuss the unique challenges multilingual parents faced with remote learning. While Hilda indicated that she was too overwhelmed by the demands of the pandemic to participate in follow-up interviews, Sara graciously agreed to share with us her experiences navigating remote learning in which she had to contend with an English-dominant instructional discourse:

> El problema es el inglés. Pues, yo no hablo inglés. Entiendo algunas cosas. Pero de repiente si [el chiquito] dice, "no sé qué dijo . . ." "ay, hijo, yo tampoco se. Vamos a ver las instrucciones." Las leemos y las traducimos. Fue la parte difícil para me, difícil para ellos. Pues no hablamos el idioma y había que detenerse a, "le traduzco a ver qué dice."

> The problem is English. Well, I don't speak English. I understand a few things. But if [the youngest] says, "I don't know what she said . . ." "Oh, son, I don't know either. Let's see the instructions." We'd read them and translate them. That was the most difficult part for me, difficult for them. We don't speak the language, and I had to rely on, "I'll translate it to see what it says."

Sara and her children's use of digital technologies, such as Google Translate, to complete academic work facilitated their ability to support each other in accessing remote learning content. As an aside, in our discussions with Sara, it became clear that she viewed her inability to speak English, rather than the teachers' inability to speak Spanish, as a problem. Unfortunately, the framing and valuation of English as the dominant language is common among multilingual and monolingual speakers alike, even in culturally responsive environments such as FVA.[44]

The valuation of Spanish as an equally valid language of discourse in the classroom was a concern Dr. Tully wanted to address, given FVA's high percentage of multilingual students. Dr. Tully discussed attempts to subvert language privilege prior to the pandemic by having teachers learn and use Spanish in the classroom. However, the onset of the pandemic pushed the

Technology as Connection

139

focus of language support squarely back on the multilingual paraprofessionals who were responsible for translating and creating content in Spanish, as described by Mr. Gabriel: "In my case, I think there is a lot more prepping because now we started doing Spanish lessons for the kids on YouTube. We shared the links with the teachers, and they can share as they feel is needed. We've done colors, days of the week, and months. This week we'll be doing body parts. We're recording videos and making it engaging." For Mr. Gabriel, the asynchronous use of YouTube to create Spanish language content was a new use of a technology he had previously used for music movement breaks in class. Paraprofessionals who were not multilingual, such as Ms. Sandy, were also involved in the making of asynchronous video content. Ms. Sandy discussed with us how she supported multilingual students by capitalizing on the accessibility features and affordances of digital technologies to create instructional content and materials that are accessible to a wide range of users, including multilingual students:

> Making the lessons inclusive at school was different doing it online. When I make the social skills lesson, it has to be accessible to everybody. We have to have options where they can read it on their own. We have to have options where they could just click a button and hear us read it for them. So, I think having all of the lessons inclusive and available for everybody is the biggest struggle and what we're all striving to do right now.

Sara corroborated Mr. Gabriel and Ms. Sandy's commentary and shared how efforts to provide multiple ways to access materials digitally made remote learning more inclusive for her family:

> Las maestras hicieron un gran trabajo en el aspecto de que grababan las clases y las tareas. Dejaban instrucción en vos y le decían, "si no puedes escribirlo, lo puedes grabar, y si no, lo puedes fotografiar, y si no, lo puedes dibujar." Entonces hubo muchas más posibilidades de poder completar esas actividades con el uso de la tecnología.

> The teachers did a great job in the sense that they audio recorded the classes and homework. They provided audio instructions and said, "If you can't write it, you can record it, and if not, you can photocopy it, and if not, you can draw it." In that sense, there were many possibilities to complete the activities using technology.

Sara's description of the multiple ways she and her family were able to access instructional content online exemplified how FVA strove to use technology to create access for their multilingual families. Essentially, both Sara and Ms. Sandy were describing the principles of UDL in practice (see chapter 3).[45] Additional and alternative modes for accessing information, such as through video/audio recordings of lectures and assignments, provided multiple means to access and engage with content for multilingual students. In the case of Sara, this included the ability to view, and review, materials on their own time, multiple times, as needed.

For Sara, the ability of her children to feel comfortable asking questions was also of paramount importance in accessing academic content, particularly due to their language status. As Sara shared with me, differences in her children's levels of comfort using English during in-person versus online instruction resulted in differences in their learning and participation:

> Hubo diferencia en el aprovechamiento del lenguaje para ellos. La más grande, ya le entiende más y ya habla más. Pero en el caso de el que va en primero, está aprendiendo inglés. Y si el hablarlo y expresarlo en la clase era complicado, en línea fue más.

> There was a difference in the advantage of language for them. The oldest one, she already understands more and speaks more. But in the case of the one who's in first grade, he's [still] learning English. And if speaking and expressing [English] was complicated in the classroom, even more so online.

As Sara notes, these differences were pronounced for her younger son, whose language resources in English were more emergent than those of his older sister. In her view, the barriers posed by remote learning were particularly pronounced for those who needed additional language support, so much so that Sara noticed her children turning to each other to receive the linguistic support missed from in-person instruction, particularly the younger brother turning to his older sister:

> Entre ellos, "¿Que dice?" "¿Como es aquí?" Si no me preguntaban a mí, entre ellos se ayudaban. En el caso del chiquito, "No le entiendo aquí. ¿Que dice?" y la grande, "Ay, es que quiere decir esto . . ." Le ayudaba traducir o le ayudaba explicarle. Y los logros, que hacían cada quien, en sus propias actividades, se los compartían.

> Between them it was, "What does this say?" "What does this mean?" If they didn't ask me, they helped each other out. In the case of the little one, "I don't understand, what does it say?" and the older one, "Well, this is what it means . . ." She helped him translate or she helped explain. And the gains that each of them made in their schoolwork, they shared with each other.

This dynamic of older multilingual students helping their younger siblings with the day-to-day navigation and translation of school life is a common

Technology as Connection

occurrence among multilingual families.[46] It is also indicative of the cultural push among many Latino families to socialize children as helpers within their collective family communities.[47]

Kindness in a Virtual World: Supporting School Community Mental Health

Prioritizing a culture of kindness during remote learning centered on supporting the mental health needs of students, parents, and staff at FVA. An increased need for social connection came about in large part due to the quarantining that schools underwent during the earlier phases of the pandemic, which for many students led to increased levels of depression, anxiety, and apprehension about the future.[48] Consequently, the onset of the pandemic instigated a substantive shift in prioritizing the mental health of students and their families.

Families' emotional struggles were of particular concern for the multilingual paraprofessionals who had more frequent interaction with parents, typically in Spanish. For staff, particularly the paraprofessionals, being attentive to students' mental health needs required an intensified focus on cultivating FVA's culture of kindness, as Ms. Yadira shared with us during her interview: "I just want everybody to be healthy. So, for me, I'm there for support. My biggest focus is making sure that the students are fine, that the parents are fine, and that I'm there as a guide. I gave them my personal numbers. I just want them to call me. I want them to feel comfortable with me and just genuinely know that we're there to support them and help them during these difficult times." In discussing the mindset that Ms. Yadira brought to her work helping families, it became apparent that prioritizing a culture of kindness in a virtual world required shifting the degree to which they made themselves available to families. While this was not a requirement asked of staff, many felt that increased connection, both inside and outside the realm of remote instruction, was necessary to safeguard families' mental health.

Using Technology to Connect with Care

Key to maintaining a caring school community was the provision of regular and diverse opportunities for students, parents, teachers, and staff to connect.[49] Teachers supported community connection in their classrooms through synchronous morning meetings that offered a predictable routine for students to engage with their classmates. Asynchronous programming facilitated in Spanish and English by paraprofessionals allowed students and parents to connect with staff in their preferred languages. Finally, synchronous coffee chats with Dr. Tully and school meetups were used to create camaraderie, engage parents, and support the broader school community through constant communication with school leadership. These approaches to using technology to connect with care helped mitigate feelings of isolation associated with the displacement from in-person schooling at FVA.

Using technology to maintain connections and mitigate isolation also occurred between staff. As an example, Ms. Carina described how Ms. Wezner used FaceTime to connect with her: "She was like, 'Hey, I'm going to FaceTime you.' Completely not work related. So, we'll just chat. I've really appreciated everyone I'm working with. Everybody's like, 'Well, we're all doing this. We're all struggling, but it's all good. We got this.'" Consistent efforts among staff to use communication technologies, such as FaceTime, to connect with each other and offer care were critical to maintaining a strong team. The use of these technologies also facilitated the building of solidarity and support for surviving the emotional stress brought on by the pandemic and navigating remote instruction during such uncertain times.

This use of communications technologies to maintain FVA's culture of care virtually also extended to students, as Mr. Gabriel demonstrated with his online math and ELA support group:

> I led a group called "Math/ELA Small Group Support" after lunch. The kids logged in, and if they had any questions for math or ELA, we would be there to help . . . Sometimes, I would stay later because I knew that some kids take more time to do their homework. And sometimes students would be very honest with me saying, "I'm scared." They use that space to see each other through their computer. I am okay with that because I know that they use that time to laugh and have a conversation with their friends.

Mr. Gabriel's patience in staying online was key to his efforts to cultivate kindness during the course of remote learning at FVA. This resulted in students' increased comfort confiding in him about their fears, in addition to creating a forum for students to be in community with each other.

Supporting Staff Who Are Also Parents

As was the case with many teachers across the United States, particularly in the case of working mothers, teachers faced additional strains due to the

Technology as Connection

need to manage the schooling of the children assigned to their classrooms along with their own children's schooling.[50] For Ms. Gomez, having a child with disabilities, while also managing a high-needs classroom, proved to be untenable:

> I think the most surprising part for me personally is just how teaching and having to be there for my students is really difficult because I also have a first grader who needs to do her lessons, and I have a child with special needs who needs to be watched at all times. And then I have a very demanding two-year-old. It's definitely been a struggle. That's why I told Dr. T, "I will not be returning this year as a teacher." Because if this is going to be our reality for this upcoming year, I will not be effective for FVA or my own family.

The forcing out of working parents, particularly women tasked with providing day-to-day support to multiple children such as Ms. Gomez, by the pandemic was unfortunately a phenomenon that took place across many communities and schools in the US.[51] Moreover, the broad lack of societal supports such as childcare and parental leave—a problem endemic to the US—pushed many working parents, particularly mothers, out of the workforce.[52]

In addition to the lack of a social safety net, such as universal childcare, FVA staff members who were also parents contended with worries about being able to address their own children's developmental needs adequately while also supporting the needs of their students. As Ms. Sandy confided, the unknown nature and impact of the COVID-19 virus itself, as well as the unknown duration of the quarantine at the time, raised many unanswered questions for parents: "I worry about my kids developmentally being stuck in the house with me. I told my son last night, 'Do you worry? Do you miss your friends?' I don't want them to regress. I'm happy they're safe. I'm happy they're not getting sick. But I do worry about what this means for them." Ms. Sandy's concerns about the long-term impacts of isolation, illness, and the continual stress brought on by the uncertainty surrounding the pandemic were echoed by multiple parents and staff at FVA. These voiced concerns were indicative of the general stressors that parents contended with across the United States as they attempted to mitigate the potential damage the pandemic might bring to their children.[53]

The Impact of First-Responder Status on Trauma and Schooling

The prioritization of a culture of kindness to support FVA staff and student families' mental health needs was particularly critical for first-responder families. For them, the horrific effects of witnessing severe COVID-19 infection, particularly prior to the availability of vaccines in 2021, were daily realities that were difficult to escape.[54] Mira shared with us the impact her husband's medical work had on the family, particularly the children, as a first responder: "My husband works at the hospital. He works with COVID patients. It was so stressful because he had to work twenty-four hours. He was so tired. The kids, they were hearing when he'd come home, they would hear about the stories, you know? . . . And so, to talk about it—it started affecting them. We had to quiet that down because it was not good for them to hear these stories he'd come home with."

Mira felt a struggle between wanting to support her husband through the daily trauma he was experiencing as a result of his work and shielding her children from the realities of the pandemic. Despite their best attempts to protect their children from the realities of Mira's husband's work as a first responder, the impact on the children was significant:

> All the patients that were really critical, he was the one to go in the room and put their PICC lines. A lot of times, he lost a lot of patients, and he would come home, and he would be depressed over it. So, we would talk about it. That's when the kids have ears, and they would hear this . . . They got really bad anxiety where my oldest daughter would cry every time we left the house because she was scared. We tried to go to a beach one day, and she just wanted to come home right away. She was scared of contracting, but more scared that she was going to give it to somebody else because we didn't know what was going on. We had to keep telling her she's safe, she's safe. Don't worry.

From our discussion with Mira, we learned that the anxiety that comes with getting a firsthand look at the impact of the virus on people's lives presented social and emotional repercussions on every aspect of daily living—true for many first responder families in the United States.[55] As Mira described, this made simple acts, such as going to the beach, anxiety-ridden endeavors that for many first-responder families and their children triggered a post-traumatic response.[56] For Mira's husband, his work connected the family to the pandemic in such as repercussive manner as to impact all aspects of daily life, including the response of her middle child, Marco, to returning to in-person school the following year:

> My middle child, Marco, he's the one that's still going through it. Going back to school has definitely been a challenge for him. He throws up before he goes to school because he has so much anxiety. He doesn't want to be at school that long.

Technology as Connection 145

He's like, "Pick me up right at 1:30. I don't want to stay any longer." So, I'm doing whatever he feels comfortable and safe with right now. We got it in his mind that if he has a cup of tea with him all the time and sips on it, it'll help his belly from getting the nervous feeling.

Marco's anxiety in not wanting to go to school was in contrast to his siblings' more enthusiastic responses to a return to schooling. Varying levels of willingness for a return to in-person schooling the following 2020–2021 school year were not uncommon for many students, families, and staff, both at FVA and across schools in the US.[57] These differences led to both regional and statewide conflicts in how quickly, or slowly, school communities across the United States were willing, and able, to make a return to in-person schooling.[58] Through it all, FVA's focus on connection was imperative to shepherding the school through the turmoil of the pandemic.

Children's Perspectives of Schooling during the Pandemic

At the time of this writing, the majority of published research focused on parents, teachers, and first responders.[59] As such, we believed it important to include the voices of FVA students themselves regarding their experiences and perspectives of the pandemic. We spoke with Marco, Mira's son, at the end of the 2019–2020 school year to gain his perspective of what the pandemic meant for him. While he chose not to discuss the anxiety Mira had previously reported to us, he was very open about his disappointment in the shift to remote learning: "I was actually pretty excited for the [in-person] Spring Jam 'cause we were working on that for a long time. And it [the pandemic] came up, and it canceled Spring Jam. Also, my birthday was the same time! I wanted to go to Legoland for my birthday. What happened? I had to cancel that plan 'cause 'no more.' A little sad."

For Marco, the cancellation of milestones, such as FVA's annual Spring Jam talent show and his own birthday, was one of the most upsetting aspects of the quarantine and shift to remote learning that occurred as a result of the pandemic. Marco's responses were broadly echoed by our child respondents in that the greatest impact and sense of loss reported included the cancellation of significant celebrations and events. This overarching sense of disappointment was felt widely across the country as countless milestones—so crucial to overall socio-emotional well-being—were canceled or deferred.[60] This led to a need to make alternative arrangements creatively, which often required using digital technologies in novel ways to support a sense of continued connection (e.g., in Marco's case, his parents ended up moving his birthday party to Zoom).[61]

The impact of the pandemic on students' mental health led to a variety of coping mechanisms—for example, in Marco's case, disappointment, anxiety, and ultimately avoidance, as detailed by Mira. For other children, such as Marco's younger brother Maddox, it led to a sense of needing to grow up faster and develop a sense of acceptance to mitigate the loss and unpredictability that came with the pandemic: "It feels pretty sad. I used to play soccer when I was not grown up. A lot. Every single break I played." What struck me about Maddox's response, difficult to capture in a transcription, was the tone of resignation with which he said "when I was not grown up." The implication being that the disappointing impact of school closures was a truncation, or acceleration, of childhood—a need to "grow up." Anecdotally, this reminded me of my own elementary-aged son's description of life before and after the pandemic: "Life before was much easier. Life with the pandemic became hard."

The disruptions in personal and social connections also created a sense of loneliness for several of our student respondents, who, like most children in the United States, were dependent on schools for most of their peer-to-peer interactions.[62] Isla, Sara's daughter, described the loneliness she felt in relation to no longer having same-age peers with whom to share her day-to-day experiences of schooling:

> Me gusto estar aquí en mi burbuja, en mi casa, y tener a mi hermano acá cerca. Pero no me gusto tanto [estar en casa] porque era menos tiempo el que me conectaba a la escuela. Sentía que me faltaba algo. Yo empecé a recompensarlo con hacer doble tarea. Mi mama me descargo unos libros de México. Estuve complementando ese tiempo con libros, pero no me gustó tanto porque no tenía a nadie con quien compartir. Lo podía compartir con mi hermano, pero no creo que lo entienda.

> I liked being here in my bubble, in my home, and having my brother nearby. But I didn't like [being home] because there was less time for me to connect with school. I felt that I was missing something. I started compensating by doing double the homework. My mother ordered books for me from Mexico. I was complimenting [my study] time with books, but I didn't like it much because I didn't have anybody to share with. I could share with my brother, but I don't think he would understand.

Isla's commentary illuminates an aspect of schooling that sometimes gets forgotten: an integral part of the school experience centers on students

Technology as Connection

147

sharing what they learn with their peers as they are learning it.[63] So, while having her younger brother and mother in her "bubble" was a comfort, it was no substitute for having same-age peers with whom to share the day-to-day aspects of schooling. For all of our child respondents, schooling *was* socialization centered on connection. Because a significant benefit of in-person learning is direct peer-to-peer interaction, for Isla, remote learning just could not compare. This sentiment was reiterated by Isla's brother, Leon:

> Al principio estaba muy bien porque podría platicar con mi hermana, salía más temprano. Pero ya, en los otros momentos, ya no me estaba gustando porque no podía hablar con la maestra, me sentía solo, quería hacer cosas, extrañaba a las maestras. Extrañe mucho hablar con mis compañeros.

> At first, it was really good because I could chat with my sister, get out [of school] early. But then, at other times, I wasn't liking it anymore because I couldn't chat with the teacher. I felt alone. I wanted to do things. I missed the teachers. I really missed chatting with my classmates.

The ramification of the loneliness and disconnect experienced by our child respondents holds implications for considering effective practices for using digital technologies to support connection during times of disconnection, such as those precipitated by the pandemic. These considerations also set the stage for chapter 7, which reflects on the roles that technology might play in children's future schooling and inclusion in a world changed by the pandemic.

7   Reflections on Technology and Inclusion in a Changing World

After concluding our in-person ethnographic work at FVA for the 2019–2020 school year, we stayed in touch and continued our collaboration with Dr. Tully and several of the teachers and parents through the 2020–2021 school year. A lot continued to change for FVA's school community during that second year—a transitory space in the mid-pandemic period when quarantine restrictions loosened and schools began taking tentative steps back toward in-person instruction. These changes, explored in follow-up interviews, conversations, and observations, centered on the residual aftereffects of surviving the first year of the pandemic and explored future hopes and dreams for the upcoming school year.

Adapting to a New Normal

Shifts in instructional practices at FVA during the 2020–2021 school year are situated in the broader context of how schools used digital technologies to navigate the changing educational landscapes precipitated by the pandemic.[1] For many schools, including FVA, the move to remote learning caused by the pandemic accelerated the road to increased digital technology adoption in classrooms.[2] For example, the number of Google Classroom users in schools increased by 250 percent from forty million in 2019 to a hundred million in 2020.[3] The accelerated and abrupt nature of pandemic-induced technology adoption often resulted in frustration for schools as they worked to build up their digital infrastructures, products, and protocols.[4] The shift to more ubiquitous technology adoption in schools also resulted in growing pains as schools strove to support families and staff in their use of digital tools for remote and, eventually, hybrid learning.[5]

Against this backdrop, the start of the 2020–2021 school year for FVA saw changes in the school population, with many families and several staff deciding to move to school environments they viewed as being either more, or less, restrictive with regard to in-person instruction. The start of fall 2020 saw a continuation of remote instruction. In winter 2021, plans were put into place to provide a hybrid model of instruction for those students deemed to have the highest need for in-person support. Due to the structure of COVID-19 pandemic regulations at that time, this consisted of the paraprofessionals and childcare professionals providing on-site support while teachers provided instruction remotely. Spring 2021 saw a shift in regulations that allowed teachers to return to classrooms for in-person instruction. This shift resulted in a revision to FVA's hybrid program, consisting of on-site in-person instruction by teachers and in-person support from paraprofessionals and service providers coupled with a real-time synchronous remote learning option. According to Dr. Tully, out of FVA's 150 families, approximately 30 percent opted for the remote option.

Hybrid Instruction at FVA

Once outside visitor restrictions were lifted, I was able to visit FVA in May 2021 to see the school's hybrid program in action. I had an opportunity to visit Ms. Wezner and check out her new classroom during a morning whole-class ELA lesson. Her classroom consisted of twelve students attending class in-person and three students attending remotely. Two paraprofessionals circulated the classroom providing support to the in-person students while Ms. Wezner provided support to the remote students during pauses in her instruction.

The students were seated at desks, masked, each three to six feet apart, separated by plexiglass dividers. From my vantage point near the back of the room, I was able to observe the actual mechanics of hybrid classroom instruction at FVA, as I outline in my observation below:

> Ms. Wezner turns on two screens: one at the front of the room that projects onto the whiteboard, and the other to the right of the class that projects onto an LCD screen.
>
> Zoom is turned on, and everyone can see the remote students on the screen and vice versa across five views: teacher view, whole-class view, and individual views for each of the three online students.
>
> Ms. Wezner begins the lesson: "We are going to read a story today. We are going to practice the new skills again with a new story. You need this paper that says my lucky day and this green page, scissors, and glue."

Reflections on Technology and Inclusion in a Changing World   151

> She projects images of both papers onto the Elmo, which is in the direct line of sight of both the online and in-person students. Ms. Wezner is observing both the screen and the classroom to see if students have located their materials. One of the remote students says that she doesn't have scissors, and Ms. Wezner says that's okay. Ms. Wezner says, "Thumbs up if you are done." All students do thumbs up in person and online. Ms. Wezner demonstrates the next step on the Elmo for the online students while the paraprofessionals circulate the classroom to support the in-person students.

Notable aspects included the synchronous and collaborative nature of the hybrid classroom. Ms. Wezner and the paraprofessionals depended on each other in their support of online and in-person students. Notably, Ms. Wezner prioritized her attention on the remote students who were not physically present. Another notable aspect was the physical setup of the hybrid classroom, which consisted of small clusters of three to four desks, distanced and separated by plexiglass. These clusters allowed for free movement between groups by the paraprofessionals while Ms. Wezner attended to supporting the online students.

The physical layout of the hybrid classroom was also notable in its intentional setup of the technology itself. The Elmo was positioned front and center in the classroom, serving as the "heart" for both the in-person and remote students. Additionally, the use of screens was multiple and accessible. One computer screen monitor was placed at the front of the classroom with Ms. Wezner, a document camera, and the Elmo. The document camera was set to a "teacher view/student view" mode that allowed the online students immediate visual access to both Ms. Wezner and the curricula and materials. This view also allowed Ms. Wezner direct visual access to the online students and their immediate laptop environment. A second computer monitor screen was placed on the right-hand side of the classroom. This monitor was set to a "classroom view/student view" mode that allowed online students visual access to their classmates and the paraprofessionals while allowing in-person students and paraprofessionals visual access to the remote learning students.

This setup promoted connection between the in-person and remote students, and I observed at least two instances in which in-person students approached remote students to observe and chat with them. Of course, the nature of this interaction was one-sided, as the remote students could not initiate this same kind of visitation. Moreover, it became evident from the missing scissors situation that remote students potentially faced barriers to access with regard to materials and hand-over-hand support, both of which could be more easily remedied in an in-person environment.

The class continued working in this back-and-forth manner for approximately an hour, at which time Ms. Wezner called for a break. As the students cleaned up, I decided to step outside to observe the students during their morning recess. I observed approximately thirty masked students, supervised by five masked paras, on the large playground. The playground structures were taped off and the students were playing tag with pool noodles to maintain some social distance—a pandemic mitigation strategy undertaken by many schools across the United States at the time. The focus of play centered on games that naturally required some distance, including a ready supply of tricycles and balls for students to play basketball and catch.

As I walked back into Ms. Wezner's classroom again after lunch, I noticed eight students inside reading silently and individual phonics work on their one-to-one Chromebooks. Outside, Ms. Wezner had pulled three students aside to do small-group guided reading. The remote students were also "with" Ms. Wezner on her laptop, which she held while instructing both the remote and in-person students. The physicality of the classroom moves stood out as notable—the remote students' movement within and across classroom environments, indoors and outdoors, as dependent on Ms. Wezner's physical positioning of the screen. This brings forth questions about the nature of embodied experiences in the classroom previously explored in chapter 6.

At an outdoor table diagonal from Ms. Wezner's small group, I also noticed what appeared to be a new SLP providing one-to-one services remotely with students via her laptop. On the left was another small group with either a paraprofessional or service provider, perhaps occupational therapy, providing services to two students in person.

For the families who chose to stay at FVA, these kinds of hybrid practices observed in Ms. Wezner's classroom were typical of the shifting modalities of instruction at FVA. The process of arriving to this point, however, was arduous and underwent several iterations and shifts from fully remote instruction in the fall, to partial in-person support for the highest needs students in the winter, and to the final implementation of the fully hybrid program in the spring of 2021. These shifts proved too much to bear for the approximately 15 percent of families who chose to leave FVA.

Family and Staff Reactions to Instructional Model Changes at FVA

Among the families in our study, Dina's family had left FVA in search of in-person schooling options for James and Daniel. While also frustrated with FVA's slow return to in-person instruction, Blake's family decided to remain. Hilda's family also decided to stay at FVA. However, the overwhelm brought on by the pandemic prompted them to opt out of continued follow-up with us during the 2020–2021 school year. Both Mira's and Sandra's families decided to stay at FVA, perhaps partly due to their children's minimal support needs compared to the more moderate support needs for Blake's and Dina's families. With that said, all three remaining families (Sara's, Mira's, and Blake's) in our study were looking forward to a new school year and the prospect of their children being able to engage in person, to whatever degree was possible, with their teachers and classmates.

Among the focal staff in our study, Ms. Gomez decided not to return to FVA as a teacher for the 2020–2021 school year, citing her son's substantive support needs as necessitating her decision to stay home as his primary caregiver, as she shared with us in chapter 6. Ms. Severin left FVA once it shifted to a hybrid model in spring 2021 due to a member of her family being immunocompromised. Ms. Severin was replaced by Ms. Petersen, who was glad to be back to in-person instruction and shared both Dr. Tully and Blake's sentiments for remote learning just to go away. The remainder of the original teachers in the study remained, of whom Ms. Wezner and Ms. Petersen were available for follow-up interviews in spring 2021.

Among service providers, Ms. Davis, the SLP, also decided not to return to FVA due to limitations and tensions in providing services remotely to align with FVA's full inclusion model. As a result, Ms. Davis returned to private practice providing speech services using a one-to-one telehealth format. The occupational therapist and physical therapists remained. Approximately 60 percent of paraprofessionals stayed at FVA. The remainder left for a similar constellation of reasons as families and teachers, as well as the transient nature of paraprofessional work. For some, there was a return to college or transition to other career opportunities. Among the four paraprofessionals who participated in interviews during the 2019–2020 school year, Mr. Gabriel and Ms. Yadira participated in follow-up interviews in spring 2021.

Affordances and Challenges in Learning with Technology

For the staff who remained at FVA, feelings toward technology use in the classroom were directly shaped by their experiences with technology during the pandemic. From our follow-up conversations, it appeared that for the younger, more technologically savvy staff, an appreciation for the affordances of technology was heightened by technology use during the pandemic. For staff who were not as accustomed to incorporating technologies into their day-to-day teaching practices, particularly teachers for whom preservice training and certification involved minimal attention to technologies, the challenges associated with teaching with technologies, outlined in chapters 5 and 6, seemed to cement prior views of technology.

For Mr. Gabriel and Ms. Wezner, two of the more technologically savvy staff at FVA, while the preference was clearly for in-person instruction— overwhelmingly the case for everyone during our follow-ups—they were able to take the lessons learned during the pandemic and tease out the aspects of their technology use that they would like to replicate in the classroom moving forward. When asked to consider the differences and similarities in his technology use with students across in-person, remote, and hybrid instructional modalities, Mr. Gabriel explained:

> I think that the kids were able to get more familiar with technology, which I think is great. It's a very good skill to have—how to create a presentation, how to write on Google Docs, how to create Google Slides, how to use certain settings, how to add video. That was a really good thing to show and for them to learn because it was new to them. That's something that I did not see in prior years where I would see little practices. So, I feel like they've benefited from having technology.

Mr. Gabriel's distinction between isolated, unplanned "little practices" with technology to coordinated, collaborative, and sustained uses of technologies, particularly for writing or instructional media production (see chapters 5 and 6), was a benefit he wanted to carry forward across in-person, hybrid, and remote instruction. Ms. Wezner reiterated the shifts in intentionally planning for using technologies to support instruction as an experience she also wanted to carry forward into the new school year. For her, this included the use of digital cloud tools, such as Google Slides, to facilitate and streamline by synchronous and asynchronous collaborative sharing and modification of classroom content and materials:

> We used [Google] Slides to anchor all of our lessons this year. So, that's really helped for the co-planning because [the co-teacher] will make ELA, I'll make

math, and then we both use them. So, it has all the plans for the lesson on it and visuals for kids and step-by-step stuff, which I would have never thought to do last year . . . It's nice to look back at that. We can reuse them. I think I would've never thought of it without the pandemic, but now it's something I'm sure we'll use more in the future. I've been trying to keep that in mind a lot with technology because we've learned so many new things on there.

For Ms. Wezner, the pandemic really shed light on the gaps in school preparedness for emergency situations, particularly those that may require schools to pivot teaching across in-person and remote modalities. A sentiment expressed by educators across the country,[6] the pandemic demonstrated weaknesses and blind spots and prompted questions about the need for preparedness, knowledge, resources, and infrastructure for future emergency situations: "It really makes us think, 'Do we need to set up an online classroom at the beginning of the year?' So that, if that happens, the kids know how to use it? Or is it something that they'll figure out at home? Now with the option of distance learning, do we need to always be prepared for it? I think there will be a big shift in learning because they have this technology. I think they'll associate computers and technology with school forever."

For other staff, including Dr. Tully, the recent experiences with remote learning prompted a desire to take a break from technology. During our follow-up visit, Dr. Tully still questioned the place and role of technology in inclusive education. And while she acknowledged its potential—and, in emergency cases, its necessity—for classroom instruction, Dr. Tully's focus was on the hope of leaving the past year behind and moving forward to reinstitute the promise of FVA's in-person inclusive education model: "Instructionally, I just think it wasn't good. I would like to let it all go, frankly. I really don't think it was good for this school's model. I think there were some positive gains for how technology can be incorporated into the classroom. However, I'm not convinced it's preferable. I'm not there yet." Dr. Tully's desires to put away remote learning, coupled with a somewhat reticent acknowledgment of the potential of technology for learning, was demonstrative of the mixed feelings many school communities felt moving through the pandemic.[7]

Dr. Tully's sentiments were reiterated by other staff, particularly the special education teachers Ms. Severin and Ms. Petersen, whose teacher training placed an exclusive premium on provision of services in person. This was coupled with minimal teacher preservice content dedicated to instructional

156   Chapter 7

best practices for the use of mainstream, educational, and assistive technologies to support the provision of services for students with diverse support needs—not uncommon in teacher education broadly and special education specialist training specifically.[8]

Family Expectations for the New School Year

The desire to move away from remote learning was also reiterated by several parents we followed up with at FVA, particularly those of students with significant support needs. For Blake, mother to Finn and Chandler, both diagnosed with autism, remote learning precluded the effective implementation of FVA's inclusion model. In her mind, the only way forward was to do away with remote learning completely, as she expressed while discussing her priorities for the upcoming 2021–2022 school year: "I think the biggest success of FVA's inclusion model is community. And we lost that. That just fell to the wayside. I think the number 1 focus is kids feeling safe and then everything else can scaffold on top of that, whatever it may be: play, therapies. I would love to see community be prioritized. And I know we need to be back in person for that. That's my answer as a parent and as a board member."

Mira, mother to Maddox, Maya, and Marco, like Blake, also desired a return to in-person learning. However, her desire was tempered by the experiences born out of being a first-responder family during the pandemic: "For the future, I do hope they get to go to school full time, but at the same time, I'm still nervous, you know, and I'm not sure I want to have my kids vaccinated yet. So, I'm still nervous about that. But I do hope that the school provides extra help for the kids . . . I'm just hoping that we can get extra help so I can get them back up there." As was true of many parents across the United States, Mira's concerns about physical and socio-emotional safety and well-being of her children persisted beyond the apex of the pandemic.[9] These concerns included the logistics of keeping students safe on campus, providing students with the academic and socio-emotional supports to reintegrate into the in-person school environment, and making decisions about whether and when to vaccinate their children.

For Sara's family, the prospective return to in-person learning for the 2021–2022 school year was met with relief, expectation, and excitement for the future:

> El año ya está por concluirse. No sé qué tanto podemos salvar . . . Esperaría que, para el siguiente año, la parte de repaso no fuera tanta. ¡Ya a lo que sigue!

Reflections on Technology and Inclusion in a Changing World

> The year is about to be over. I don't know how much we can salvage . . . I'd hope that for next year, the review period isn't too long. On to the next thing!

The desire to move onward was echoed by Sara's children, Leon and Isla, who were looking forward to FVA's future campus expansion, which we learned about in June 2021, as Isla expressed here:

> Yo deseo que haya salones más grandes, más compañeros. Tal vez un poquito más de tarea [riendo]. Y tal vez, un campus más grande.

> I hope that we have larger classrooms, more classmates. Perhaps a bit more homework [giggles]. And maybe, a larger campus.

With the exception of Marco, who was still anxious about a return to in-person instruction, both Mira's and Blake's children were also eager to return to FVA, with the primary motivator being that they would be able to engage with their classmates and school community so that, as Leon shared, "Ya podemos estar en contacto" (we can be together again).

Looking Forward: Hopes and Goals for Rebuilding

Just prior to the end of the 2020–2021 school year, Dr. Tully informed me that FVA would be adding a second school site for the upcoming year. There was a mix of exhaustion, relief, and hope in her voice for this latest endeavor, both to overcome the challenges of the past year and to expand upon the promise of FVA's inclusion model.

Several months later, right before the 2021 winter break, Dr. Tully invited me to visit the new site. She gave me a tour and explained the latest happenings at FVA, including how they had tried to recover from the pandemic and move forward with new initiatives. For example, just that month, staff began leading retention conferences with families to discuss plans for students' academic and socio-emotional recuperation the following year. It also included structural leadership and programming shifts, as Dr. Tully described during our follow-up: "I'm planning to have everyone on campus every day, full-time learning with the least restrictions as possible on their movements . . . We'll be operating across two sites next year. So, I'm planning to face those new challenges that will be emerging with that. I hired two assistant principals. Very excited! I'm hoping to move into the executive director position more fully." Dr. Tully also shared that FVA already had the two campus sites fully staffed and that school leadership was planning extended learning opportunities. This included an intervention-focused after-school program to mitigate the failures in instructional access that occurred during the 2020–2021 school year. Dr. Tully also reflected on what she had learned the prior year, particularly as it related to tensions between receiving guidance from the state and striving to achieve a new normal. Dr. Tully shared that she anticipated the need for future health-and-safety measures, which she felt would impede how FVA's inclusive education program was designed initially.

At the same time, Dr. Tully also indicated that she felt the FVA school community would be better able to accommodate any restrictions more effectively the second time around if it came to that. And despite the trepidation and unknowns of the 2021–2022 school year, Dr. Tully concluded our time together by sharing her hopes and dreams for the following year:

> I'm hoping to rebuild our sense of community with the staff and the families. I'm planning to reengage with our foundational model of inclusion and co-teaching and co-planning, and then continue walking our path. I don't think we're going to put this year behind us. I do expect to do a lot of work rebuilding our community from the ground. I hope to get back to a place where kids can come and feel well . . . I want to keep my eyes on that. And reengage with what was working before, which is a very close-knit community of caring individually. I think that's actually a good remedy for this.

Dr. Tully's belief in better days for FVA spoke of her hope for the future—a hope that many of us share as educators, caregivers, and members of our own extended communities. It is with these thoughts that we now turn to part III of the book, consisting of chapters 8 and 9, to present a relational framework for understanding how technologies could be used to support connection and to discuss future considerations and implications for supporting inclusive education at the intersection of language, literacy, and technology.

III

8 Interdependence: A Relational Framework for Exploring Inclusive Education

In this chapter, we present interdependence—a state in which people collaborate toward shared goals—as a relational framework for exploring inclusive education.[1] Using this framework, we argue that a significant social value in people's use of digital technologies lies in their potential to mediate interdependent collaboration—a departure from previous work centering technology use as primarily one to one.[2] We discuss inclusion, and by extension inclusive uses of digital technologies, across medical and social models of disability (see chapter 2).[3] This includes a discussion of the independence movement that sprang from social models of disability.[4] We explain how the independence movement positioned the use of digital technologies as critical tools for supporting independence, as well as how the movement was a precursor to interdependence.[5]

Moreover, we discuss how the independence movement's traditional aims of promoting autonomy—tied with the original goals of assistive one-to-one technologies—may be insufficient in promoting the full social inclusion of people with disabilities.[6] We cite this critique as partly leading to the proliferation and introduction of interdependence as an alternative framework for understanding disability and inclusive uses of digital technologies.[7] This foregrounds our usage of interdependence to explore disability in the context of inclusive education and inclusive uses of digital technologies, illustrated with examples taken from the preceding chapters, to provide further analysis of the meaning making that took place among students, parents, teachers, and staff at FVA.

Inclusive Technology Use across Models of Disability

Technology Use in Relation to the Medical Model of Disability

Digital technologies are traditionally designed for one-to-one use to support individual users.[8] For example, technologies designed with the needs of disabled users in mind are typically placed under the umbrella of one-to-one assistive technologies, such as for those who are minimally speaking (see chapter 5).[9] Providers might engage in one-to-one clinical practice to train individual users on how to use the technology—for example, during one-to-one speech therapy—to remedy perceived deficits in the disabled user.[10] This positioning of technology is consistent with the medical model of disability (see chapter 2).

In these circumstances, technology is seen as a clinician's tool to remediate a deficit of the individual user with the goal of increasing their ability to function. In this view, disability is positioned as a condition in need of rectification, and the technology is positioned as the tool to do the rectifying.[11] Within the medical model, the disabled user is often positioned as dependent on the technology, with minimal cross-training done between teachers, caregivers, and other significant people in the disabled user's life.[12]

Technology Use in Relation to Social Models of Disability

Uses of digital technologies aligned with social models of disability include multiple users using technology collaboratively. For example, at FVA, Conrad used the LAMP communication program installed on his iPad device in small-group settings to engage with his classmates (see chapter 5). What made this interaction memorable was that all the students, not just Conrad, learned how to use the device and were engaged in using it with Conrad. In this case, we have a group of individuals using a device, originally intended for individual use, collaboratively.

Social and collaborative uses of technology at FVA allude to a broader picture of how we can position technology use to support inclusive education. Exploring social uses of technologies enables an expansion in our understanding of what digital technologies can entail and the role they may play in promoting inclusion. Adopting an interdependent framing allows us to see relations in technology use to move beyond one-to-one uses informed by a medical model of disability to include collaborative uses aligned with social models of disability (see chapter 2).

Interdependence

Finally, a social view of disability places greater emphasis on identifying external, rather than internal, barriers to access—the premise being that people are disabled by barriers in their environment rather than by individual impairment (see chapter 2).[13] A social view of disability therefore centers inclusive technology use as minimizing environmental barriers to access..

The Independence Movement as Social Imperative

The shift toward social views of disability led to the independence movement as socially imperative for inclusion (see chapter 2).[14] Central to the movement was reimagining the use of assistive technologies to promote independent access to previously inaccessible spaces—a critical moment in disability advocacy and scholarship.[15] The independence movement advocated for supports and processes that enabled disabled individuals to make decisions about their own care as a counterpoint to dependency.[16]

However, the independence movement has more recently faced the critique of falling short of emphasizing practices that cultivate the social capital necessary for full participation and inclusion.[17] Several within the disability advocacy and research community, including activists (e.g., Mia Mingus and Dom Chatterjee) and disabilities studies scholars (i.e., Al Condeluci and Glen White) have critiqued that independence is not enough, and instead call for a more synergistic orientation within social models of disability. Accordingly, the independence perspective may not account for collaborative uses of resources and tools, including digital technologies, to create community and engage disabled people as active agents, creators, and members.

Ultimately, interdependence as a framework for exploring inclusion was born partly as a response to this critique. Moreover, interdependence moves beyond an independence lens to illuminate and to amplify collaborative strategies disabled people engage in navigating their lives. Toward this goal, disability activist, Mia Mingus, shares: "With disability justice, we want to move away from the 'myth of independence,' that everyone can and should be able to do everything on their own. I am not fighting for independence, as much of the disability rights movement rallies behind. I am fighting for an interdependence that embraces need and tells the truth: no one does it on their own and the myth of independence is just that, a myth."[18] The prioritization of an independence framing positions interdependence, an inherently relational framework for organizing behavior, at odds with the Western focus on autonomy and individual advancement.[19]

In Cranmer's words, "The challenge then is to consider how schools can change to become more inclusive. Yet, current policy on inclusion is undermined by competitive individualism within wider society and an ethos of marketization and neoliberalism."[20]

In her discussion of public policy regarding the inclusion of disabled children into mainstream educational settings, Cranmer sets forth the argument that policy enables a society to understand its values.[21] In the case of Western nations, ample evidence exists that independence, marked by individualism, is a primary social value.[22] This is in contrast to Eastern nations, as well as more socially oriented Western nations, that adopt a more collective, interdependent approach as the primary social value.[23] As a result, in cultures where independence is valued as the primary marker of a functioning society, there is a danger of individualism being championed and valued over inclusion.[24] So, while independence is an important and crucial aspect of enabling well-being, it is not, in and of itself, enough to support a move toward more fully inclusive models of education.[25]

We position interdependence as a natural extension of the independence movement, complementary to social models of disability. Specifically, an interdependence framing endorses the extension of independent living skills learned to a variety of social and community contexts without replacing independent living goals.[26] We present interdependence as an inherently relational framework that is congruent with shifts in the disability communities toward community-centered approaches to understanding disability.

Interdependence as a Framework for Exploring Inclusive Education

Motivation for the development of an interdependence paradigm centers on the assertion that people with higher levels of social capital in their communities lead more successful lives.[27] A crucial premise of the interdependence paradigm, as Glen White and Al Condeluci envision, is that services and supports for disabled individuals should focus on building social capital, given that disabled people systematically have less access to social capital, are less likely to be integrated in civic and social community endeavors, and are more likely to be isolated.[28] Moreover, relationship building is the focus of interdependence, with the goal of brokering social capital to promote community engagement and inclusion.[29] In her semi-autobiographical monologue, "Interdependency (Excerpts from Several Talks)," Mia Mingus

Interdependence   165

reveals how relationship building is key to interdependency: "Interdependency is not just me 'dependent on you.' It is not you, the benevolent oppressor, deciding to 'help' me. Interdependency is both 'you and I' and 'we.' It is solidarity, in the best sense of the word. It is inscribing community on our skin over and over and over again. Because the truth is: we need each other. We need each other. And every time we turn away from each other, we turn away from ourselves."[30] For Mingus, interdependency means being in relationships with the people who have the potential to provide support, assistance, or accessibility, whether it be asking a stranger to open a container or a physical therapist if they are able to work overtime. To be successful, this requires that disabled people cultivate relationship-building and maintenance skills. This relationship and skill building goes hand in hand with the cultivation of social capital.[31]

Disabled researcher Cynthia Bennett takes from Mingus's views to adopt interdependence as a framework for assessing the moves that disabled individuals engage in with *each other* and nondisabled individuals in their collaborative uses of technologies. Specifically, Bennett and colleagues provide a roadmap for how an interdependence framework can be used to understand the relations between individuals, interactions, and assistive uses of technologies. In short, Bennett and colleagues assert that an interdependence frame "(1) focuses on relations, (2) helps us make sense of multiple forms of assistance happening simultaneously, (3) draws out the often-underwritten contributions of people with disabilities, and (4) can help disassemble hierarchies that prefer ability." In their conceptualization, seeing relations refers to "a coming together of people and things in a particular moment in time."[32] As such, interdependence centers relations and can provide a heuristic for how accessible a situation is with regard to the contextual factors.

Adopting an interdependence framework also allows us to acknowledge the relational nature of simultaneous actions, customs, and behaviors. This understanding was essential to us in assessing the inclusive team-teaching approach undertaken at FVA, as well as the integration of parents into the community ecology of the school. Applying an interdependence framework included paying particular attention to instances where individuals both provide and receive support, including what Bennett and colleagues refer to as "multiple types of access support." As a result, adopting an interdependence framework afforded us a structure for breaking down individual moves to better understand how each member of the FVA school community both provided and received assistance.[33] (Throughout this chapter, we use "participant moves" to refer to the varied ways people navigate and use their resources for social and communicative purposes.)[34]

Finally, interdependence provides an empowerment framework for acknowledging the work done by people with disabilities—a critical concept we engaged with in studying FVA's inclusive school practices (see chapter 4). Interdependence as a mechanism for empowerment is built on the premise that all people and things in interaction with each other are mutually reliant.[35] Thus, an interdependent framework can reveal the work done by, and for, members of disability communities.

As we explore inclusive education at the intersection of language, literacy, and technology, we use interdependence to understand how families and staff came together at FVA to support inclusive LLT practices—ultimately cultivating students' access to social capital. In the remainder of the chapter, we elaborate on Bennett's application of interdependence to build an argument for using *interdependence* as a framework for (1) assessing participant moves to support inclusion, (2) adopting intersectional approaches to understanding inclusion, and (3) exploring inclusive uses of digital technologies in relation to disability and education.[36]

Interdependence as a Framework for Assessing Participant Moves to Support Inclusion

Inclusion is social in nature and requires a participatory element. Moreover, precedence exists for using interdependence as a frame for understanding the moves participants make to support inclusion. Bennett and colleagues, as well as Branham and Kane, discuss using an interdependence framing to assess and understand the moves people with disabilities make in relation to their uses of assistive technologies.[37] White and colleagues, and Mingus, explore interdependence as a way to understand the moves people with disabilities make in relating to each other as well as nondisabled individuals, positioning interdependence as essential to surviving and thriving in a world not designed for disabled people.[38]

We extend these applications to include interdependence as a frame for assessing the moves that participants make to support inclusive educational practices. As discussed in chapter 2, we use "inclusion" to refer to structures

Interdependence

of access and participation and "inclusive" to refer to integrative actions. In this context, inclusive classrooms are those that, in implementing inclusive practices, support an integrated inclusive education environment where all students are equitably supported and valued (see chapter 2).[39] This marries "inclusion as act" with "interdependence as engagement," making inclusion as participant action compatible with interdependence as engagement.

At FVA, we saw this in the effects of interdependent behavior on disabled people's participatory inclusion. Thus, as we observed the moves that students, parents, teachers, and staff made at FVA, we began to notice common threads—notably that the most inclusive moments occurred at the times that the community adopted an interdependent approach to engagement. The culmination of students' inclusion at FVA partly lay in their interconnected support of each other. Interdependence provides a compelling frame for exploring and understanding the moves participants made to support inclusive education at FVA.

Interdependence as a Framework for Intersectional Approaches to Inclusive Education

Interdependence as a theoretical framework for understanding interpersonal behavior is by nature intersectional because it requires a willingness by participants to take unique perspectives, approaches, and assets into account. Moreover, interdependent thinking requires participants to understand the ways that multiple identities and contexts interrelate. Adopting interdependence as an approach requires contextual understanding of how differing, sometimes competing, contingencies impact and hold influence over each other, particularly toward the accomplishment of shared endeavors. Intersectionality as theory also places great focus on contextual understanding, particularly as it relates to using such understanding to accomplish broader-reaching societal goals.

Kimberle Crenshaw was the first to conceptualize intersectionality as a qualitative framework for discussing structural identities in relation to systems of oppression and power. Intersectionality provides a framework for understanding how facets of a person's identity—for example, race, gender, disability, and class—influence discrimination and privilege.[40] A primary objective of the intersectional approach is to identify, and dismantle, systemic causes of oppression that afford advantage and disadvantage, disproportionately impacting historically marginalized groups.[41] Broadening from its roots in first- and second-wave feminism, which largely focused on the experiences of white middle-class women, through Black feminist theory (e.g., Jennifer C. Nash), intersectionality has since shifted beyond identity as an accounting of power.[42]

Feminism introduced intersectionality into the study of disability with the acknowledgment that systems of oppression relating to race, gender, and class also intersected with disability.[43] Intersectional research is now more focused on the interlocking impact of belonging to more than one historically marginalized group—for example, multilingual students with disabilities—and how multiple group membership can lead to multiple forms of advantage or discrimination.[44]

Given FVA's culturally and developmentally diverse population, our exploration of disability and inclusion had to take participants' intersectional identities into account for our assessment to be nuanced. Integrating an intersectional approach to our study of interdependence at FVA thus allowed us to see how "disability is imbricated with other categories of 'difference,' such as race, gender, nationality, age, sexuality, poverty, etc., categories that previously seemed so clear-cut, but are in reality complex, interwoven and embedded in space and time."[45]

Adopting an intersectional approach to the application of interdependence as a relational frame allowed us to cultivate an understanding of the individual and collective contextual impacts on technology use and how those related to the inclusion of students at FVA. It also allowed us to see how personal contingencies across multiple axes of difference interacted to amplify students' inclusion at FVA.

Interdependence as a Framework for Exploring Technology Use across Disability

Our presentation of interdependence as a framework for exploring technology use in relation to disability is threefold: (1) to serve as a relational frame for understanding more fully inclusive uses of technologies, (2) to afford a conceptual heuristic for observing the moves that people make with each other in their use of technology, and (3) to position interdependence as a relational framework for understanding how technologies can be used collaboratively to promote inclusive education practices through the creation of social capital (see chapter 5).

Interdependence

As illustrated in figure 8.1, we use an interdependence framing to interrogate the notion that dependent one-to-one uses centered on medical models of disability, or even independent one-to-one uses aligned with social models, are not the most salient ways that digital technologies can be used inclusively. Moreover, we make the claim that an interdependent approach to technology use supports inclusive education practices through the creation of social capital—an important component of inclusion.[46]

Adopting an interdependent approach to exploring LLT practices at FVA allowed us to better understand how technologies were collaboratively used by students to express themselves, connect with classmates and teachers, and demonstrate competencies and understanding in the classroom. Adopting an interdependent approach in studying LLT practices at FVA also afforded a fuller appreciation of the socially empowering potential students' technology use held for giving voice to their ambitions, thoughts, and feelings, as well as for removing barriers to participation and expression.

Cultivating Interdependence in Schools

Interdependence provides an empowerment framework for acknowledging, and building upon, the work done by students, teachers, and staff within schools. As we explore engagement with each other, and with digital technologies, we can use interdependence to better understand how students

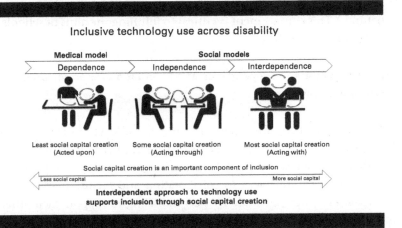

Figure 8.1
Framework for understanding inclusive technology use across models of disability.

model for each other to create accessibility. Interdependence provides a framework for exploring how school communities can achieve inclusion by engaging in collaborative practices that cultivate engagement and increase social capital.

Interdependence in schools is complex, characterized by multiple simultaneous actions and practices within the classroom environment. In the examples in this book, we have seen the improvisational nature and flexibility required in cultivating a joyful and interdependent classroom community. This attunement and flexibility to the socio-emotional needs of students enabled teachers to maintain connection with students.

A distinguishing quality in inclusive schools is the deep interdependence among students and staff in forming the school community. Interdependence at FVA, particularly in relation to their full inclusion model, manifested as a commitment to intentionally work, play, and learn together—in the process, being mindful to support maximum participation. Interdependence materialized in the collaboration and assistance that students and staff bestowed upon each other. The quality of this collaboration and assistance was continuous and comprehensive—occurring before, during, and after class.

Throughout our time at FVA, we saw many behaviors meant to create access, community, and inclusion for students with diverse abilities, backgrounds, and needs. Adopting an interdependent frame allowed us to better understand the ways that the broader FVA community engaged in inclusive education practices across the school. We learned that being a member of the FVA community meant "we are in *all of this* together. Nobody gets left behind." This commitment is critical to fulfilling the aims of schools wanting to be more inclusive.

Revisiting FVA: Interdependence as a Foundation for an Inclusive Education Community

A commitment to interdependence requires a level of care between community members not typically seen in segregated school settings.[47] That it frequently presented at FVA, we assert, was a direct result of integration with a commitment to collaboration and inclusion. We saw this at FVA—for example, in students' peer modeling to support each other's participation. This level of care between students with and without disabilities contrasts with the isolation disabled students often experience in other

Interdependence

schools, as Ms. Davis points out: "What I love the most about FVA, that's different from traditional schools, is that I consistently see all the kids playing together, and they help each other. At other schools, I'd see kids sitting at a different table for lunch or not being included in some activities. FVA doesn't do that."[48] Vulnerability and learning to rely on one another are integral to the delivery of a school's inclusive education program. Promoting reliance between members of a school community also serves a greater goal of ensuring that members have agency in supporting each other to participate to their fullest capacity, bringing to mind the kinds of outcomes that result when marginalized community members work together toward shared goals.[49] This acknowledgment—and acceptance—of vulnerability and inter-reliance is key to a relational understanding of interdependence as "being in this together," as expressed here by Ms. Carina:

> You need to be able to work with other people. So, that's just an adjustment—being able to communicate effectively with all the adults in the classroom . . . Learning to rely on other people and not just, "I can do it on my own" because, I mean, you can't. You need the support. We all need the support. Communicating with all the people all the time is good because there's going to be times where I feel like overwhelmed, but it's not "Oh, I'm overwhelmed and I'm alone." It's "Okay, we're all overwhelmed together."

Ms. Carina describes the challenge in making the shift to an interdependence framing as not being accustomed to seeking support but rather, in her words, defaulting to "doing it alone." This relational shift in how we work means sharing the burden of problem solving together. Being "overwhelmed together" in our feelings, behaviors, and practices of collaboration, as Ms. Carina describes, makes relating an inclusive and humanizing experience. Adopting an interdependent frame in the delivery and conceptualization of inclusion allows for the full humanization of all community members, as Mr. Gabriel shared in his description of what it means to be inclusive:

> When we usually go to a typical student school, you don't get to see the reality of our entire population. We don't get to see that true community that you live in. And so, when you grow up and you see, kids or human beings, in the market with special needs, you kind of, well, tend to just look at them weird . . . I feel like being in a full inclusion school, you get to see and you get to know that person. And just because that person might act a different way and might look a different way than you do, it doesn't make that person any less than you are. So, I feel like the students who go to full inclusion have a better understanding of who this person is. His ideas.

Mr. Gabriel points out the rarity of this level of inclusion—where everyone matters equally without judgement—saying that people don't usually "see the reality of our entire population" because people with disabilities tend to be made invisible, with systemic structures, practices, and attitudes preventing full integration.[50] He makes the important distinction that not only is true inclusion *not* common, it is also not reflective of a "true community." In other words, without the inclusion of disabled community members, we don't have a comprehensive representation of society. Acceptance of this is integral to an interdependent vision of inclusive education in which *all* members of a community have equal access, visibility, and voice.

We also used interdependence as a framework to understand more deeply FVA's community of care. This resulted in the analysis of FVA's inclusive education model across four principles, first introduced in chapter 4: (1) creativity and innovation, (2) autonomy and choice, (3) culture of kindness, and (4) an intersectional vision of inclusion. These four principles formed the foundation of FVA's inclusive community. This application of interdependence is congruent with ecological community-centered approaches to understanding inclusion in school communities as relational. Adopting an interdependence frame afforded us a way to understand the ecological and relational nature of the practices and customs at FVA.[51] This, in turn, allowed us to explore more fully the four principles of inclusion that we identified at FVA.

Creating a Collaborative Community of Creativity and Innovation

Operationalizing a vision for inclusive education within schools requires the development of a collaborative learning community that clearly defines its roles and responsibilities to students. In *Am I My Brother's Keeper? Educational Opportunities and Outcomes for Black and Brown Boys*, Adriana Villavicencio states, "Embarking on the transformative work in a school requires a community of students committed to the same goals who can serve as mentors, confidants and creative partners."[52] At FVA, this was an effort spearheaded by Dr. Tully to leverage the trust garnered from FVA's strong culture of kindness toward the creation of a collaborative and innovative professional learning environment.

Staff collaboration and innovation, as evidenced at FVA, should focus on shared messaging and allowance of time for professional development and preparation. It should also include provision of regular formative observation and feedback of teaching practice, as was practiced by

Dr. Tully—herself a master teacher and "practitioner leader," as described by Ms. Gomez. Time and again, the staff discussed how Dr. Tully supported their growth as active professionals,[53] centering collaboration from a place of social justice underlying FVA's inclusive values.

Finally, the intentional integration of paraprofessionals and service providers, as we saw at FVA, into curriculum planning and implementation is critical to developing a collaborative professional community centered on inclusion. Collaboration refutes the relegation of responsibility for students with disabilities onto others and pushes against practices that "refer out" disabled students to paraprofessionals and service providers.[54]. It requires, instead, a focus on integrating service providers and paraprofessional staff into general education settings and including both general and special education teachers as central to that endeavor.[55]

Collaboration also tackles the gap between beliefs, values, and attitudes underpinning inclusive education and the lack of guidance offered to teachers and providers about how inclusion should be enacted in schools. Cultivating teacher and provider buy-in for collaborative models of teaching requires developing staff's understanding of the benefits of inclusive teaching strategies.[56] Collaborative endeavors toward inclusive education practices involve supporting general teachers in believing in their ability to support *all* children, not needing to "hand off" certain children to others.

One co-teaching combination that creatively embraced collaboration was Ms. Wezner, a general education teacher at FVA who also happened to hold a special education teaching credential, and Ms. Severin, a special education teacher at FVA and the only staff member, other than Dr. Tully, to have previously taught at another full inclusion school. Ms. Wezner discusses her unique partnership with Ms. Severin in their provision of inclusive instruction:

> Being able to come from a side that actually knows how to write goals and all the legal parameters, I think that we collaborate on goals a lot for the kids. Just bouncing ideas off of each other like, "How can they meet that goal?" Or if she finds something for one kid's specific goal, then I'll be like, "Oh, actually that'd be great for our whole class. Let's use it as a whole lesson for everyone because everyone can use that graphic organizer." So, I think just being able to plan with the goals in mind and then adapting it to really benefit *everyone* rather than just that one kid.

Ms. Wezner speaks of how her unique background in special education supports her ability to collaborate with Ms. Severin in the development and application of IEP goals. This is relatively uncommon for general education teachers to collaborate so closely with teachers providing specialized education services in the development of IEP goals—a disconnect that could create barriers to creating more inclusive collaboration across the various members of IEP teams in typical school settings.[57]

As such, creating an inclusive professional community requires institutional buy-in for infrastructures that support collaborative practices in the classroom. This requires that district and school leadership support for teacher and staff professional development as collaborative be explicit. This also requires redefining the role of paraprofessionals as bridges, using explicit training and organization to support comprehensive integration of paraprofessionals into classroom planning and instruction. Finally, teachers need to be supported in designing lessons to be more inclusive, rather than trying to build in inclusion after the fact. This includes support for collaboration with paraprofessionals and service providers preemptively being built into teacher and staff preparation time.

Empowering Participation by Cultivating Autonomy and Choice

In our discussions of what inclusion meant at FVA, families and staff repeatedly shared that helping students build autonomy required helping them to acquire the life skills needed to make good choices, cultivate social capital, negotiate relationships, and engage in their communities. Autonomy and choice were made possible through the presumption of competence and the allowance of multiple forms of participation. Empowering participation through autonomy and choice are prerequisites for inclusion and essential components of participative school communities.

At FVA, the cultivation of autonomy and choice centered on helping students cultivate the relational tools needed to navigate day-to-day living. Ms. Severin alluded to the role interdependence plays in cultivating autonomy and supporting the relational tasks of working, living, and problem solving in society:

> One of my professors hammered it home to me in my teaching program. All of the kids on my caseload—even the ones with the most significant disabilities—I want them to be able to go into a shop, and order a sandwich, and be able to pay for it, and hopefully be there with friends. So, they're with a group of friends, they order a sandwich, the shop makes the sandwich wrong. They can go back and say, "Excuse me, you put onion on my sandwich. I really don't want onion. Can you redo this again?" Make the change, do all that, sit with their friends, have a sandwich, and then get home. And home is maybe where they live with their

> friends 'cause they're like eighteen or twenty-one. And they have a fun social life, and they have a meaningful job, and they feel like they are contributing.

In this excerpt, a connection is made between interdependence and sources of social capital, which Ms. Severin defines as the ability to advocate for oneself, make and keep friendships, and live a happy and productive life. Developing students' abilities to garner social capital—crucial to the social integration of people with disabilities—touches on an essential objective of full inclusion education programs: to prepare students to lead fulfilling lives as contributing members of their communities.[58] Ultimately, by adopting interdependent approaches to cultivating the inclusion of students with disabilities, schools can support students' abilities to sustain integrated lives within their communities.

A desire for autonomy and choice for students with disabilities was also reiterated by parents at FVA. Parents came to believe in the right of their children to have the choice to be educated in an inclusive general education setting. As a result, integration should be seen as necessary for supporting students' autonomy and potential. This includes presuming competence, dispelling myths about disability, and believing in students' true potential, which we saw with Madeline's commentary about her daughter Star's capabilities. Madeline, like many parents at FVA, came to reject presumptions made about students with disabilities, coming to believe instead that children's growth and inclusion centers on presuming competence.

Finally, we found that technology use is most inclusive when its affordances are used to amplify student agency and voice and support participation in the school community. At FVA, this included allowing students choices in their multimodal uses of technology for personal expression, as we saw with Star. Empowering autonomy and choice also means using technology to remove barriers to expression. A major example at FVA was students' collaborative use of AAC technologies to express themselves, connect with classmates and teachers, and demonstrate competencies and understanding within the classroom. Students' collaborative uses of digital technologies afforded opportunities to grow their social capital by amplifying their voice within the classroom community, as we observed with Tammy's use of Proloquo2Go. Applying an interdependent framework allowed us to understand better the ways that technologies were inclusively used by students to be known within their classroom communities as active participants.

Institutionalizing a Culture of Kindness

The cultivation of interdependent approaches to inclusion involves developing the social skills needed to advocate for, and sustain, meaningful relationships. Critical to this work is institutionalizing a culture of kindness as a means of creating spaces "centered on love, care, and joy." In *Am I My Brother's Keeper?*, Villavicencio discusses the importance of creating a community of care to counter the harmful messages students face about themselves and to affirm their identities and self-expression: "Protective spaces like these, established over time with attention to building trust and modeling vulnerability, can help schools develop meaningful relationships among teachers and students while generating a sense of brotherhood and of family among students."[59]

Mr. Gabriel provided a compelling example of a staff member who truly encapsulated Villavicencio's conceptualization of the necessity for protective spaces in cultivating equity and inclusion. When asked what he most wished for the students at FVA, he centered his messaging on the importance of cultivating a culture of kindness as a cornerstone for building an inclusive interdependent school community:

> I would like them to succeed and for them to just explore and do whatever they feel is right. I would love to see them be successful and be loving and caring and be gentle with the world. I feel like our community has a better sense of taking care of your community and your friends compared to the typical learning school. And not to say that they don't have a sense of, you know, consciousness of that, but I feel we really put that out there in our community. So, I don't know, it's a very heavy question for me to think about.

Creating a culture of kindness also requires a recognition of agency and connection as critical components for being interdependent: to truly connect, schools need to understand and affirm the agencies students bring as individuals to the collective classroom. This requires positioning students as active agents within their school communities.[60] Affording agency instills in students the knowledge that they can use their assets and skills to contribute to the school community. This includes allowing for student interests and questions to shape the pedagogies that inform classroom instruction within schools, including the use of digital technologies.[61] Moreover, relationships centered on kindness empowers and includes students, allowing them to realize their agency and connection within their classroom communities.

Interdependence

Championing an Intersectional Vision of Inclusive Education

Finally, FVA strove to meet its mission by demonstrating a commitment to an intersectional vision of inclusive education. In this book, we have connected the ways in which FVA families and staff strove to consider students' multiple identities in the implementation of FVA's inclusive education model. We found that staff and families' multiple identities and perspectives informed their views and approaches to inclusion, particularly as they related to students' intersecting needs across language and disability.

Examples of students' intersecting identities influencing service delivery were particularly evident in the speech and language therapy work that took place with multilingual students with disabilities at FVA. Intersecting needs across language and disability were also evident in FVA's attempts to include multilingual language supports for students during school-wide celebrations, performances, and events that brought linguistically diverse families and staff together. Also significant was the positioning of paraprofessionals, who were mostly multicultural and multilingual, as cultural brokers within FVA, thus leveraging the affordances of staff members' intersecting identities as essential to supporting the inclusion of multilingual students with disabilities.

Finally, we explored families own intersectional perspectives, revealing specific beliefs about the intersecting relations between the needs of multilingual and disabled students. This included the need for differentiated instruction, as Hilda, mother to a multilingual student with a learning disability, noted in her interview with us. It also means taking into account the potential overlaps in needs between language and disability, as Sara, mother to two neurotypical multilinguals, noted in supporting effective practices to meet the needs of multilingual students with disabilities. Sara's reframing of language status and disability as both distinct and interconnected complements an interdependent approach to understanding the relational commonalities multilinguals and students with disabilities could potentially share.

Moving Forward: Supporting a Fuller Vision of Inclusive Education

The past century has brought humanity into an increasingly interconnected and globalized world where concepts of independence no longer hold the same power they once did in the industrial era.[62] In an increasingly interconnected world, individual actions have ripple effects on the greater ecosystem, and as we have seen with countries' policy responses to global emergencies (e.g., climate change, the pandemic), ignoring this reality can come with great cost.

Countries' collective responses to global problems serve as real-world examples of the importance of moving toward an interdependent frame of thinking for our collective growth, health, and survival. In the final chapter, we will continue to apply an interdependent approach to discuss policy and practices into schools to actualize a fuller vision of inclusive education.

9 Looking to the Future

Reform-minded proponents of inclusive education have moved toward school-wide inclusion models in which all students are seen as permanent members of the general education classroom.[1] This has increasingly resulted in the inception of schools such as FVA where a commitment to inclusive education supports students with disabilities as valued members of the school community. There has, however, been room for interpretation in defining inclusive education and determining what inclusive practices might look like in integrated general education classrooms, including those facilitated by digital technologies at the intersection of language and literacy.[2] This room for interpretation includes gaps in beliefs about the value of inclusive education, how best to support infrastructures for inclusive LLT practices, as well as a lack of guidance for constituents invested in cultivating inclusive schools.[3]

This lack of prescriptive clarity poses challenges for school communities seeking to coordinate and implement inclusive education programming that thoughtfully integrates LLT practices—a term we defined in chapters 1 and 5 to describe integrated approaches for examining language, literacy, and technology as interconnected practices and literacies.[4] As a result, this book was written partly in response to the call for more research and policy suggestions for amplifying inclusive LLT practices relating to disabled children's uses of digital technologies in schools.[5] Toward this endeavor, we synthesize our findings to offer suggestions for inclusive education policy and practice at the intersection of language, literacy, and technology.

A comprehensive vision of inclusive education requires a substantive paradigm shift by policymakers, school leadership, teachers, and parents in understanding and mitigating how principles of inclusion have historically played out in schools. Using FVA as a case study, we outline key recommendations for realizing a fuller vision of inclusive education integrating inclusive LLT practices and digital pedagogies. Moreover, this chapter encourages a rethinking of the ways that schools' digital technology use can contribute to the inclusion of students with disabilities in the classroom, arguing for a perspective of interdependence emphasizing the relational and contextual nature of people's engagement with each other via their technology use.[6] Throughout the book, examples of students' LLT practices have been synthesized using an interdependent lens to extrapolate how advocates can support policies and practices that foster the inclusion of disabled children in school and society.

Inclusive LLT Practices in Schools: Understanding the Successes and Challenges

The purpose of this book was to explore FVA's full inclusion model to reveal how schools might support children's inclusion via inclusive LLT practices. In chapters 4–7, we explored FVA's framework for inclusive education, LLT practices, and assistive uses of digital technologies to support students' agency and engagement in the classroom. Through this journey, we discovered numerous dimensions of inclusive education practice at FVA, including participants' perceptions and approaches to inclusion and the factoring of their LLT practices across school and home contexts. We synthesized the results of our in-person observations and interviews at FVA to outline recommendations about how to mobilize an inclusive pedagogy that incorporates digital technologies in schools to support inclusion. We situated this discussion within the framework of examining successes and challenges at FVA to support a deeper understanding of effective practices for using digital technologies to support students' inclusion in schools.

As described in chapter 4, major successes at FVA included participants' ability to cultivate and operationalize a framework for inclusive education centering on interdependence as a cornerstone of inclusion. This presented itself across four dimensions that we conceptualized as FVA's framework for inclusion: supporting creativity and innovation, enabling autonomy and choice, cultivating a culture of kindness, and committing to an intersectional vision of inclusion that accounts for families' diverse identities and experiences as cultural assets.

Looking to the Future 181

As we described in chapter 5, a major success was FVA's ability to support the inclusion of minimally speaking students in the classroom through students' assistive uses of digital technologies. This included students' own, and collaborative, use of AAC technologies to share their voices and engage with peers. This also included students' use of assistive features in word-processing tools to facilitate their writing process. Our observation of students' LLT practices afforded the opportunity to explore thematically the affordances of using digital technologies to support students' agency as readers and writers, as well as illuminate how students' uses of digital technologies afforded alternative modes of identity and expression.

However, alongside these successes, challenges integrating digital technologies into FVA's in-person classroom practice arose. Except for assistive uses of AAC technologies, there was unevenness in technology uptake and integration into the classroom. Moreover, we found that technologies were mostly used to support the daily functions of teaching rather than being used tranformatively to expand access and engagement with the curriculum. Inconsistencies in technology use often centered on variability in teacher understanding of the technologies themselves, differing perceptions of the utility in integrating digital technologies into classrooms, as well as gaps in resources and technical support. These factors can lead to tensions in decisions about when, where, and how to allow and use digital technologies in schools.[7] As Cranmer notes in *Disabled Children and Digital Technologies*, technology use in schools tends toward the pedestrian in support of the mechanics of teaching rather than being used to expand students' critical thinking and engagement.[8]

Differences in the attitudes and values that parents, teachers, support staff, and students placed on the use of technologies in the classroom also posed challenges. Parents and teachers were more likely to view technologies as potential disruptors, while paraprofessionals, service providers, and students were more likely to view technologies as mediators for communication and connection. In the latter view, connection and expression—along with what Garcia describes in *Good Reception* as the cultural wealth that students bring to the classrooms in their use of digital technologies—are but several of the affordances that the use of classroom technologies could hold for learning and engagement.[9]

182   Chapter 9

Inclusion across Contexts: Remote and Hybrid Uses of Technology to Support Connection

The sudden shifts to remote and hybrid learning across US schools commencing in the spring of 2020 led to a new set of challenges, as well as opportunities, for reflection and reinvention. Specifically, at FVA, exploring how digital technologies were used to facilitate shifts in boundaries, priorities, and roles was key to understanding how technologies could be used to support connection and inclusion during times of uncertainty in the educational landscape of the pandemic. Exploring these technology-enabled shifts in chapters 6 and 7 was at the heart of developing a better understanding of the challenges and affordances of the increased, often improvised, uses of digital technologies during the pandemic.

Remote interviews with FVA's families and staff shed light across four considerations: reconceptualizing new ways to use previously existing technologies, negotiating and shifting boundaries and roles between schools and students' homes in the implementation of remote and hybrid learning, and prioritizing mental health to redefine how FVA chose to be inclusive. We found that these shifts in technology use centered on reconceptualizing the originally intended uses of digital technologies to meet unanticipated social needs brought on by the pandemic. Shifting the use of digital teleconferencing applications, such as Zoom, from primarily a conference tool to a digital forum for remote classroom instruction and service delivery was a primary example of this. The repurposing of digital technologies resulted in technology applications not originally designed for remote classroom instructions, such as Zoom, affording widely available and cost-effective platforms for supporting large numbers of districts and schools.[10] These unanticipated uses of digital technologies for alternative and improvised purposes, while imperfect, nevertheless enabled essential interactions between students, parents, and teachers that allowed schools to maintain connected during the pandemic.[11]

Additionally, we discussed the negotiations that staff and families undertook to invite staff into students' homes and parents into teachers' classrooms through the eye of the camera. Resulting tensions of the former included apprehension, as evidenced by students turning off their cameras, while the latter led to teacher anxiety caused by the direct viewing of teachers' real-time classroom practices. With that said, affordances included parents and teachers more intensively collaborating to support student

Looking to the Future

learning. Increased understanding of day-to-day classroom instruction was also facilitated by parents' access to their children's classrooms via the camera, which lent itself to an increased awareness between teachers and parents of the circumstances and challenges inherent in teaching and learning.

We also explored a redefining of boundaries between what constituted school versus home environments, which in some cases resulted in the blending of the two. These shifts in boundaries were coupled with changes in attitudes among parents and staff regarding interest, and willingness to use digital technologies in novel and collaborative ways to support remote and hybrid instruction. These shifts in attitudes, including perceived affordances of the utility of incorporating digital technologies into classroom instruction, were critical to the increased uptake of staff's technology use during the pandemic. Finally, FVA's shift in prioritizing a culture of kindness virtually included a heightened focus on supporting students' socioemotional health and safety. These concerns, which have persisted and become amplified beyond the apex of the pandemic, include a reevaluation of the supports and resources students need to reintegrate into school environments transformed by the pandemic.[12]

Key Questions for Inclusive LLT Practices in Schools

Research questions (see appendix A) used to explore inclusive LLT practices at FVA were *process* oriented toward addressing case-study empirical goals.[13] Research questions included:

What do inclusive school and classroom practices look like in an inclusive school community?

How do students, staff, and parents engage in literacy activities and use digital technologies in an inclusive school community?

How do LLT practices support (or hinder) students' inclusion as fully engaged members in their school community?

While our research questions allowed us to synthesize findings reflective of inclusive LLT practices, they also afforded a frame for arriving at practical questions to guide our discussion of why this research matters. Practical questions were derived from the research process that we undertook at FVA and are meant to inform recommendations for effective practice. Practical questions include:

How can school communities make schools more inclusive?

How can school communities use digital technologies to support students' inclusion, agency, and connection across in-person, remote, and hybrid settings?

How can school communities cultivate inclusive LLT practices to empower students' voices as creators?

These practical questions guide our discussion of disabled students' inclusion, facilitated through collaborative uses of digital technologies embedded within LLT practices.

We consider a school community's usage of technology to be inclusive when it supports inclusive education more broadly through the cultivation of creativity and innovation, autonomy and choice, a culture of kindness, and an intersectional vision of inclusion. We also consider digital technology use to be inclusive when it is collaboratively used to support language and literacy practices, enable the presumption of competence, support multimodal forms of expression, and amplify student voice. Moving beyond this heuristic, enabling inclusive uses of digital technologies requires reflecting on the myriad contextual factors influencing schools' uses and experiences with digital technologies across specific contexts—critical to the cultivation of an inclusive pedagogy.[14]

Defining a Vision for Inclusive Digital Pedagogy

Widespread beliefs abound about the power of digital technologies to transform schools. However, the practical institutional and classroom-level practices that could bring schools closer to that reality on a broader scale are often absent.[15] As such, engaging in inclusive digital pedagogy starts with understanding that technology-enabled learning is not just about the technologies themselves but rather the connected learning that occurs when digital technologies are used to support inclusion.[16]

An expanded view of inclusive digital pedagogy as social and relational aligns with our interdependence framing and considers the sociocultural impacts of using technology in school communities. As Cranmer shares, understanding technology as a mechanism for access requires the view that access "be the result of a set of complex and interrelated qualities, human and social resources and relationships alongside the digital."[17] Understanding

Looking to the Future

technology as a mechanism for creating access and inclusion involves viewing its use as encompassing multiple social resources and relationships.[18]

Ultimately, a model of inclusive digital pedagogy entails viewing digital inclusion as embedded across multiple people and contexts.[19] These contexts include intentional whole-school mobilization integrating technology use in collaborative ways that extend beyond one-to-one uses to empower agency, as illustrated in figure 9.1. These sociocultural and relational qualities of twenty-first-century technology use are amplified across a convergence of mainstream, educational, and assistive technologies to promote increased engagement between users and their worlds.

As such, an inclusive digital pedagogy uses technology to create access and inclusion by engaging with the affordances of collaborative technology use. Inclusive digital pedagogy requires a supportive infrastructure to engage *all* students universally in using digital technologies to connect and learn about their world.[20] In part II of the book, we discussed the first two contexts: (1) principles for intentional whole-school mobilization of inclusive practice, and (2) LLT practices that support collaborative technology use. In the follow section, we discuss the final context relevant to creating an inclusive digital pedagogy: the need for empowering infrastructures that support student, teacher, and parent agency. This final context requires addressing barriers to adoption, understanding discrepancies in attitudes

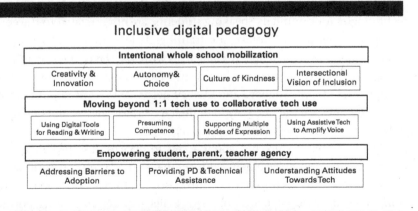

Figure 9.1
Framework for understanding inclusive digital pedagogy across contexts.

186   Chapter 9

toward technology uptake, and providing consistent professional development and technical assistance.

Address Barriers to Adoption

Barriers to adoption of digital technologies that support inclusive LLT practices at FVA included challenges in balancing provision of services with the goal of piloting FVA's inclusive education program. More broadly, competing priorities and barriers to adoption are also coupled with a lack of institutional guidance at the district, state, and federal levels for how best to integrate digital technologies into classrooms. At FVA, this presented within the scope of needing to navigate the constraints placed by a prevailing medical viewpoint of service delivery not always aligned with the values and goals of full inclusion, as Dr. Tully shared: "Inclusive service delivery has been just a battle the entire time, and we're still battling it out now . . . Honestly, almost all of the structures of special education simultaneously advocate for full inclusion and constrain the practice of it." Moreover, consistent and coordinated uses of digital technologies, particularly for disabled students, are often scuttled by costs, insufficient material and time resources, and lack of professional development, outreach, and support. When infrastructure supports are in place for technologies to be consistently used to support students' inclusion, students are empowered to engage more fully in the classroom.

Inconsistencies in the use of digital technologies, particularly assistive technologies for minimally speaking students, are often related to the competing priorities in staff uptake and training. At FVA, these competing priorities sometimes created uptake challenges with Ms. Davis, the SLP, and Ms. Alexa, who wanted to incorporate assistive technologies more consistently to support students' language and literacy needs. As is common in schools, staff sometimes see the integration of digital technologies as separate from, rather than integral to, inclusive practice.

Digital inclusion is not just about access to devices, it is also about unified messaging and engagement with the belief that the thoughtful adoption of collaborative technology use into classroom instruction is an essential component of inclusive education. This belief requires cultivating positive views toward the integration of digital technologies into classroom practice to inclusively to support students' language and literacy engagement. As such, inclusive education practice involves including teachers, parents, and service

Looking to the Future

providers in the consultation of how technologies can be adopted and integrated into students' LLT practices, including specific discussion of children's use of AAC devices and assistive features already prevalent in mainstream and educational technologies. Inclusive education practice also requires normalizing the use of assistive features in digital technologies to support students' LLT practices—for example, supporting teachers and parents in allowing students' use of speech-to-text or text-to-speech digital tools.

Understand Discrepancies in Attitudes toward Technology Uptake

Promoting coordinated and consistent use of digital technologies requires taking inventory of school community members' attitudes toward inclusive uses of digital technologies in the classroom. Consultation and assessing of attitudes require being mindful of the common assumptions, including not assuming that teachers, providers, and parents know more than they actually do about how to inclusively integrate digital technologies into the classroom to support inclusive LLT practices. It also involves not making assumptions and overestimations of students' comfort levels in using digital technologies to support their engagement in the classroom—a common pitfall being to assume that all of today's generation of students are digital natives. For digital technology interventions and initiatives to be successful, understanding attitudes toward technology adoption is essential. This includes understanding the level of security or insecurity that school community members might feel regarding their competencies for using technologies.

In many schools, as was the case at FVA, disconnects in attitudes and roles occur between the home and school contexts with regards to students' digital technology use, including those used to support students' language and literacy engagement.[21] Parent attitudes can sometimes be impacted by the disconnect between different levels of use, and knowing how technologies are used, across the home and school contexts. For example, when we pivoted to discussing the role of technology in supporting Star's literacy practices at school, Madeline was very intentional in the ways that she used technology at home (see chapter 5). However, she was not familiar with how technology was being used with Star at school:

Interviewer: You mentioned PE. Do you take your iPad with you?

Star: Yeah.

Madeline: No. Star, for PE you don't use a computer, right? You don't take a computer to PE, do you?

Star: No.

Interviewer to Madeline: I know sometimes they'll give iPads [AAC devices] to the kids.

Madeline: Oh yeah?

Interviewer: With programs like Proloquo2Go.

Madeline: Oh, okay.

Interviewer: I don't know if they're doing that with her.

Madeline: Yeah, I don't know either.

I later confirmed that Star's classroom did indeed use technology in the classroom for GoNoodle sensory breaks—Star's version of PE. Given the level of Madeline's involvement with Star's education, we were a bit surprised to learn that her use of technology with Star was divorced from the digital activities of the school. Disconnects between home and school in the uses of digital technologies with disabled students is not uncommon and can have repercussions for students for whom consistent uses of technologies across home and school are beneficial.[22]

We also noticed a disconnect in technology preference and use in our interview with Blake, Finn's mother. In her interview, Blake indicated that while certain digital apps were used to support reading, there was reticence to incorporate technology into Finn's writing routines. Similar to other families we interviewed, Blake reported that technology was used primarily as a source of entertainment: "We don't use a lot. Both of them have, what is it? The Kindle Fire . . . But that's more for traveling and entertainment. We'll use that to stream a movie on the airplane. I do have an app on my iPhone that I'll let them use called "Endless Alphabet." It's a fun app that helps with reading and writing, and it's interactive and you drag the letters to spell. That's the only one they like. I wouldn't say they use a lot of technology for reading and writing." Blake viewed Finn's need for tactile stimulation as more compatible with the physical reading of books rather than reading digitally. While at times she indicated Finn's enjoyment in using digital literacy applications, they were usually used as entertainment and not necessarily positioned as an intrinsically important LLT practice. Blake's sentiments revealed a disconnect between home and school practices that added to her ambivalence around digital technology use and which were in contrast to what we observed in Finn's use of digital technologies in the classroom.

Looking to the Future   189

At FVA, teacher viewpoints of the affordances of using digital technologies to support students' LLT practices tended to align with those of parents. However, many paraprofessional perceptions, such as Ms. Carina's in chapter 5, aligned with students' primarily positive reception of digital technologies. The majority of teacher viewpoints at FVA aligned with common viewpoints held by teachers generally toward the use of technologies for LLT practices. These include a preference for the physical experience of holding and feeling a physical book, as well as a concern with the negative effects of digital technologies on children's cognition—attitudes and perceptions commonly expressed by parents and teachers about the impacts of screens on students' attention and retention.[23]

Finally, competing attitudes, viewpoints, and buy-in among school community staff almost always reflect those of school leadership. In the case of FVA, while Dr. Tully was supportive of the possibilities of using digital technologies to support inclusion and LLT practices, she didn't feel confident about how best to integrate technologies into classrooms. As a result, identifying how best to integrate digital technologies into a school's inclusive education model of instruction was a primary objective of our research-practice partnership work with FVA.

To conclude, assessing the attitudes of school community members toward technology is critically important to sustainable integration of digital technologies in classrooms.[24] Making necessary shifts toward a collective messaging of the affordances of digital technologies for inclusive LLT practices involves assessing school community member assumptions and knowledge gaps and assisting constituents in viewing technology use more holistically.[25] This includes supporting an understanding of how school communities can use technology to amplify personal language and expression, particularly for students with disabilities.[26] As Alper discusses in *Giving Voice*, practical ways to support productive understandings among families and staff of the affordances of digital technologies include surveying and conversing early on in the school year. This includes understanding how attitudes influence beliefs about potential affordances digital technologies could play in students' lives within the school community ecosystem.[27]

Provide Consistent Professional Development and Technical Assistance
School community member attitudes, implementation, and messaging also relate to technical knowledge and comfort with using digital technologies

to support inclusive LLT practices. We saw this in our attempts to bring digital storytelling, defined as the multimodal uses of digital tools to tell stories, to FVA during the fall of 2019.[28] Digital storytelling as an inclusive LLT practice was embraced by Dr. Tully and the staff. However, once we began training staff in using WeVideo (see appendix B) to make digital stories, issues with teachers' level of comfort surfaced.

Differences in comfort level using technology, coupled with teachers' competing priorities to focus on lesson planning and implementation of FVA's full inclusion model, were underestimated by us and resulted in challenges implementing digital storytelling at FVA. This resulted in participating teachers being unsure of how to incorporate digital storytelling into their actual curricula, despite believing in the value of it as an inclusive LLT practice. Compounded by teachers' lack of technical familiarity with the WeVideo technology itself, attempts to integrate digital storytelling at FVA at the teacher level stalled.

Our experiences attempting to integrate digital storytelling into the inclusive teaching practices at FVA suffered from not having an infrastructure for ongoing professional development and technical support. As a result, incorporating digital storytelling became untenable. These results align with prior research demonstrating that despite best intentions, if technology interventions are not systematically supported with adequate professional development and technical assistance, they are more likely to fail.[29]

With that said, we were pleasantly surprised to learn later that two of the paraprofessionals who participated in the training—Mr. Kellan, an English-speaking paraprofessional of European descent in his first year, and Mr. Gabriel—had taken up digital storytelling at FVA to document the daily life, special occasions, and celebrations of the school community. These digital stories were used as documentation of FVA's cultural practices and values, content for promotional and celebratory materials, and a creative and empowering outlet for the paraprofessionals to engage in and support FVA's school community.

As Mr. Gabriel was one of the most tech-savvy staff members at FVA, providing technical assistance to the school, including the digital storytelling endeavors, fell largely on him. Without schools being afforded the resources to contract extended technical assistance, the task of providing that support often falls on the staff members who identify as most technologically proficient. In this respect, we fell victim to the common occurrence of offering

Looking to the Future

an LLT intervention without also supporting FVA in developing a plan for funding and technical assistance to support implementation.

One of the purposes in having introduced digital storytelling at FVA as an inclusive LLT practice was to encourage staff to move beyond functional uses of technologies toward integrative uses that support content creation, expression, and empowerment. We felt digital storytelling would allow students to develop their individual writing skills, as well as afford them opportunities for collaborative synchronous and asynchronous peer writing.[30] Of course, our primary oversight in the launching of digital storytelling at FVA lay in not fully realizing the extent to which require continual professional development, funding, and technical assistance. Were it not for Mr. Gabriel's resourcefulness and technical knowledge, with support from Mr. Kellan, the fate of digital storytelling at FVA might have been bleak. Launching inclusive digital pedagogies, such as those encapsulated by digital storytelling, requires professional development addressing both the influence of first-order (i.e., access) and second-order (i.e., attitudes) factors influencing the uptake of digital technologies in schools.[31] This includes discussion of how limiting factors can constrain uses of digital technologies as assets that support students' LLT practices.

Conclusion

This book aimed to build upon prior works in its relational view of participant social practice in the use of digital technologies to support the inclusion of students in the classroom at the intersection of language and literacy. In the tradition of Cranmer, Livingstone and Sefton-Greene, Alper, and Schuelka and Carrington, we engaged in research on both the formal and informal learning that occurs within school community ecosystems via parent and practitioner uses of digital technologies to support the inclusive education of disabled children. Building on the existing literature, we also aimed to differentiate this from previous works by extending research on engagement with digital technologies to demonstrate how direct observation of both online and offline LLT practices engaged in by disabled children, along with their teachers and caregivers, converge across school and home contexts to support inclusion.

This exploration of LLT practices in support of an inclusive digital pedagogy is situated within what Livingstone and Sefton-Greene refer to as "a particularly interesting point in late modernity, in which the contrary forces of socio-technological innovation and the reproduction of traditional structures (the school, the family, social class) threaten to pull young people in different directions."[32] As such, we situate our observing of how students engage with digital technologies knowing that the conditions under which students grow and learn are impacted by twenty-first-century shifts of substantive sociocultural significance.

The unique challenges children must face in growing up in the twenty-first century cannot be ignored, nor can the fact that these futures depend on how school communities choose to integrate digital technologies to support inclusive education practices into students' lives.[33] Aligned with the ideals laid forth by our relational framing of interdependence, equitable uses of digital technologies in the twenty-first century hold potential promises for connection and creative thinking, and act as a bridge between more traditional and newer LLT practices for social change.[34]

At their best, the affordances of digital technologies offer powerful access and connection.[35] From this perspective, digital affordances can facilitate communication that is "creative, civic, collaborative, and experimental, potentially linking spaces, respecting voices, building self—efficacy, supporting interests, acknowledging expertise, and scaffolding learning."[36] By exploring the ways in which students, families, and schools engage in LLT practices, we reveal what Livingstone and Sefton-Greene call "the processes of social reproduction" to illuminate and enact aspects of disabled children's identities that might overwise be made invisible and to reveal how school communities use technological resources to enact alternatives for inclusive education practice.[37] Studying the lives of students with disabilities, along with their teachers and caretakers, reveals aspects of their social worlds that might otherwise remain marginalized.

Using FVA as a case study, we intended to shed light on inclusive education practices that enable an interdependent vision of inclusion at the intersection of language, literacy, and technology. As school communities begin shifting toward inclusive models of education, understanding technology's role in this process is critical to the success of inclusion efforts to create access and equity in schools. This book seeks to add to the interdisciplinary study of disability, education, and technology by examining the ways in which digital technologies can support inclusive LLT practices for

Looking to the Future

culturally and linguistically diverse students with and without disabilities. Toward this end, we strove to illuminate the kinds of social organization that allow for inclusive school communities to thrive, particularly through the deployment of digital technologies to help students express agency and voice. We hope that insights gained from FVA's example lead to a greater understanding and adoption of interdependent approaches that support inclusive education—aspiring to a future where *all* student voices extend beyond the margins.

Appendix A: Methods for Investigating Inclusive Education

This appendix presents an overview of the methods that form the basis for the findings discussed in this book. It begins with a discussion of the selection of FVA as a study site and continues with a description of the context surrounding data collection and analysis at FVA. We discuss the rationale for using case-study and ethnographic approaches to collect and analyze interview, focus group, and classroom observation data.[1] We detail how we used three levels of analysis at the school, classroom, and focal family level to select a diverse range of families and staff for interviews varying across grade level, socioeconomic background, abilities and areas of need, and experiences with literacy and technology. We then describe the sources of data collected during the 2019–2020 and 2020–2021 school years that allowed us to address our research inquiries. Finally, we detail our use of qualitative approaches to analyze the interview, classroom observation, and document data including both first- and second-cycle coding and content analysis.[2]

Selection of FVA as Study Site

This study was primarily concerned with exploring and understanding (1) inclusive best practices in support of LLT practices, (2) how digital technologies were used to scaffold student agency and engagement within the classroom, and (3) how students used digital technologies to amplify their voice as readers and writers. FVA classrooms are ideal environments to explore these questions due to their integrated and inclusive settings with diverse students, varied and constant uses of technologies, teachers and staff who were interested in inviting us into the classroom, and families invested in supporting LLT practices at home.

FVA's unique school culture and organization (see chapter 4) afforded an ideal environment for analyzing the ways in which schools could use digital technologies to support student inclusion while developing their language and literacy skills. Moreover, FVA's developmentally and culturally diverse mix of students, which included minimally speaking students learning to use digital communication devices, illustrate the potential of technology to embody and empower student agency and voice. FVA as a study site also provided an opportunity to observe the affordances of using digital technologies to support the literacy practices of students with sensory processing needs—for example, those requiring additional support in engaging in cognitively demanding tasks such as writing.

Finally, FVA was an excellent site in that it gave us an opportunity to observe both challenges in implementation specific to FVA's unique inclusive setting, such as those related to consistent integration and use of assistive communication device for minimally speaking students. Observations at FVA also afforded a view into the challenges more commonly seen in lower-resourced schooling environments attempting to integrate digital technologies into classroom practice, including those related to uses of one-to-one laptops and mobile media for students.[3]

Study Design

Remaining true to our origins as a research-practice partnership, we collaborated with FVA's executive director in the implementation of the project. This included incorporating her feedback into the study design, data-collection procedures, and participant sampling and recruiting for the study.

In consultation with the executive director, we decided on the use of an embedded case-study design and ethnographic methodologies to analyze interview and classroom observation data.[4] In this design, we used three levels of analysis at the school level (one case), combo class grade level (four cases), and focal family level (six cases; see table A.1).

We chose the case-study approach because it is appropriate for exploratory, descriptive studies, in which the goal is to develop a better understanding of contexts and processes—in this case, how the school used technologies to support inclusion. Choosing an embedded case-study approach allowed us to develop a better understanding of inclusive best practices and ways in which students utilized technologies to support language and literacy

Appendix A

Table A.1
Embedded units of analysis

Unit of Analysis	Case(s)
School	One (FVA)
Grade	Four (K, 1/2, 2/3, 4/5 grade combos)
Families	Six (children per grade: K: 4; 1/2: 3; 2/3: 3; 4/5: 2)

practices within the full inclusion setting. Taking an ethnographic approach allowed us to explore, describe, and interpret participants' shared, and distinct, practices and perspectives—in this case, the ways that students experienced themselves, their peers, and the greater school community at school and at home.

At the school level, we explored the practices that the school community engaged in during whole-school events and recess/lunch breaks through an analysis of school observation data collected in person in fall 2019 and winter 2020 (see Sources of Data). At the classroom level, we explored students' and teachers' uses of digital technologies in the classroom through analysis of weekly in-person classroom observation data in fall 2019 and winter 2020, as well as remote asynchronous classroom instruction in spring 2020. During this time, we also collected writing samples and artifacts in coordination with teachers and staff.

We also explored staff's perceptions of their inclusive classroom practices and use of digital technologies through analysis of staff interviews conducted remotely via Zoom or in person in spring 2020 and spring 2021 (see Sources of Data). Finally, at the focal family level, we explored families' perceptions of inclusion as well as their uses of digital technologies in home and community settings through analysis of family interviews. Family interviews were conducted in person at FVA in winter 2020 and either remotely or in person in spring 2021 (see Sources of Data). All staff and family interviews were audio recorded, transcribed, and anonymized. All participants were de-identified using pseudonyms.

Research Questions
Guiding research questions were used to explore inclusive LLT practices at FVA. We define guiding research questions as those which are *process* oriented and support the intellectual and practical goals of an inquiry or

study. This contrasts with what Maxwell refers to as *variable*-oriented questions more common to quantitative approaches.[5] Our guiding research questions were:

What do inclusive school and classroom practices look like in an inclusive school community?

How do students, staff, and parents engage in literacy activities in an inclusive school community?

How do students, staff, and parents use digital technologies in an inclusive school community?

How do LLT practices support (or hinder) students' inclusion as fully engaged members in their school community?

Maxwell discusses the utility of flexibly using research questions in qualitative research to explore meaning and process, stating that such questions should evolve over time and advance the goals of the research at hand. As such, our guiding research questions were revisited often and were used to inform the development of our observation and interview protocols, and subsequent data analysis, to align with our stated goals and theoretical framework outlined in chapters 1, 8, and 9.

Protocol Development
The observation protocol used to collect data at the school and class levels was adapted by our team from the Teaching Dimensions Observation Protocol (TDOP).[6] The TDOP is a classroom observation protocol designed to provide nuanced descriptions of teaching practice rather than an evaluative judgment of the quality of teaching. The TDOP can be used by researchers and educators under a limited educational license, is designed to measure critical dimensions of teaching behavior, and is customizable to fit specific research and instructional needs.

I piloted the observation protocol in spring 2019 prior to officially starting the research project in fall 2019. Initial piloting is a useful tool for developing and testing protocol items, developing a better understanding of participants' perspectives and behaviors, and supporting refinements to the theoretical framework.[7] During this pilot phase, I used informal classroom observations to refine the protocol iteratively to capture better the behaviors seen at FVA that could provide insight into answering our guiding research questions for the project. The refined protocol was used to collect classroom and observation data during fall 2019 and winter 2020 (see table A.2).

Appendix A 199

Table A.2
Selected observation protocol items

Guiding Question	Category	Sample Codes
What do inclusive school and classroom practices look like in an inclusive school community?	Special education services	**Structured Academic Instruction (SAI):** Teacher or service provider provides specialized help individually or in small groups
		Speech therapy: One-to-one, pair, or small-group services aimed at supporting speech development
		Occupational therapy: One-to-one, pair, or small-group services aimed at supporting gross and fine-motor development
		Reading/writing intervention: One-to-one, pair, or small-group instruction aimed at supporting reading/writing development
		Social skills/behavioral supports: One-to-one, pair, or small-group interventions aimed at supporting student social and behavioral goals
	Co-teaching practices for inclusion	**One teach, one assist:** One teacher provides whole-group instruction while other teacher provides individual assistance
		Station (center) teaching: Student groups rotate between teachers and/or staff as they move from station to station as a group
		Parallel teaching: Students are split into two groups and provided either the same or complementary lessons in their smaller groups
		Team teaching: Teachers coordinate and plan together to provide instruction together to students within the same classroom
How do students, staff, and parents engage in literacy activities in an inclusive school community?	Literacy activities	**Listening to connected text:** Students are engaged in listening to text read by the teacher or audio
		Reading comprehension: Students are engaged in talking or writing about the meaning of text
		Writing: Students are composing a specific piece of extended writing
		Language development: Teachers help students attend to studying language, including figurative language, idioms, and grammar

(continued)

Table A.2
(continued)

Guiding Question	Category	Sample Codes
How do students, staff, and parents use digital technologies in an inclusive school community?	Instructional technology	**Demonstration equipment:** Overhead projector, Elmo, digital slides, clickers, TV screen, smartboard/whiteboard, other
		Devices (teacher and/or student): Tablet (i.e., iPad), desktop computer, laptop computer (i.e., Chromebook), other
		Digital content: Visual media (e.g., movie, documentary, video clips), social media (e.g., YouTube), education apps, games, websites, other
	Assistive technology	**Mobility aids:** Wheelchairs, scooters, walkers, canes, crutches, prosthetic devices, and orthotic devices
		Software/hardware: Communication apps (i.e., Proloquo2Go), voice recognition, screen readers, and screen enlargement apps
		Digital features: Closed captioning, speech-to-text/text-to-speech functions, hot spots, adjustable font
		Environmental modifications: Playground equipment, class supplies, ramps, grab bars, wider doorways to enable access
How do LLT practices support (or hinder) students' inclusion as fully engaged members in their school community?	Classroom engagement	**Making connections:** Students are given examples (either verbally through illustrative stories or graphically through movies or pictures) that clearly and explicitly link class material to popular culture, the news, and other common student experiences
		Problem solving: Students are asked to solve a problem actively (e.g., work out a mathematical equation) through explicit (e.g., "Please solve for X") or written (e.g., worksheets) requests to solve a problem
		Creating: Students are provided with tasks where the outcome is open-ended rather than fixed (e.g., students are asked to generate their own ideas rather than finding a specific solution)

Appendix A

201

We used insights gained from school and classroom observations, along with informal conversations with students, parents, and staff, to inform the development of staff and family interview protocols (see table A.3). The development of interview questions centered on exploring emerging themes and ideas that were becoming apparent from classroom observations, as well as tapping into noticed patterns and tensions. As with the classroom

Table A.3
Selected interview protocol items

Category	Type	Sample Questions
Family	Parent	What adjustments have you needed to make in how you engage with school moving from a more "typical" environment to a full inclusion environment?
		How has the push-in structure at FVA benefited/challenged your child?
		What kinds of things does your family like to read or write about at home? In your opinion, how does your child feel about reading and writing? With and without technology? Is there a preference?
	Student	What do you like about FVA? What makes FVA special to you? Can you tell me your favorite parts of the day?
		Let's talk about computers. Do you use computers for reading and writing? What is your favorite thing to do on the computer?
Staff	Teacher/paraprofessional	What makes FVA different, or similar, to other schools? What did you expect? What surprised you?
		What have been the benefits/challenges of integrating technology into the full inclusion model? How is this similar/different from your use of tech in "typical" classroom environments?
	Speech/service provider	What adjustments have you needed to make in your delivery of services in a full inclusion environment using a push-in structure? How do you consult and collaborate with team members to meet students' IEP goals?
		In your opinion, how do your students feel about communicating with and without technology? Is there a preference? Why?
	Administrative	What brought you to FVA? Could you share your reasons for working at FVA?
		Could you share your hopes and dreams for students at FVA?

observation protocol, we did our best to ensure that interview questions aligned with the guiding questions for the project. This approach resulted in the interviews being used as semi-structured conversational tools for exploring and allowing families and staff to share their stories and experiences at FVA, particularly in relation to how technology could be used to support the inclusion of students as readers and writers at the school.

Participants

School Demographics

Table A.4 details school demographic information for FVA in comparison to the school demographics of the surrounding county. While FVA's school population was representative of the socioeconomic and cultural diversity found in the surrounding county (see chapter 4), FVA's enrollment of lower-income students of color, second-language students, and students with disabilities was higher compared to the surrounding county.

Families at FVA

Within the broader school population, we identified focal families with whom to conduct interviews (see Sampling and Recruitment). Selected families were representative of the socioeconomic and cultural backgrounds of the broader FVA school population. The families also presented with a range

Table A.4
FVA school demographics

Demographic	Future Visions Academy	Surrounding County
Students	120	450,000
Gender	52% female, 48% male	52%, 48% male
Race/ethnicity	81% minority enrollment (64.2% Latinx, 19.2% white, 13.3% multiracial, 1.7% Asian, 1.7% Hawaiian/Pacific Islander)	75% minority enrollment (49.1% Latinx, 25% white, 16.9% Asian, multiracial 4.3%, Filipino 2%, Black 1.3%, 0.3% Hawaiian/Pacific Islander)
Disability	21%	13%
English language student	37%	22%
Free/reduced price meals	63%	50%

Appendix A

of perspectives about, and rationale for, enrolling at FVA. Parent participants tended to be self-selecting, committed to the principles of full inclusion, and strong advocates and supporters of FVA's instructional model.

Table A.5 details demographic information for FVA families who participated in interviews during the 2019–2020 and 2020–2021 academic school years. Eighty percent of families self-identified as BIPOC, 67 percent of families had at least one child with a disability and identified as either working or middle class, and 50 percent of families spoke a language other than English at home.

Staff at FVA

Table A.6 details demographic information for FVA teachers and staff who participated in in-person classroom observations, as well as remote and in-person interviews, during the 2019–2020 and 2020–2021 academic school years. Twenty-one total staff participated, of whom 42 percent were paraprofessionals, 36 percent were teachers, 11 percent were service providers, and 11 percent were administrative staff. One hundred percent participated in school/classroom observations, and 47 percent participated in interviews. Fifty-seven percent of teachers were experienced, with at least five years of teaching, and forty-two percent were in their first or second year

Table A.5

Family interview participants

Parent	Child(ren)	Ethnic Self-ID	Disability	Economic Status	Home Language	Grade (Class)
Madeline	Star	European and Filipino	Down syndrome	Upper middle class	English	2 (Ohlin)
Dina and Noah	James Daniel	Mexican and Pacific Islander	Down syndrome	Working class	English/ some Spanish	3 (Wezner) K (Macias)
Hilda	Leonardo Luigi	Mexican	Learning disability	Working class	Spanish/ ELL	1 (Ohlin) 4 (Gomez)
Mira	Maddox Maya Marco	Filipino	None	Middle class	English/ some Tagalog	K (Jarvis) 4 (Gomez) 2 (Wezner)
Sara	Leon Isla	Mexican	None	Middle class	Spanish/ ELL	K (Macias) 3 (Wezner)
Blake	Finn Chandler	European	Autism	Upper middle class	English	2 (Ohlin) K (Macias)

Table A.6
Staff participants

Name	Position	Class	Experience	Ethnic Self-ID	Language
Ms. Jarvis*	General ed teacher	TK/Kinder	Experienced teacher	European	English
Ms. Macias*	General ed teacher	K	Experienced teacher	Latina	English and Spanish
Ms. Ohlin*	General ed teacher	1/2	Second-year teacher	European	English
Ms. Wezner**	General ed teacher	2/3	First-year teacher	European	English
Ms. Gomez**	General ed teacher	4/5	Experienced teacher	Latina	English and Spanish
Ms. Haberly*	Special ed teacher	K and 4/5	Second-year teacher	European	English
Ms. Severin**	Special ed teacher	TK/K, 1/2, 2/3	Experienced teacher	European	English
Ms. Davis**	SLP	All classes	Experienced provider	Multiracial	English
Ms. Alexa*	SLPA	All classes	First-year provider	Latina	English
Ms. Carina**	Paraprofessional	2/3 and 3/4	Second-year paraprofessional	Latina	English and Spanish
Mr. Gabriel**	Paraprofessional	K and TK/K	First-year paraprofessional	Latino	English and Spanish
Ms. Sandy**	Paraprofessional	2/3 and 3/4	First-year paraprofessional	European	English
Ms. Yadira**	Paraprofessional	TK/K and 1/2	Second-year paraprofessional	Latina	English and Spanish
Ms. Holly*	Paraprofessional	TK/K and 2/3	First-year paraprofessional	European	English
Mr. Kellan*	Paraprofessional	1/2 and 2/3	First-year paraprofessional	European	English
Mr. Anthony*	Paraprofessional	K and 1/2	Second-year paraprofessional	Latino	English and Spanish
Ms. Belinda*	Paraprofessional	1/2	Second-year paraprofessional	Latina	English and Spanish
Mr. Bernardo*	Paraprofessional	TK/K Boys and Girls Club Program	Second-year paraprofessional	Latino	English and Spanish
Ms. Petersen**	Special ed teacher	TK/K, 1/2, 2/3	Experienced teacher	European	English
Dr. Tully**	Executive director	All classes	Experienced teacher and administrator	European	English
Ms. Cindy*	Office administration	All classes	Experienced administrator	Latina	English and Spanish

*Observation only. **Observation and interview.

Appendix A

of teaching. All of the paraprofessionals were new to their positions, with all being in their first or second year. With the exception of the SLPA, all administrative, services, and support staff had at least five years of experience in education.

Recruitment

Staff at FVA

After securing approval from FVA's school board and our university Institutional Review Board, we conducted an informational meeting at FVA at the start of the 2019–2020 academic school year to introduce the research team, discuss the study with the staff, and answer questions. FVA staff were recruited in person and via email by FVA directly prior to this informational meeting.

We then contacted staff who self-selected and agreed to participate via email to finalize participation, secure informed consent, and schedule classroom observations and interviews (see Sources of Data). None of the staff were paid for their participation in the study, and their participation extended through the 2019–2020 and 2020–2021 academic school years. Staff participated in-person classroom observations conducted by me in fall 2019, winter 2020, and spring 2021. Staff participated in interviews in person at FVA or remotely via Zoom in spring 2020 and spring 2021 (see Sources of Data).

Families at FVA

We consulted with the executive director and teachers to recruit families using maximum variation sampling.[8] Our goal in using maximum variation sampling was to select as diverse a range of participants as possible across cultural, linguistic, disability, and socioeconomic dimensions. This sampling method allowed us to explore a range of perspectives across a variety of families from diverse backgrounds—affording a more robust view into students' and parents' perspectives.

We conducted informational meetings with families at FVA at the start of the 2019–2020 academic school year to introduce the research team, discuss the study, and answer questions about all aspects of the study. Prior to the meeting, FVA distributed an opt-out letter explaining the study with an opportunity to opt out of the study. Parents who did not wish for their child to be in the study, as part of either classroom observations or interviews, were asked to opt out by returning the signed opt-out letter or contacting their child's teacher or us. Two families at FVA returned opt-out letters in total.

We also coordinated with the executive director and teachers to visit each classroom at the start of the 2019–2020 academic school year to explain the study, secure assent, and answer students' questions. Assenting and consented students were included in in-person school and classroom observation data collected by me in fall 2019 and winter 2020. Any students who did not assent, or whose parents did not wish for them to participate, engaged in classroom activities but were not included in classroom observation data and did not participate in interviews.

Families identified by us, in coordination with the executive director and staff, for interviews received a parent interview recruitment and consent letter. These letters were sent home with children by their teachers. Parents indicating that they were interested in participating in family interviews were then contacted by me to set an interview appointment. Focal students whose parents provide informed consent to be interviewed were also asked to provide assent using a child assent protocol developed by us, in coordination with FVA staff, to meet the communication needs of each student. Consenting families were interviewed by me after school at FVA in winter 2020 and remotely via Zoom in spring 2021 (see Sources of Data).

Sources of Data

Data sources collected using the protocols described above included (1) detailed field notes, taken in ten-minute intervals, of forty-nine weekly sixty-minute in-person passive classroom and school observations, conducted fall 2019 through winter 2020, as well as spring 2021; (2) verbatim transcriptions of fourteen initial and follow-up audio-recorded, semi-structured staff interviews (four teachers, four paraprofessionals, one SLP, and one administrator, thirty minutes each), conducted remotely or in person in spring 2020 and spring 2021; (3) verbatim transcriptions of twenty-six audio-recorded, semi-structured family interviews (seven parents and twelve children, thirty minutes each) conducted in person in the winter and spring of 2020 and remotely in spring 2021; and (4) school-, teacher-, and student-produced documents and artifacts, including writing samples, video, and photographs of digital technologies used in classrooms, as well as synchronous

Appendix A

and asynchronous paper-based and digital instructional content. Collection of data for school observations, staff interviews, and family interviews is detailed below and in tables A.7, A.8, and A.9, respectively.

School and Classroom Observations

Participating staff experienced me coming into their classrooms to conduct weekly in-person classroom observations during the fall and winter of the 2019–2020 school year, as well as the spring of the 2020–2021 school year once students returned to in-person learning (see table A.7). Sixty-minute classroom observations were scheduled in coordination with participating teachers in person and via email. During classroom observations, I passively observed interactions between students and teachers, students and students, and students and supporting staff. On occasion, students would approach me to ask a question or say hi. I would briefly say hello and immediately redirect them to their assigned class/group activity.

During these observations, I collected preliminary information and took notes on student, teacher, and supporting staff interactions in ten-minute intervals using the observation protocol described above, paying particular attention to when, why, how, and with whom students and teachers engaged in literacy activities with and without technology, as well as when and how they were included and engaged in classroom activities. During shifts in classroom activity—for example, during centers—I would rotate across the classroom to acquire a better view of the observed activities. On occasion, the class would leave the classroom to conduct an outdoor activity, at which time I would shadow them and continue taking field notes until the sixty-minute observation period concluded.

At the conclusion of each observation, I wrote post-observation analytic memos noting any overarching observations, analysis, and thoughts specific to incidents or activities of particular interest that may have occurred during the session. These memos, along with the observational data recorded in ten-minute intervals, provided the school and classroom observation data to be analyzed for the study (see Analysis section).

During the course of my visits to FVA to conduct classroom observations, the teachers and staff would recommend additional activities, class times, and school events for me to observe. So, in addition to regularly scheduled classroom observations, I also observed whole-school activities, such as FVA's Winter Wonderland celebration, as well as recess and lunch breaks.

208   Appendix A

Table A.7
Classroom and school observations

Location	Teachers	Supporting Staff	Number, Date, and Type
TK/Kinder	Ms. Jarvis Ms. Severin	Paras: Ms. Yadira, Mr. Gabriel, Ms. Holly, Mr. Bernardo Speech: Ms. Davis, Ms. Alexa	Literacy centers (10/28/19, 11/18/19), speech and language goals/literacy centers (1/9/20, 1/23/20, 2/13/20)
Kinder	Ms. Macias Ms. Haberly	Paras: Mr. Anthony, Mr. Gabriel, Mr. Bernardo Speech: Ms. Davis, Ms. Alexa	Phonics/silent reading (10/21/19), math centers (10/28/19), speech and language goals/literacy centers (1/9/20, 1/30/20, 2/6/20, 2/13/20), speech and language goals/literacy centers (2/19/20)
1/2 combo class	Ms. Ohlin Ms. Severin	Paras: Ms. Yadira, Mr. Kellan, Mr. Anthony, Ms. Belinda Speech: Ms. Davis, Ms. Alexa	Math centers (10/28/19), Literacy centers (11/4/19, 11/11/19), speech and language goals/social skills whole group (2/13/20), speech and language goals/literacy centers (2/26/20)
2/3 combo class	Ms. Wezner Ms. Severin	Paras: Ms. Carina, Ms. Sandy, Mr. Kellan, Ms. Holly Speech: Ms. Davis, Ms. Alexa	Storytime (10/21/19), Math centers (11/4/19), Independent and whole-group writing (11/18/19, 5/26/21), reading whole group (12/2/19, 5/26/21), speech and language goals/ phonics whole group (1/9/20), speech and language goals/literacy centers (1/23/20, 5/26/21), speech and language goals/social skills whole group (2/26/20)
4/5 combo class	Ms. Gomez Ms. Haberly	Paras: Ms. Carina, Ms. Sandy, Ms. Holly Speech: Ms. Davis, Ms. Alexa	Independent writing (10/21/19), science whole group (11/4/19), independent writing (11/18/19), writing whole group (12/2/19), speech and language goals/ social skills whole group (1/9/20, 1/30/20, 2/13/20), speech and language goals/grammar whole group (2/6/20)
Whole school	All staff	All staff	Team collaboration meeting (10/11/19), flag day and class rotations (10/14/19), staff lounge (10/21/19, 11/18/19, 1/23/20), digital storytelling PD (10/24/19– 10/25/19), front office/staff lounge (10/28/19, 10/30/19, 5/26/21), holiday assembly (12/19/19), recess (2/13/20, 5/26/21)

Appendix A

I was also invited to spend time in the staff lounge. While in the staff lounge, I had the opportunity to chat with staff about their experiences at FVA, building a more complete picture of life at the school.

The transition to remote learning in the spring of 2020 was a sudden one. I received an email from the executive director in March, stating that in-person class instruction and therefore classroom observations would need to cease. At this time, we agreed that the best way forward was to take a pause while FVA sorted out how it was going to move forward with remote learning for the remainder of the year. In April 2020, I had a follow-up meeting with the executive director via Zoom, and we decided that I would reach out to participating teachers to ask to be granted access to their asynchronous Google Classroom platforms.

Two teachers, Ms. Wezner and Ms. Gomez, agreed to grant me remote access to their Google Classroom platforms, and I reviewed asynchronous content for the grade 2/3 and 3/4 combo classrooms in the spring of 2020. Ms. Wezner also invited me into her classroom for additional classroom observation during spring 2021 upon the return of in-person instruction at FVA. While no formal data collection occurred in the fall and winter quarters of the 2020–2021 academic school year, I initiated and supervised the provision of pandemic remote learning support, facilitated by undergraduates from our partner university, as part of our extended research-practice partnership work.[9]

Staff Interviews

The unanticipated move to emergency remote learning in March 2020 resulted in initial staff interviews being conducted by me during spring and summer 2020, and again the following year in spring 2021 upon the school's return to in-person instruction. Initial and follow-up semi-structured staff interviews were conducted remotely via Zoom from our respective workplaces or in person at FVA, depending on staff preference (see table A.8). All interviews were audio-recorded, anonymized, and transcribed.

Interviews were scheduled in coordination with participating staff via email. During interviews, I actively listened for repeating and diverging themes in participant responses to questions outlined in the interview protocol described above and asked follow-up questions accordingly. This process also included asking participants to comment on points of interest and tension brought up by other interviewees as themes began to surface.

Table A.8
Staff interviews

Staff	Position (Class)	Location (Date)
Ms. Wezner	General education teacher (2/3 combo)	Remote (4/20/20), in person (4/23/21)
Ms. Gomez	General education teacher (4/5 combo)	Remote (5/21/20)
Ms. Severin	Special education teacher (TK/K, 1/2, 2/3 combo)	Remote (5/6/20)
Ms. Petersen	Special education teacher (TK/K, 1/2, 2/3 combo)	In person (4/30/21)
Ms. Davis	SLP (All classes)	Remote (5/4/20)
Ms. Carina	Paraprofessional (2/3 and 3/4 combo)	Remote (4/27/20)
Mr. Gabriel	Paraprofessional (K and TK/K combo)	Remote (4/20/20), remote (5/20/21)
Ms. Sandy	Paraprofessional (2/3 and 3/4 combo)	Remote (4/22/20)
Ms. Yadira	Paraprofessional (TK/K and 1/2 combo)	Remote (4/20/22), in person (4/23/21)
Dr. Tully	Executive director (all classes)	Remote (6/2/20), remote (6/3/21)

I always concluded each interview by asking participants to share additional commentary of their choosing and responded to any questions they had or felt I should ask.

Since interviews were audio-recorded, I focused my attention on actively engaging with participants, resulting in rich conversational interview content. For all interviews, I wrote notes, both during the interview and after, as unstructured memos in a project notebook reserved solely for this purpose. Informal memos were used to document surfacing themes, points for further inquiry, and follow-up questions and to-do items.

The decision to conduct follow-up staff interviews in the spring of 2021 was made after initial interviews were completed and was informed by several factors. First, many of the staff were in their first year of either teaching or working as a paraprofessional, and the team was curious to see how their practices and perspectives would change over time. Second, it became evident that the approach to incorporating digital technologies into instruction was impacted by competing priorities related to FVA being in the piloting phase of implementing the full inclusion program

Appendix A

(see chapters 4–7). Finally, the shift to remote learning prompted additional inquiry into how digital technologies were used to support language and literacy practices.

Family Interviews

Initial family interviews were conducted in winter 2020 and again the following year during spring 2021. Initial and follow-up semi-structured family interviews were conducted remotely via Zoom from our respective homes or in-person at FVA or in the family's home, depending on family preference (see table A.9). All interviews were audio-recorded, anonymized, and transcribed.

Family interviews were scheduled in coordination with participating families in person after school or by phone. As with staff interviews, during family interviews, I actively listened for repeating and diverging themes and asked follow-up questions accordingly. I always concluded each interview by asking participants to share additional commentary or questions of their choosing and responded to any questions they either had of the research project or felt I should ask participants.

The family interview process itself entailed interviewing the children first, with the parent usually sitting nearby occasionally offering support or redirection, depending on the child's age and needs during the

Table A.9
Family interviews

Parent	Child (Grade/Class)	Location (Date)
Madeline	Star (2nd/Ohlin)	In person (1/28/20)
Dina and Noah	James (3rd/Wezner) Daniel (K/Macias)	In person (2/6/20)
Hilda	Leonardo (1st/Ohlin) Luigi (4th/Gomez)	In person (2/10/20)
Mira	Maddox (K/Jarvis) Maya (4th/Gomez) Marco (2nd/Wezner)	In person (2/25/20), remote (5/5/21)
Sara	Leon (K/Macias) Isla (3rd/Wezner)	In person (3/6/20), remote (5/4/21)
Blake	Finn (2nd/Ohlin) Chandler (K/Macias)	In person (6/6/21)

interview. After the child portion of the interviews, I would interview the parents. During the parent portion of the interview, the children would typically sit nearby, attending to games and educational technology applications on a parent's mobile phone. On occasion, if the interview was held at home or near FVA's school playground, the children would venture outside to play while waiting for their parent to complete their portion of the interview.

During family interviews, I focused my attention on actively engaging with participants, and included breaks and modifications to the protocol as needed. This flexible approach was meant to create a comfortable environment for the families, the result of which was rich conversational interview content. Unlike staff interviews, I opted early on to write notes after, and not during, the family interviews to avoid the distraction they sometimes caused for the children. Notes were written in the form of informal memos and were used to document surfacing themes, points for further inquiry, and follow-up questions and to-do items.

The decision to conduct follow-up family interviews in the spring of 2021 was made after initial interviews were completed and was influenced by factors similar to those informing our decision to conduct follow-up staff interviews. As with staff, we were curious to see how families' practices and perspectives regarding using digital technologies to support language and literacy practices might change, particularly in relation to the shift to remote learning.

Analysis

In our case-study design, we incorporated qualitative approaches to analyze interview, classroom observation, and document data as follows:[10]

First- and second-cycle coding We first randomly selected a sampling of data to identify themes and categories across the data using initial coding.[11] We used this first cycle of coding to identify all resulting codes that could pertain to inclusive practices, language and literacy activity, and uses of digital technologies in the classroom. We then used a second cycle of coding to refine, consolidate, and subsume these codes into categories and themes. These results were used to develop a codebook for analyzing the remainder of the data using content analysis.

Appendix A

Content analysis We used the codebook developed in step 1 to conduct a directed content analysis of the data.[12] Directed content analysis is a sweeping analytic strategy that allows expeditious coding of broader segments of data in relation to the selected theoretical perspectives.

Analytic description As we engaged with students, teachers, staff, and parents in the process of collecting observation and interview data, we also noted our resulting thoughts, reflections, analyses, and descriptions of setting and interaction through analytic memo writing.[13] These analytic memos were triangulated with analysis from coding and content analysis to form a basis for descriptions of culture sharing, meaning making, social groupings and interactions, and surfacing cross-case themes.

Ensuring Trustworthiness

We ensured trustworthiness using multiple methodological strategies to minimize researcher bias and address reliability and validity concerns as they related to our collection, implementation, and analysis of data. First, we used a constant comparative method of analysis to discuss the results of first- and second-cycle coding with the research team and the executive director at the school to mitigate researcher bias and reliability concerns related to the development, revision, and application of a coding scheme to data.[14]

Next, we used a modified application of the Weber protocol to mitigate coding reliability concerns. The Weber protocol consists of defining units of analysis, categories, and codes to create a coding scheme; applying the coding scheme to a data sample; and assessing and revising the coding for accuracy.[15]

We addressed truthfulness and validity of findings using respondent validation, in which we invited study participants to comment on whether identified themes and concepts accurately reflect their experiences.[16] We also addressed truthfulness and validity by continuing to recruit and conduct interviews, as well as observations, until we reached saturation, which we noted once we kept seeing a repetition of topics, themes, patterns, and behaviors.[17] Finally, we used triangulation using multiple data sources and analytic methods to approximate more comprehensive findings.[18]

Appendix B: Technologies Used at FVA

Assistive Technologies Designed to Create Access

Technology	Chapter(s)	Definition
LAMP	3, 5, 7	LAMP uses a speech-generating device to expose students to core words with auditory feedback. LAMP can be used with several speech-generating digital applications and dedicated devices. However, FVA exclusively used LAMP Words for Life for iOS on iPad devices. It was designed to be used by people with autism. However, now it is used by minimally speaking individuals across a range of disabilities.[1]
PECS	3, 5	PECS is a common low- to mid-tech intervention used independently or in conjunction with Proloquo2Go. PECS uses pictures of preferred and high-frequency objects and actions as exchange items that students can use with a communicative partner to comment, make requests, and answer questions. The goal of PECS is to teach functional communication, with more advanced users often transitioning to AAC applications and speech-generating devices. PECS was initially developed for students diagnosed with autism. However, today it is used with students of all ages facing communication challenges across multiple disabilities.[2]
Proloquo2Go	1, 3, 5, 8	Proloquo2Go is a high-tech, symbol-based communication app for iOS designed to be used by minimally speaking individuals as a daily communication tool.[3] Proloquo2Go can be customized with high-frequency keywords organized thematically in folders and uses text-to-speech child and adult voices across multiple languages, including the ability to switch languages mid sentence for bilingual users. It is designed to be used by minimally speaking individuals across all ability levels in need of AAC support.

(continued)

Appendix B

Universally Designed Educational Technologies

Technology	Chapter(s)	Definition
Endless Alphabet	8	Endless Alphabet is an educational app built for children as young as two years old. Players are given letters scattered across the screen and an outline of a word they must spell. As they drag letters to their appropriate placeholder in the outline, the letters make their phonic sound. When a word is completed, users receive visual feedback and encouragement. The app was designed to limit stress by not providing high scores or failures within the game, and it can be found in the Apple App Store, as well as Google Play, Windows, and Amazon.[4]
Epic	3, 5	Epic is a digital reading platform, giving families and educators access to an extensive library of thousands of books, audiobooks, graphic novels, and educational videos meant to engage every type of reader. The application helps build students' vocabulary and reading skills using learning tools such as comprehension quizzes, speech-to-text functions, and dictionary features. On this platform, both parents and educators can track a student's progress and assign readings from a variety of subjects and topics (ELA, science and arts, socio-emotional learning, math, and more).[5]
Everyday Speech	5	Everyday Speech videos, games, and activities are designed to cultivate students' social communication and social-emotional learning skills. The social learning platform's therapy materials are used by SLPs, special education teachers, psychologists, parents, and anyone looking to work on social skills in one-on-one or group settings. Users can access the video-modeled curriculum on their iPads or through the Everyday Speech website.[6]
Flip (aka Flipgrid)	6	Flip (formerly known as Flipgrid) is a video-based discussion tool that allows teachers to post and share topics with students through videos accompanied by text. Students are then prompted to respond through further video posts, giving them a platform to share their voice, connect with peers, and express their creativity with the addition of emojis, stickers, drawings, and more. The service can be accessed on nearly any device with camera capabilities either through a web browser or through the Flip app.[7]

Appendix B

Universally Designed Educational Technologies

Technology	Chapter(s)	Definition
IXL	3	IXL is a personalized digital learning program that uses insights from student work within the K–12 curriculum to generate guidance and action plans for each student through real-time diagnostics. The website has thousands of math, science, social studies, and language practice questions that can also be accessed through app versions on Chrome, iOS, and Android.[9]
Kahoot	5	Kahoot is a game-based learning platform where students and teachers can create trivia quizzes on any topic through either live games or remote challenges so students can complete them at their own pace. To join a game, players will access a unique PIN on their own device to answer the questions displayed on their host's screen. Users have the ability to create and share their own quizzes, or search readily made games on a variety of topics through a web browser or access it on a mobile device.[10]
Lexia	3, 5	Lexia Learning is an interactive reading program that offers individualized literacy instruction to students based on diagnostic data. After a series of online assessments, students work on online activities presented visually or auditorily, focused on the skills they find challenging. If students continue to struggle with a particular skill, the Lexia program alerts teachers and provides them with scripted lesson and paper-and-pencil activities.[11]
Prodigy	5	Prodigy's math and English multiplayer games use adaptive algorithms to identify students' strengths and weaknesses, while also allowing students to review prerequisite skills when they struggle in a certain area. The games create personalized pathways for students to develop key skills, and teachers and parents can assign curriculum-based practice and pinpoint learning gaps.[12]
ReadWorks	5	The ReadWorks website provides educators with reading comprehension texts and instructional materials meant for digital classes, print, or smartboard presentations. Along with student progress dashboards for teachers, the platform offers StepReads, audio versions of passages, vocab support, and Spanish cognates to make assigned readings more accessible to students.[13]

(continued)

218 Appendix B

Universally Designed Educational Technologies

Technology	Chapter(s)	Definition
Seesaw	6	With the interactive Seesaw platform, teachers can search through hundreds of lessons on STEM topics, early literacy, and history, or create their own activities to share with students. While completing assignments, students can build a portfolio of their learning through photos, drawings, videos, and more. The platform includes built-in translations for more than a hundred languages for families to track student progress and leave feedback for their students and teachers so they can stay in the loop with their child's learning.[14]
Smarty Ants	5	Smarty Ants is an adaptive learning environment that builds foundational reading skills by providing students with animated lessons and activities. While teachers are given lesson ideas for large- and small-group instruction, students can grow English and Spanish literacies by singing songs, recording their own read-aloud practice, and developing fine-motor skills through game play and sensory exploration.[15]

Mainstream Technologies Designed with Accessible Features

Technology	Chapter(s)	Definition
FaceTime	6	FaceTime is a video and audio chat application for iPhone, iPad, and Mac users, allowing them to communicate one-on-one or in small groups. iOS users can create and share a link to a FaceTime call via messages or mail with non-Apple devices. Along with filtered background sounds and live-captioning tools, FaceTime has improved its accessibility by allowing users to share their screen to look at photos and watch videos together.[16]
Google Workspace (aka G Suite)	1, 3, 5, 6	Google Workspace (formerly known as G Suite) includes custom emails for businesses and institutions and collaborative web-based tools, including Calendar, Translate, Docs, Sheets, Slides, and Jamboard. With Google Docs, users can synchronously or asynchronously collaborate and comment on shared documents with a screen reader, type with their voice, use keyboard shortcuts and spell-check functions, and use braille displays. Similarly, Google Slides allows users to create and collaborate on presentations with a screen reader and use live captions and a braille display. Finally, Google's Jamboard is an interactive whiteboard app, allowing users to add pictures, written text/drawings, and Post-it notes to share ideas effectively.[17]

Appendix B

Mainstream Technologies Designed with Accessible Features

Technology	Chapter(s)	Definition
WeVideo	6, 8	WeVideo is an online video editing software that allows users to prepare scripts to tell their digital stories. Content is created using video projects with an array of editing tools to facilitate revision and finalization of digital video stories. This multimedia creation platform also facilitates communication in teams with its real-time collaboration and screen-recording features.[18]
YouTube	3, 5, 6	YouTube is a social media platform and video-sharing service that allows users to share, like, comment on, and upload videos. YouTube can be accessed on web browsers and on mobile devices, allowing users to reach YouTube communities through prerecorded videos or live streaming. The platform offers auto-generated subtitles and captions for audiences, where users can edit the language, size and color of font, and location of text within the video frame.[19]
Zoom	3, 6, 8	Zoom is an online video telephony software program that can be used for video- and audio-based meetings, screen sharing, and instant messaging. Zoom offers live transcriptions, closed captioning, keyboard shortcuts, and screen reader supports. Users and hosts can also spotlight participants using custom view, such as a sign language interpreter so they can always be in audience view during meetings.[20]

Notes

Chapter 1

1. Matthew J. Schuelka and Suzanne Carrington, "Innovative and Global Directions for Inclusive Education in the 21st Century," in *Global Directions in Inclusive Education*, ed. Matthew J. Schuelka and Suzanne Carrington (London: Routledge, 2021), 6.

2. UNESCO, *A Guide for Ensuring Inclusion and Equity in Education* (Paris: UNESCO, 2017), https://unesdoc.unesco.org/ark:/48223/pf0000248254; UNESCO, *Global Education Monitoring Report 2020—Inclusion and Education: All Means All* (Paris: UNESCO, 2020), https://unesdoc.unesco.org/ark:/48223/pf0000373718; Schuelka and Carrington, "Innovative and Global Directions for Inclusive Education," 1–26.

3. Schuelka and Carrington, "Innovative and Global Directions for Inclusive Education," 1–26.

4. Steve Silberman, *NeuroTribes: The Legacy of Autism and the Future of Neurodiversity* (New York: Penguin, 2015).

5. National Council on Disability, *IDEA Series: The Segregation of Students with Disabilities* (Washington, DC: National Council on Disability, 2018), https://ncd.gov/sites/default/files/NCD_Segregation-SWD_508.pdf.

6. UNESCO, *Global Education Monitoring Report 2020*; Schuelka and Carrington, "Innovative and Global Directions for Inclusive Education," 1–26.

7. Closing the Gap, accessed April 21, 2023, https://www.closingthegap.com/conference/.

8. Closing the Gap; Schuelka and Carrington, "Innovative and Global Directions for Inclusive Education," 1–26.

9. Dave L. Edyburn, "2003 in Review: A Synthesis of the Special Education Technology Literature," *Journal of Special Education Technology* 19, no. 4 (2004): 57–80, https://doi.org/10.1177/016264340401900407; Michael J. Kennedy and Donald D. Deshler, "Literacy Instruction, Technology, and Students with Learning Disabilities:

Research We Have, Research We Need," *Learning Disability Quarterly* 33, no. 4 (2010): 289–298, https://doi.org/10.1177/073194871003300406; David H. Rose, Anne Meyer, and Chuck Hitchcock, eds., *The Universally Designed Classroom: Accessible Curriculum and Digital Technologies* (Cambridge, MA: Harvard Education Press, 2005).

10. Peggy Coyne et al., "Literacy by Design: A Universal Design for Learning Approach for Students with Significant Intellectual Disabilities," *Remedial and Special Education* 33, no. 3 (2012): 162–172, https://doi.org/10.1177/0741932510381651; Weiqin Chen, "Multitouch Tabletop Technology for People with Autism Spectrum Disorder," *Procedia Computer Science* 14 (2012): 198–207; Curt Dudley-Marling and Mary B. Burns, "Two Perspectives on Inclusion in the United States," *Global Education Review* 1, no. 1 (2014): 14–31, https://files.eric.ed.gov/fulltext/EJ1055208.pdf; Festus E. Obiakor et al., "Making Inclusion Work in General Education Classrooms," *Education and Treatment of Children* 35, no. 3 (2012): 477–490, https://doi.org/10.1353/etc.2012.0020.

11. Edyburn, "2003 in Review," 57–80; Kennedy and Deshler, "Literacy Instruction," 289–298; Rose et al., *The Universally Designed Classroom*.

12. Dudley-Marling and Burns, "Two Perspectives on Inclusion," 14–31; Obiakor et al., "Making Inclusion Work," 477–490; Michael Solis et al., "Collaborative Models of Instruction: The Empirical Foundations of Inclusion and Co-Teaching," *Psychology in the Schools* 49, no. 5 (2012): 498–510, https://doi.org/10.1002/pits.21606.

13. Obiakor et al., "Making Inclusion Work," 477–490; Solis et al., "Collaborative Models of Instruction."

14. Dudley-Marling and Burns, "Two Perspectives on Inclusion," 14–31; Obiakor et al., "Making Inclusion Work," 477–490; Rose et al., *The Universally Designed Classroom*.

15. AnnMarie D. Baines, *(Un)Learning Disability: Recognizing and Changing Restrictive Views of Student Ability* (New York: Teachers College Press, 2014), 107.

16. Jean Lave and Etienne Wenger, *Situated Learning: Legitimate Peripheral Participation* Cambridge University Press, 1991).

17. Brian V. Street, "Introduction: The New Literacy Studies," in *Cross Cultural Approaches to Learning*, ed. Brian V. Street (Cambridge University Press, 1993), 1–21.

18. Mike Oliver, "The Individual and Social Models of Disability" (paper presented at the Joint Workshop of the Living Options Group and the Research Unit of the Royal College of Physicians, London, UK, July 1990).

19. Cynthia L. Bennett, Erin Brady, and Stacy M. Branham, "Interdependence as a Frame for Assistive Technology Research and Design," in *Proceedings of the 20th International ACM SIGACCESS Conference on Computers and Accessibility* (New York: ACM, 2018), 161–173, https://doi.org/10.1145/3234695.3236348.

Notes to Chapter 1

20. Sue Cranmer, *Disabled Children and Digital Technologies: Learning in the Context of Inclusive Education* (London: Bloomsbury Academic, 2020); Sonia Livingstone and Julian Sefton-Green, *The Class: Living and Learning in the Digital Age* (New York: New York University Press, 2016).

21. For a discussion of critical disability theory, see Edlyn V. Peña, Lissa D. Stapleton, and Lenore M. Schaffer, "Critical Perspectives on Disability Identity," *New Directions for Student Services* 2016, no. 154 (2016): 85–96, https://doi.org/10.1002/ss.20177.

22. For a discussion of the application of social constructivist perspectives to education, see A. Sullivan Palincsar, "Social Constructivist Perspectives on Teaching and Learning," *Annual Review of Psychology* 49 (1998): 345–375.

23. Alice Wong, ed., *Disability Visibility: First-person Stories from the Twenty-first Century* (New York: Vintage, 2020); Emily Ladau, *Demystifying Disability: What To Know, What To Say, and How To Be an Ally* (Berkeley, CA: Ten Speed Press, 2021).

24. Wong, *Disability Visibility*; Ladau, *Demystifying Disability*.

25. Schuelka and Carrington, "Innovative and Global Directions for Inclusive Education," 1–26.

26. Baines, *(Un)Learning Disability*; Sheelagh Daniels-Mayes, Gary Fry, and Karen Sinclair, "Is Inclusive Education Enough for Australian Aboriginal Students?: Making the Case for Belonging Education to Disrupt the Normalised Agenda of Assimilation," in *Global Directions in Inclusive Education*, ed. Matthew J. Schuelka and Suzanne Carrington (London: Routledge, 2021), 99–115.

27. Baines, *(Un)Learning Disability*; Daniels-Mayes et al., "Is Inclusive Education Enough for Australian Aboriginal Students?"; Schuelka and Carrington, "Innovative and Global Directions for Inclusive Education," 1–26.

28. Schuelka and Carrington, "Innovative and Global Directions for Inclusive Education," 1–26.

29. Cranmer, *Disabled Children and Digital Technologies*.

30. Cranmer, *Disabled Children and Digital Technologies*; Steve Matthewman, *Technology and Social Theory* (London: Macmillan International Higher Education, 2011).

31. Cranmer, *Disabled Children and Digital Technologies*.

32. Cranmer, *Disabled Children and Digital Technologies*, 24–25.

33. Julie Causton-Theoharis and George Theoharis, "Creating Inclusive Schools for All Students," *School Administrator* 65, no. 8 (2008): 24–25, https://www.aasa.org/SchoolAdministratorArticle.aspx?id=4936; Wayne Sailor and Blair Roger, "Rethinking Inclusion: School Wide Applications," *Phi Delta Kappan* 86, no. 7 (2005): 503–509, https://doi.org/10.1177/003172170508600707.

34. Derrick Armstrong, Ann C. Armstrong, and Ilektra Spandagou, "Inclusion: By Choice or By Chance?," *International Journal of Inclusive Education* 15, no. 1 (2011): 29–39, https://doi.org/http://dx.doi.org/10.1080/13603116.2010.496192; Dudley-Marling and Burns, "Two Perspectives on Inclusion," 14–31.

35. Edyburn, "2003 in Review," 57–80.

36. Kennedy and Deshler, "Literacy Instruction," 289–298.

37. Mark Warschauer, *Technology and Social Inclusion: Rethinking the Digital Divide* (Cambridge, MA: MIT Press, 2004).

38. Bennett et al., "Interdependence as a Frame," 161–173.

Chapter 2

1. Obiakor et al., "Making Inclusion Work," 477–490.

2. Bob Algozzine and James E. Ysseldyke, *The Fundamentals of Special Education: A Practical Guide for Every Teacher* (Thousand Oaks, CA: Corwin Press, 2006); Kathy Hall et al., "SATurated Models of Pupildom: Assessment and Inclusion/Exclusion," *British Educational Research Journal* 30, no. 6 (2004): 801–817, https://doi.org/10.1080/0141192042000279512.

3. Dudley-Marling and Burns, "Two Perspectives on Inclusion," 14–31; Obiakor et al., "Making Inclusion Work," 477–490.

4. Coyne et al., "Literacy by Design," 162–172; Chen, "Multitouch Tabletop Technology," 198–207; Dudley-Marling and Burns, "Two Perspectives on Inclusion," 14–31; Obiakor et al., "Making Inclusion Work," 477–490.

5. Obiakor et al., "Making Inclusion Work," 477–490; Solis et al., "Collaborative Models of Instruction," 498–510; Rose et al., *The Universally Designed Classroom.*

6. Jay W. Rojewski, In Heok Lee, and Noel Gregg, "Causal Effects of Inclusion on Postsecondary Education Outcomes of Individuals with High-Incidence Disabilities," *Journal of Disability Policy Studies* 25, no. 4 (2015): 210–219.

7. Schuelka and Carrington, "Innovative and Global Directions for Inclusive Education," 1–26; Baines, *(Un)Learning Disability.*

8. Dudley-Marling and Burns, "Two Perspectives on Inclusion," 14–31.

9. Obiakor et al., "Making Inclusion Work," 477–490; Solis et al., "Collaborative Models of Instruction," 498–510.

10. Schuelka and Carrington, "Innovative and Global Directions for Inclusive Education," 1–26.

Notes to Chapter 2

11. Silberman, *NeuroTribes*; Barbara Boroson, "Inclusive Education: Lessons from History," *Educational Leadership* 74, no. 7 (2017): 18–23.

12. Peter Mundy and Ann Mastergeorge, *Educational Interventions for Students with Autism*. UC Davis MIND Institute Autism for Educators Series (Hoboken, NJ: Jossey Bass, 2012).

13. Dudley-Marling and Burns, "Two Perspectives on Inclusion," 14–31.

14. Dudley-Marling and Burns, "Two Perspectives on Inclusion," 14–31.

15. Dudley-Marling and Burns, "Two Perspectives on Inclusion," 14–31.

16. Solis et al., "Collaborative Models of Instruction," 498–510.

17. Tracy Gershwin Mueller and Anna Moriarity Vick, "An Investigation of Facilitated Individualized Education Program Meeting Practice: Promising Procedures that Foster Family–Professional Collaboration," *Teacher Education and Special Education* 42 (2019): 67–81.

18. Mundy and Mastergeorge, *Educational Interventions for Students with Autism*; Silberman, *NeuroTribes*.

19. Mundy and Mastergeorge, *Educational Interventions for Students with Autism*.

20. Solis et al., "Collaborative Models of Instruction," 498–510.

21. Solis et al., "Collaborative Models of Instruction," 498–510.

22. Schuelka and Carrington, "Innovative and Global Directions for Inclusive Education," 1–26.

23. UNESCO, "The Salamanca Statement and Framework for Action on Special Needs Education" (adopted by the World Conference on Special Needs Education: Access and Quality, Salamanca, Spain, June 7–10, 1994).

24. Schuelka and Carrington, "Innovative and Global Directions for Inclusive Education," 1–26.

25. Max Roser and Esteban Ortiz-Ospina, "Global Education," *Our World in Data* (2016), https://ourworldindata.org/global-education.

26. Schuelka and Carrington, "Innovative and Global Directions for Inclusive Education," 1–26; UNESCO, *EFA Global Monitoring Report 2015—Education for All 2000–2015: Achievements and Challenges* (Paris: UNESCO, 2015).

27. Baines, *(Un)Learning Disability*; Cranmer, *Disabled Children and Digital Technologies*; Schuelka and Carrington, "Innovative and Global Directions for Inclusive Education," 1–26.

28. Ladau, *Demystifying Disability*.

29. Pamela Fisher and Dan Goodley, "The Linear Medical Model of Disability: Mothers of Disabled Babies Resist with Counter-Narratives," *Sociology of Health and Illness* 29 (2007): 66–81, https://doi.org/10.1111/j.1467-9566.2007.00518.x.

30. Glen W. White et al., "Moving from Independence to Interdependence: A Conceptual Model for Better Understanding Community Participation of Centers for Independent Living Consumers," *Journal of Disability Policy Studies* 20, no. 4 (2010): 233–240. https://doi.org/10.1177%2F1044207309350561.

31. White et al., "Moving from Independence to Interdependence," 233–240.

32. Cranmer, *Disabled Children and Digital Technologies*; Oliver, "The Individual and Social Models of Disability"; Mia Mingus, "Access Intimacy, Interdependence and Disability Justice," *Leaving Evidence* (blog), April 12, 2017, https://leavingevidence.wordpress.com/2017/04/12/access-intimacy-interdependence-and-disability-justice/.

33. Cranmer, *Disabled Children and Digital Technologies*; Oliver, "The Individual and Social Models of Disability."

34. Cranmer, *Disabled Children and Digital Technologies*; Oliver, "The Individual and Social Models of Disability"; Ladau, *Demystifying Disability*.

35. Gerben M. DeJong, "Independent Living: From Social Movement to Analytic Paradigm," *Archives of Physical Medical Rehabilitation* 60 (1979): 435–446, http://citeseerx.ist.psu.edu/viewdoc/download?doi=10.1.1.879.20&rep=rep1&type=pdf; White et al., "Moving from Independence to Interdependence," 233–240.

36. Ladau, *Demystifying Disability*.

37. DeJong, "Independent Living," 435–446; White et al., "Moving from Independence to Interdependence," 233–240.

38. DeJong, "Independent Living," 435–446; White et al., "Moving from Independence to Interdependence," 233–240.

39. DeJong, "Independent Living," 435–446.

40. Lex Frieden, "Independent Living Models," *Rehabilitation Literature* 41, no. 7–8 (1980): 169–173; White et al., "Moving from Independence to Interdependence," 233–240; DeJong, "Independent Living," 435–446.

41. Ladau, *Demystifying Disability*; Silberman, *NeuroTribes*.

42. Mingus, "Access Intimacy"; Wong, *Disability Visibility*; Silberman, *NeuroTribes*; Naoki Higashida, *The Reason I Jump: The Inner Voice of a Thirteen-Year-Old Boy with Autism* (Toronto: Knopf Canada, 2013); Ladau, *Demystifying Disability*.

43. James M. Kauffman et al., *Special Education: What It Is and Why We Need It* (New York: Routledge, 2018).

Notes to Chapter 2

44. Larry Weimer, *Crossroads: Harrison A. Williams, Jr. and Great Society Liberalism, 1959–1981: An Exhibition* (New Brunswick, NJ: Rutgers University Libraries, 2009), https://doi.org/doi:10.7282/T3GX48H9.

45. Douglas Biklen, *Achieving the Complete School: Strategies for Effective Mainstreaming* (New York: Teachers College Press, 1985), 3.

46. Dudley-Marling and Burns, "Two Perspectives on Inclusion," 14–31.

47. Dudley-Marling and Burns, "Two Perspectives on Inclusion," 26.

48. Causton-Theoharis and Theoharis, "Creating Inclusive Schools," 24–25; Ane Qvortrup and Lars Qvortrup, "Inclusion: Dimensions of Inclusion in Education," *International Journal of Inclusive Education* 22, no. 7 (2018): 803–817.

49. Sailor, Wayne, and Blair Roger. "Rethinking Inclusion: School Wide Applications." Phi Delta Kappan 86, no. 7 (2005): 503–509. https://doi.org/10.1177/003172170508 600707.

50. Sailor and Roger, "Rethinking Inclusion," 503–509.

51. Dudley-Marling and Burns, "Two Perspectives on Inclusion," 14–31.

52. Dudley-Marling and Burns, "Two Perspectives on Inclusion," 14–31.

53. Causton-Theoharis and Theoharis, "Creating Inclusive Schools," 24–25; Sailor and Roger, "Rethinking Inclusion," 503–509; Laura Green, Paula Chance, and Melissa Stockholm, "Implementation and Perceptions of Classroom-Based Service Delivery: A Survey of Public School Clinicians," *Language, Speech, and Hearing Services in Schools* 50, no. 4 (2019): 656–672.

54. Dudley-Marling and Burns, "Two Perspectives on Inclusion," 14–31.

55. Obiakor et al., "Making Inclusion Work," 477–490; Solis et al., "Collaborative Models of Instruction," 498–510.

56. Mundy and Mastergeorge, *Educational Interventions for Students with Autism*; Obiakor et al., "Making Inclusion Work," 477–490; Solis et al., "Collaborative Models of Instruction," 498–510.

57. Mundy and Mastergeorge, *Educational Interventions for Students with Autism*; Solis et al., "Collaborative Models of Instruction," 498–510.

58. Obiakor et al., "Making Inclusion Work," 477–490; Solis et al., "Collaborative Models of Instruction," 498–510.

59. Sharon Vaughn, Jeanne S. Schumm, and Maria E. Arguelles, "The ABCDEs of Co-Teaching," *Teaching Exceptional Children* 30, no. 2 (1997): 4–10; Obiakor et al., "Making Inclusion Work," 477–490.

60. Obiakor et al., "Making Inclusion Work," 477–490; Solis et al., "Collaborative Models of Instruction," 498–510; Vaughn et al., "The ABCDEs of Co-Teaching," 4–10.

Notes to Chapter 2

61. Armstrong et al., "Inclusion: By Choice or By Chance?," 29–39; Dudley-Marling and Bridget Burns, "Two Perspectives on Inclusion," 14–31.

62. Armstrong et al., "Inclusion: By Choice or By Chance?," 29–39.

63. Dudley-Marling and Burns, "Two Perspectives on Inclusion," 14–31; David Scanlon and Diana Baker, "An Accommodations Model for the Secondary Inclusive Classroom," *Learning Disability Quarterly* 35, no. 4 (2012): 212–224.

64. Beth A. Ferri, "Undermining Inclusion? A Critical Reading of Response to Intervention (RTI)," *International Journal of Inclusive Education* 16, no. 8 (2012): 863–880; Green et al., "Implementation and Perceptions of Classroom-Based Service Delivery," 656–672.

65. Dudley-Marling and Burns, "Two Perspectives on Inclusion," 14–31; Lynda Miller, *What We Call Smart: A New Narrative for Intelligence and Learning, School-Age Children Series* (San Diego, CA: Singular Publishing Group, 1993).

66. Dudley-Marling and Burns, "Two Perspectives on Inclusion," 14–31; Miller, *What We Call Smart.*

67. Kenneth J. Gergen, "Social Understanding and the Inscription of Self," in *Cultural Psychology: Essays on Comparative Human Development*, ed. James W. Stigler, Richard A. Schweder, and Gilbert Herdt (Cambridge, UK: Cambridge University Press, 1990), 569–606; Rosemary C. Kalenga and Elsa Fourie, "Trekking Back to Mainstream for Inclusive Education, Is It There?" *Educational Studies* 38, no. 2 (2012): 175–187.

68. Douglas Biklen, *Autism and the Myth of the Person Alone* (New York: New York University Press, 2005); Grace Blum, Megan Wilson, and Yelena Patish, "Moving Toward a More Socially Just Classroom through Teacher Preparation for Inclusion," *Catalyst: A Social Justice Forum* 5, no. 1 (2015): article 4.

69. Dudley-Marling and Burns, "Two Perspectives on Inclusion," 24.

70. Phyllis E. Horne and Vianne Timmons, "Making It Work: Teachers' Perspectives on Inclusion," *International Journal of Inclusive Education* 13, no. 3 (2009): 273–286; Green et al., "Implementation and Perceptions of Classroom-Based Service Delivery," 656–672.

71. Gary Bunch and Kevin Finnegan, "Values Teachers Find in Inclusive Education," in *Proceedings of the 5th International Special Education Conference* (Manchester, UK: University of Manchester, 2000); Norman E. Fox and James E. Ysseldyke, "Implementing Inclusion at the Middle School Level: Lessons from a Negative Example," *Exceptional Children* 64 (1997): 81–98; Blum et al., "Moving Toward a More Socially Just Classroom."

72. Larry G. Daniel and Debra A. King, "Impact of Inclusion Education on Academic Achievement, Student Behavior and Self-Esteem, and Parental Attitudes,"

Notes to Chapter 2

The Journal of Educational Research 91, no. 2 (1997): 67–80; Caroline Moore, Debra Gilbreath, and Fran Maiuri, "Educating Students with Disabilities in General Education Classrooms: A Summary of the Research," (paper was published in Education Resources Information Center (ERIC), Washington D.C., 1998), https://eric.ed.gov /?id=ED419329; Blum et al., "Moving Toward a More Socially Just Classroom."

73. Obiakor et al., "Making Inclusion Work," 477–490.

74. María Cristina Cardona Moltó, "Teacher Education Students' Belief of Inclusion and Perceived Competence to Teach Students with Disabilities in Spain," *International Journal of Special Education* 10 (2009): 33–41; Obiakor et al., "Making Inclusion Work," 477–490.

75. Marloes Koster et al., "Being Part of the Peer Group: A Literature Study Focusing on the Social Dimension of Inclusion in Education," *International Journal of Inclusive Education* 13, no. 2 (2009): 117–140; Joseph M. Strayhorn and Philip S. Strain, "Social and Language Skills for Preventive Mental Health: What, How, Who and When," in *Children's Social Behavior: Development, Assessment and Modifications*, ed. P. S. Strain, M. J. Guralnick, and H. Walker (New York: Academic Press, 1996), 287–330; Michael Campbell, "An Application of the Theory of Planned Behavior to Examine the Impact of Classroom Inclusion on Elementary School Students," *Journal of Evidence-Based Social Work* 7, no. 3 (2010): 235–250.

76. Marloes Koster et al., "The Social Position and Development of Pupils with SEN in Mainstream Dutch Primary Schools," *European Journal of Special Needs Education* 22, no. 1 (2007): 31–46; Koster et al., "Being Part of the Peer Group," 117–140; Turki Alquraini and Dianne Gut, "Critical Components of Successful Inclusion of Students with Severe Disabilities: Literature Review," *International Journal of Special Education* 27, no. 1 (2012): 42–59.

77. Janette K. Klingner and Sharon Vaughn, "Students' Perceptions of Instruction in Inclusion Classrooms: Implications for Students with Learning Disabilities," *Exceptional Children* 66, no. 1 (1999): 23–37; Solis et al., "Collaborative Models of Instruction," 498–510.

78. Klingner and Vaughn, "Students' Perceptions of Instruction in Inclusion Classrooms," 23–37.

79. Judith Wiener, "Do Peer Relationships Foster Behavioral Adjustment in Children with Learning Disabilities?" *Learning Disability Quarterly* 27 (2004): 21–30; Debby Zambo and Carter Davidson, "Ostracism and Adolescents with Learning and Behavioral Disabilities: Preventing and Lessening its Effects," *Intervention in School and Clinic* 48, no. 3 (2013): 178–183.

80. Sharon S. Coben and Naomi Zigmond, "The Social Integration of Learning Disabled Students," *Journal of Learning Disabilities* 19, no. 10 (1986): 614–618; Stephanny F. N. Freeman and Marvin C. Alkin, "Academic and Social Attainments of

Children with Mental Retardation," *Remedial and Special Education* 21, no. 1 (2000): 3–18; Hollace Goodman, Jay Gottlieb, and Robert H. Harrison, "Social Acceptance of EMRS Integrated into a Non-Graded Elementary School," *American Journal of Mental Deficiency* 76, no. 4 (1972): 412–417; Michael Kuhne and Judith Wiener, "Stability of Social Status of Children with and without Learning Disabilities," *Learning Disability Quarterly* 23 (2000): 64–75; Mara Manetti, Barry H. Schneider, and Gary Siperstein, "Social Acceptance of Children with Mental Retardation: Testing the Contact Hypothesis with an Italian Sample," *International Journal of Behavioral Development* 25, no. 3 (2001): 279–286; Malka Margalit and Meira Efrati, "Loneliness, Coherence and Companionship among Children with Learning Disorders," *Educational Psychology* 16 (1996): 69–79; Karl J. Skårbrevik, "The Quality of Special Education for Students with Special Needs in Ordinary Classes," *European Journal of Special Needs Education* 20, no. 4 (2005): 387–401.

81. Koster et al., "Being Part of the Peer Group," 117–140; Alquraini and Gut, "Critical Components of Successful Inclusion," 42–59.

82. Horne and Timmons, "Making It Work," 273–286; Campbell, "An Application of the Theory of Planned Behavior," 235–250.

83. Thomas E. Scruggs and Margo A. Mastropieri, "Teacher Perceptions of Mainstreaming/Inclusion, 1958–1995: A Research Synthesis," *Exceptional Children* 63, no. 1 (1996): 59–74.

84. Horne and Timmons, "Making It Work," 273–286; Scruggs and Mastropieri, "Teacher Perceptions of Mainstreaming/Inclusion," 59–74.

85. Scruggs and Mastropieri, "Teacher Perceptions of Mainstreaming/Inclusion," 59–74.

86. Elias Avramidis and Brahm Norwich, "Teachers' Attitudes towards Integration/Inclusion: A Review of the Literature," *European Journal of Special Needs Education* 17, no. 2 (2002): 129–147; Horne and Timmons, "Making It Work," 273–286; Solis et al., "Collaborative Models of Instruction," 498–510.

87. Scruggs and Mastropieri, "Teacher Perceptions of Mainstreaming/Inclusion," 59–74.

88. Scruggs and Mastropieri, "Teacher Perceptions of Mainstreaming/Inclusion," 59–74.

89. Alquraini and Gut, "Critical Components of Successful Inclusion," 42–59.

90. Elena Marin, "Are Today's General Education Teachers Prepared to Face Inclusion in the Classroom?" *Procedia Social and Behavioral Sciences* 142 (2014): 702–707.

91. Green et al., "Implementation and Perceptions of Classroom-Based Service Delivery," 656–672.

Notes to Chapter 3

92. James Ryan, "Establishing Inclusion in a New School: The Role of Principal Leadership," *Exceptionality Education International* 20, no. 2 (2010): 6–24.

93. Marilyn Friend et al., "Co-Teaching: An Illustration of the Complexity of Collaboration in Special Education," *Journal of Educational and Psychological Consultation* 20, no. 1 (2010): 9–27.

94. Qvortrup and Qvortrup, "Inclusion," 803–817.

95. Blum et al., "Moving Toward a More Socially Just Classroom"; Avramidis and Norwich, "Teachers' Attitudes towards Integration/Inclusion," 129–147.

96. Horne and Timmons, "Making It Work," 273–286; Lorna Idol, "Key Questions Related to Building Collaborative and Inclusive Schools," *Journal of Learning Disabilities* 30, no. 4 (1997): 384–394; Alquraini and Gut, "Critical Components of Successful Inclusion," 42–59.

97. Horne and Timmons, "Making It Work," 273–286; Fox and Ysseldyke, "Implementing Inclusion at the Middle School Level," 81–98.

98. Horne and Timmons, "Making It Work," 273–286; Solis et al., "Collaborative Models of Instruction," 498–510.

Chapter 3

1. Edyburn, "2003 in Review," 57–80; Matthew T. Marino, "Defining a Technology Research Agenda for Elementary and Secondary Students with Learning and Other High-Incidence Disabilities in Inclusive Science Classrooms," *Journal of Special Education Technology* 25 (2010): 1–27.

2. Kennedy and Deshler, "Literacy Instruction," 289–298.

3. Bennett et al., "Interdependence as a Frame," 161–173; Kennedy and Deshler, "Literacy Instruction," 289–298.

4. Schuelka and Carrington, "Innovative and Global Directions for Inclusive Education," 11.

5. Carnegie Corporation of New York, *The Opportunity Equation: Transforming Mathematics and Science Education for Citizenship and Global Economy* (Princeton, NJ: Institute for Advanced Study, 2009).

6. Marilyn Jager Adams, *Beginning to Read: Thinking and Learning about Print* (Cambridge, MA: MIT Press, 1994); James P. Byrnes and Barbara A. Wasik, *Language and Literacy Development: What Educators Need to Know* (New York: Guilford Press, 2019); Catherine E. Snow, M. Susan Burns, and Peg Griffin, eds., *Preventing Reading Difficulties in Young Children* (Washington, DC: National Research Council, National Academy Press, 1998).

7. Sathiyaprakash Ramdoss et al., "Use of Computer-Based Interventions to Improve Literacy Skills in Students with Autism Spectrum Disorders: A Systematic Review," *Research in Autism Spectrum Disorders* 5, no. 4 (2011): 1306–1318.

8. Penny Ur, *A Course in Language Teaching: Practice and Theory* (Cambridge University Press, 1996).

9. Ur, *A Course in Language Teaching*; Adams, *Beginning to Read*.

10. Snow et al., *Preventing Reading Difficulties in Young Children*.

11. Keith Stanovich, "Matthew Effects in Reading: Some Consequences of Individual Differences in the Acquisition of Literacy," *Reading Research Quarterly* 21, no. 4 (1986): 360–407.

12. Adams, *Beginning to Read*; Snow et al., *Preventing Reading Difficulties in Young Children*; Byrnes and Wasik, *Language and Literacy Development*.

13. Kristie Asaro-Saddler, "Using Evidence-Based Practices to Teach Writing to Children with Autism Spectrum Disorders," *Preventing School Failure: Alternative Education for Children and Youth* 60, no. 1 (2016): 79–85; Chen, "Multitouch Tabletop Technology," 198–207.

14. Chen, "Multitouch Tabletop Technology," 198–207; Coyne et al., "Literacy by Design," 162–172; Robert C. Pennington et al., "Using Simultaneous Prompting and Computer-Assisted Instruction to Teach Story Writing to Students with Autism," *Assistive Technology Outcomes and Benefits* 7 (2011): 24–38.

15. Pennington et al., "Using Simultaneous Prompting," 24–38; Kristie Asaro-Saddler, "Writing Instruction and Self-Regulation for Students with Autism Spectrum Disorders," *Topics in Language Disorders* 36, no. 3 (2016): 266–283; Asaro-Saddler, "Using Evidence-Based Practices," 79–85.

16. Amy Gillespie and Steve Graham, "A Meta-Analysis of Writing Interventions for Students with Learning Disabilities," *Exceptional Children* 80, no. 4 (2014): 454–473; Steve Graham, Karen R. Harris, and Lynn Larsen, "Prevention and Intervention of Writing Difficulties for Students with Learning Disabilities," *Learning Disabilities Research and Practice* 16, no. 2 (2001): 74–84; Steve Graham and Karen R. Harris, "Writing Instruction," in *Learning about Learning Disabilities*, 3rd ed., ed. B. Wong (San Diego, CA: Elsevier Science, 2004), 281–313.

17. Asaro-Saddler, "Writing Instruction and Self-Regulation," 266–283.

18. Robert C. Pennington and Monica E. Delano, "Writing Instruction for Students with Autism Spectrum Disorders: A Review of Literature," *Focus on Autism and Other Developmental Disabilities* 27, no. 3 (2012): 158–167; Asaro-Saddler, "Writing Instruction and Self-Regulation," 266–283; Steve Graham and Karen R. Harris, "Improving the Writing Performance of Young Struggling Writers: Theoretical and Programmatic

Notes to Chapter 3

Research from the Center on Accelerating Student Learning," *The Journal of Special Education* 39, no. 1 (2005): 19–33.

19. Asaro-Saddler, "Writing Instruction and Self-Regulation," 266–283; Pennington and Delano, "Writing Instruction for Students with Autism Spectrum Disorders," 158–167.

20. Karen R. Harris and Steve Graham, "Self-Regulated Strategy Development in Writing: Premises, Evolution, and the Future," *British Journal of Educational Psychology* 6 (2009): 113–135.

21. Asaro-Saddler, "Writing Instruction and Self-Regulation," 266–283, and "Using Evidence-Based Practices," 79–85; Pennington et al., "Using Simultaneous Prompting," 24–38; Pennington and Delano, "Writing Instruction for Students with Autism Spectrum Disorders," 158–167.

22. Asaro-Saddler, "Writing Instruction and Self-Regulation," 266–283, and "Using Evidence-Based Practices," 79–85; Pennington et al., "Using Simultaneous Prompting," 24–38; Pennington and Delano, "Writing Instruction for Students with Autism Spectrum Disorders," 158–167.

23. Asaro-Saddler, "Writing Instruction and Self-Regulation," 266–283, and "Using Evidence-Based Practices," 79–85.

24. Pennington et al., "Using Simultaneous Prompting," 24–38; Pennington and Delano, "Writing Instruction for Students with Autism Spectrum Disorders," 158–167.

25. Pennington and Delano, "Writing Instruction for Students with Autism Spectrum Disorders," 158–167.

26. Asaro-Saddler, "Using Evidence-Based Practices," 79–85; Pennington and Delano, "Writing Instruction for Students with Autism Spectrum Disorders," 158–167.

27. Graham and Harris, "Writing Instruction," 281–313; Asaro-Saddler, "Writing Instruction and Self-Regulation," and "Using Evidence-Based Practices," 79–85.

28. Asaro-Saddler, "Writing Instruction and Self-Regulation," 266–283, and "Using Evidence-Based Practices," 79–85.

29. Vince Connelly and Julie Dockrell, "Writing Development and Instruction for Students with Learning Disabilities: Using Diagnostic Categories to Study Writing Difficulties," in *Handbook of Writing Research*, ed. Charles A. MacArthur, Steve Graham, and Jill Fitzgerald (New York: Guilford Press, 2016), 349–363.

30. Connelly and Dockrell, "Writing Development and Instruction for Students with Learning Disabilities," 349–363.

31. Asaro-Saddler, "Using Evidence-Based Practices," 79–85.

32. Pennington and Delano, "Writing Instruction for Students with Autism Spectrum Disorders," 158–167; Asaro-Saddler, "Using Evidence-Based Practices," 79–85.

33. Graham et al., "Prevention and Intervention of Writing Difficulties," 74–84.

34. Graham et al., "Prevention and Intervention of Writing Difficulties," 74–84.

35. Asaro-Saddler, "Writing Instruction and Self-Regulation," 266–283; Pennington and Delano, "Writing Instruction for Students with Autism Spectrum Disorders," 158–167.

36. Kennedy and Deshler, "Literacy Instruction," 289–298.

37. Kennedy and Deshler, "Literacy Instruction," 289–298.

38. Edyburn, "2003 in Review," 57–80; Kennedy and Deshler, "Literacy Instruction," 289–298.

39. Kennedy and Deshler, "Literacy Instruction," 289–298.

40. Dave L. Edyburn, "Critical Issues in Advancing the Special Education Technology Evidence Base," *Exceptional Children* 80, no. 1 (2013): 7–24, https://doi.org/10.1177/001440291308000107.

41. Cynthia M. Okolo and Emily C. Bouck, "Research about Assistive Technology: 2000–2006. What Have We Learned?" *Journal of Special Education Technology* 22, no. 3 (2007): 19–33.

42. Sumita C. Ghosh, *Technology for Inclusion: Special Education, Rehabilitation, for All* (Ronkonkoma, NY: Linus Learning, 2017); Susan E. Anderson and Rebecca S. Putman, "Special Education Teachers' Experience, Confidence, Beliefs, and Knowledge about Integrating Technology," *Journal of Special Education Technology* 35, no. 1 (2020): 37–50; Mark Warschauer, *Electronic Literacies: Language, Culture, and Power in Online Education* (New York: Routledge, 1998).

43. Cranmer, *Disabled Children and Digital Technologies*; Kylie A. Peppler and Mark Warschauer, "Uncovering Literacies, Disrupting Stereotypes: Examining the (Dis) Abilities of a Child Learning to Computer Program and Read," *International Journal of Learning and Media* 3, no. 3 (2011): 15–41; Warschauer, *Electronic Literacies*.

44. Charles A. MacArthur et al., "Technology Applications for Students with Literacy Problems: A Critical Review," *The Elementary School Journal* 101, no. 3 (2001): 273–301.

45. Adams, *Beginning to Read*; Snow et al., *Preventing Reading Difficulties in Young Children*.

46. MacArthur et al., "Technology Applications for Students with Literacy Problems," 273–301.

47. Carol Sue Englert et al., "Scaffolding the Writing of Students with Disabilities through Procedural Facilitation: Using an Internet-Based Technology to Improve Performance," *Learning Disability Quarterly* 30, no. 1 (2007): 9–29.

Notes to Chapter 3

48. MacArthur et al., "Technology Applications for Students with Literacy Problems," 273–301; Englert et al., "Scaffolding the Writing of Students with Disabilities," 9–29.

49. Min Wook Ok and Kavita Rao, "Digital Tools for the Inclusive Classroom: Google Chrome as Assistive and Instructional Technology," *Journal of Special Education Technology* 34, no. 3 (2019): 204–211; MacArthur et al., "Technology Applications for Students with Literacy Problems," 273–301.

50. Jenell Krishnan et al., "Supporting Online Synchronous Collaborative Writing in the Secondary Classroom," *Journal of Adolescent and Adult Literacy* 63, no. 2 (2019): 135–145; Gillespie and Graham, "A Meta-Analysis of Writing Interventions," 454–473; Karen R. Harris et al., "Turning Broccoli into Ice Cream Sundaes," in *Write Now! Empowering Writers in Today's K–6 Classroom*, ed. Kathy Ganske (Newark, DE: International Reading Association, 2014), 87–108.

51. Randall Boone and Kyle Higgins, "The Role of Instructional Design in Assistive Technology Research and Development," *Reading Research Quarterly* 42, no. 1 (2007): 135–140; Rolf B. Fasting and Solveig-Alma Halaas Lyster, "The Effects of Computer Technology in Assisting the Development of Literacy in Young Struggling Readers and Spellers," *European Journal of Special Needs Education* 20, no. 1 (2005): 21–40; Sharon Walpole and Michael C. McKenna, *Differentiated Reading Instruction: Strategies for the Primary Grades* (New York: Guilford Press, 2007); Theodore A. Barker and Joseph K. Torgesen, "An Evaluation of Computer-Assisted Instruction in Phonological Awareness with Below Average Readers," *Journal of Educational Computing Research* 13, no. 1 (1995): 89–103.

52. Edyburn, "Critical Issues in Advancing the Special Education Technology Evidence Base," 7–24.

53. Technology-Related Assistance Act for Individuals with Disabilities, US Code 29 (1988); Assistive Technology Act, US Code 29 (1998), §§ 3002 et seq.

54. Individuals with Disabilities Act, US Code 20 (2004), §§ 1401 et seq.

55. Ghosh, *Technology for Inclusion*; Meryl Alper, *Giving Voice: Mobile Communication, Disability, and Inequality* (Cambridge, MA: MIT Press, 2017).

56. Ghosh, *Technology for Inclusion*; Alper, *Giving Voice*.

57. Ghosh, *Technology for Inclusion*; Mike Blamires, ed., *Enabling Technology for Inclusion* (Thousand Oaks, CA: SAGE, 1999).

58. Alper, *Giving Voice*.

59. The Center for AAC and Autism, accessed March 3, 2022, https://www.aacandautism.com/.

60. Alper, *Giving Voice*; Asaro-Saddler, "Using Evidence-Based Practices," 79–85; Pennington et al., "Using Simultaneous Prompting," 24–38.

61. Asaro-Saddler, "Using Evidence-Based Practices," 79–85; Pennington et al., "Using Simultaneous Prompting," 24–38.

62. Ok and Rao, "Digital Tools for the Inclusive Classroom," 204–211.

63. Bennett et al., "Interdependence as a Frame," 161–173.

64. Rita C. Richey, "Reflections on the 2008 AECT Definitions of the Field," *Tech-Trends* 52 (2008): 24–25, https://doi.org/10.1007/s11528-008-0108-2; Donn R. Garrison and Terry Anderson, *E-Learning in the 21st Century: A Framework for Research and Practice* (London: Routledge, 2003); Al Januszewski and Michael Molenda, eds., *Educational Technology: A Definition with Commentary* (New York: Routledge, 2013).

65. Benjamin Herold, "Technology in Education: An Overview," *Education Week* 20, no. 7 (2016): 129–141.

66. David H. Rose and Anne Meyer, *Teaching Every Student in the Digital Age: Universal Design for Learning* (Alexandria, VA: Association for Supervision and Curriculum Development, 2002).

67. Dudley-Marling and Burns, "Two Perspectives on Inclusion," 14–31.

68. Michael Cole, *Cultural Psychology: A Once and Future Discipline* (Cambridge, MA: Harvard University Press, 1998); James Paul Gee, *Social Linguistics and Literacies: Ideology in Discourses*, 2nd ed. (Bristol, PA: Falmer Press, 1996); Ray McDermott and Hervé Varenne, "Culture as Disability," *Anthropology and Education Quarterly* 26, no. 3 (1995): 324–348.

69. Dudley-Marling and Burns, "Two Perspectives on Inclusion," 14–31.

70. David H. Rose and Anne Meyer, *A Practical Reader in Universal Design for Learning* (Cambridge, MA: Harvard Education Press, 2006); Rose et al., *The Universally Designed Classroom*.

71. Center for Applied Special Technology, accessed September 8, 2022, https://www.cast.org/.

72. Chuck Hitchcock and Skip Stahl, "Assistive Technology, Universal Design, Universal Design for Learning: Improved Learning Opportunities," *Journal of Special Education Technology* 18, no. 4 (2003): 45–52.

73. Rose and Meyer, *A Practical Reader in Universal Design for Learning*.

74. Yenda Prado, *PBS KIDS Digital Features for DEIA Accessibility*, PBS KIDS, 2021.

75. Prado, *PBS KIDS Digital Features for DEIA Accessibility*.

76. Sheryl Burgstahler, "The Role of Technology in Preparing Youth with Disabilities for Postsecondary Education and Employment," *Journal of Special Education Technology* 18, no. 4 (2003): 7–19.

77. Ghosh, *Technology for Inclusion*; Blamires, *Enabling Technology for Inclusion*.

Notes to Chapter 3

78. Jennifer Cullen, Stephen B. Richards, and Catherine Lawless Frank, "Using Software to Enhance the Writing Skills of Students with Special Needs," *Journal of Special Education Technology* 23, no. 2 (2008): 33–44.

79. Asaro-Saddler, "Using Evidence-Based Practices," 79–85.

80. Ok and Rao, "Digital Tools for the Inclusive Classroom," 204–211.

81. Pennington and Delano, "Writing Instruction for Students with Autism Spectrum Disorders," 158–167; Asaro-Saddler, "Writing Instruction and Self-Regulation," 266–283; Graham and Harris, "Improving the Writing Performance of Young Struggling Writers," 19–33.

82. Asaro-Saddler, "Using Evidence-Based Practices," 79–85, and "Writing Instruction and Self-Regulation," 266–283; MacArthur et al., "Technology Applications for Students with Literacy Problems," 273–301.

83. Viet Vu et al., "Digital Storytelling for Academic Literacy: Culturally Responsive Multimodal Composition Course Design," in *Learning Critical Thinking Skills Beyond the 21st Century for Multidisciplinary Courses*, ed. Zehilia B. Wilhite (San Diego, CA: Cognella, 2021), 172–190.

84. MacArthur et al., "Technology Applications for Students with Literacy Problems," 273–301.

85. Asaro-Saddler, "Using Evidence-Based Practices," 79–85.

86. Ok and Rao, "Digital Tools for the Inclusive Classroom," 204–211.

87. Charles A. MacArthur et al., "Spelling Checkers and Students with Learning Disabilities: Performance Comparisons and Impact on Spelling," *The Journal of Special Education* 30 (1996): 35–57.

88. Fasting and Lyster, "The Effects of Computer Technology," 21–40.

89. Kennedy and Deshler, "Literacy Instruction," 289–298; MacArthur et al., "Technology Applications for Students with Literacy Problems," 273–301.

90. Dorothy Chun, Richard Kern, and Bryan Smith, "Technology in Language Use, Language Teaching, and Language Learning," *The Modern Language Journal* 100, no. S1 (2016): 64–80.

91. Ok and Rao, "Digital Tools for the Inclusive Classroom," 204–211.

92. Kennedy and Deshler, "Literacy Instruction," 289–298; Srikala Naraian and Mark Surabian, "New Literacy Studies: An Alternative Frame for Preparing Teachers to Use Assistive Technology," *Teacher Education and Special Education* 37, no. 4 (2014): 330–346.

93. Ok and Rao, "Digital Tools for the Inclusive Classroom," 204–211; Fasting and Lyster, "The Effects of Computer Technology," 21–40.

94. Alper, *Giving Voice*; Cranmer, *Disabled Children and Digital Technologies*.

Chapter 4

1. National Alliance for Public Charter Schools, accessed April 21, 2023, https://www.publiccharters.org/; Federico R. Waitoller, *Excluded by Choice: Urban Students with Disabilities in the Education Marketplace* (New York: Teachers College Press, 2020).

2. Waitoller, *Excluded by Choice*.

3. For an in-depth discussion of charters as education models, see Waitoller, *Excluded by Choice*.

4. Alfredo J. Artiles, Federico R. Waitoller, and Rebecca Neal, "Grappling with the Intersection of Language and Ability Differences: Equity Issues for Chicano/Latino Students in Special Education," in *Chicano School Failure and Success: Past, Present, and Future*, ed. Richard R. Valencia (New York: Routledge, 2010), 213; Waitoller, *Excluded by Choice*.

5. Joshua D. Angrist, Parag A. Pathak, and Christopher R. Walters, "Explaining Charter School Effectiveness," *American Economic Journal: Applied Economics* 5, no. 4 (2013): 1–27; Albert Cheng et al., "'No Excuses' Charter Schools: A Meta-Analysis of the Experimental Evidence on Student Achievement," *Journal of School Choice* 11, no. 2 (2017): 209–238; Eric Crane, Brian Edwards, and Noli Brazil, *California's Charter Schools: Measuring their Performance* (Mountain View, CA: EdSource, 2007), https://www.wested.org/resources/californias-charter-schools-measuring-their-performance/#.

6. Erica Frankenberg, "NEPC Review: *Segregation, Race, and Charter Schools: What Do We Know?*" (Boulder, CO: National Education Policy Center, 2016); Julia S. Rubin and Mark Weber, "Charter Schools' Impact on Public Education: Theory versus Reality," in *The Risky Business of Education Policy*, ed. Christopher H. Tienken and Carol A. Mullen (New York: Routledge, 2021), 72–87; Waitoller, *Excluded by Choice*.

7. Bethany M. Hamilton-Jones and Cynthia O. Vail, "Preparing Special Educators for Collaboration in the Classroom: Pre-Service Teachers' Beliefs and Perspectives," *International Journal of Special Education* 29, no. 1 (2014): 76–86.

8. Hamilton-Jones and Vail, "Preparing Special Educators," 76–86.

9. A. Banotai, "Classroom Collaboration Offers Benefits to Students, Teachers and Clinicians," *Advance Online Edition for Speech–Language Pathologists and Audiologists* 16, no. 33 (2006): 6; Kellie L. Bauer et al., "20 Ways for Classroom Teachers to Collaborate with Speech–Language Pathologists," *Intervention in School and Clinic* 45, no. 5 (2010): 333–337.

10. Betty Kollia and Christopher Mulrine, "Collaborative Practice Patterns for Included Students among Elementary Educators and Speech and Language Pathologists," *Journal of Education and Human Development* 3, no. 4 (2014): 33–44; Bauer et al., "20 Ways for Classroom Teachers to Collaborate," 333–337.

Notes to Chapter 4

11. Yenda Prado et al., "Dual-Language Engagement: Concerted Cultivation of Spanish use among Students, Teachers, and Parents," *Bilingual Research Journal* 45, no. 2 (2022): 159–179; Sofía Chaparro, "School, Parents, and Communities: Leading Parallel Lives in a Two-Way Immersion Program," *International Multilingual Research Journal* 14, no. 1 (2020): 41–57; Deborah Palmer et al., "Team Teaching among Mixed Messages: Implementing Two-Way Dual Language Bilingual Education at Third Grade in Texas," *Language Policy* 15, no. 4 (2016): 393–413.

12. Qvortrup and Qvortrup, "Inclusion," 803–817.

13. Obiakor et al., "Making Inclusion Work," 477–490.

14. Green et al., "Implementation and Perceptions of Classroom-Based Service Delivery," 656–672.

15. Naomi Zigmond, "Where Should Students with Disabilities Receive Special Education Services? Is One Place Better than Another?" *The Journal of Special Education* 37, no. 3 (2003): 193–199.

16. Alquraini and Gut, "Critical Components of Successful Inclusion," 42–59.

17. Zigmond, "Where Should Students with Disabilities Receive Special Education Services?" 193–199.

18. Zigmond, "Where Should Students with Disabilities Receive Special Education Services?" 193–199.

19. Frank Fitch, "Inclusion, Exclusion, and Ideology: Special Education Students' Changing Sense of Self," *The Urban Review* 35, no. 3 (2003): 233–252.

20. For a discussion of ecological perspectives in education program implementation, see Prado et al., "Dual-Language Engagement."

21. Susan B. Palmer et al., "Foundations for Self-Determination in Early Childhood: An Inclusive Model for Children with Disabilities," *Topics in Early Childhood Special Education* 33, no. 1 (2013): 38–47.

22. Ms. Wezner later explained that she used to monitor behavior from the front of the classroom but switched to the back because the students got very proficient at self-regulating with a visual reminder.

23. Hamilton-Jones and Vail, "Preparing Special Educators," 76–86.

24. Fitch, "Inclusion, Exclusion, and Ideology," 233–252.

25. Obiakor et al., "Making Inclusion Work," 477–490. See also medical model of disability in chapter 1.

26. Boroson, "Inclusive Education," 18–23.

27. Alquraini and Gut, "Critical Components of Successful Inclusion," 42–59.

28. Jean P. Hall, "Narrowing the Breach: Can Disability Culture and Full Educational Inclusion Be Reconciled?" *Journal of Disability Policy Studies* 13, no. 3 (2002): 144–152.

29. Cheryl M. Jorgensen, Michael McSheehan, and Rae M. Sonnenmeier, "Presumed Competence Reflected in the Educational Programs of Students with IDD before and after the Beyond Access Professional Development Intervention," *Journal of Intellectual and Developmental Disability* 32, no. 4 (2007): 248–262; Douglas Biklen and Jamie Burke, "Presuming Competence," in *Beginning with Disability: A Primer*, ed. Lennard J. Davis (New York: Routledge, 2018), 269–288.

30. Lan Liu-Gitz and Devender R. Banda, "A Replication of the RIRD Strategy to Decrease Vocal Stereotypy in a Student with Autism," *Behavioral Interventions: Theory and Practice in Residential and Community-Based Clinical Programs* 25, no. 1 (2010): 77–87; Oksana V. Zashchirinskaia, "Modern Ideas about Intellectual Disability in Medical Psychology in the Context of Non-Verbal Communication of Primary School Children," *Journal of Intellectual Disability-Diagnosis and Treatment* 8, no. 4 (2020): 594–601.

31. Alquraini and Gut, "Critical Components of Successful Inclusion," 42–59; Zoe E. Samborski, "Educator Perceptions of the Social Benefits from Peer to Peer Interactions between General and Special Education Students" (PhD diss., California State University, Sacramento, CA, 2021); John McDonnell and Pam Hunt, "Inclusive Education and Meaningful School Outcomes," in *Equity and Full Participation for Individuals with Severe Disabilities: A Vision for the Future*, ed. Martin Agran et al. (Baltimore, MD: Paul H. Brookes, 2014), 155–176.

32. Hall, "Narrowing the Breach," 144–152.

33. McDonnell and Hunt, "Inclusive Education and Meaningful School Outcomes," 155–176; Hall, "Narrowing the Breach," 144–152.

34. John Lanear and Elise Frattura, "Getting the Stories Straight: Allowing Different Voices to Tell an 'Effective History' of Special Education Law in the United States," *Education and the Law* 19, no. 2 (2007): 87–109.

35. Brandt Chamberlain, Connie Kasari, and Erin Rotheram-Fuller, "Involvement or Isolation? The Social Networks of Children with Autism in Regular Classrooms," *Journal of Autism and Developmental Disorders* 37, no. 2 (2007): 230–242; Coral Kemp and Mark Carter, "The Social Skills and Social Status of Mainstreamed Students with Intellectual Disabilities," *Educational Psychology* 22, no. 4 (2002): 391–411.

36. Qvortrup and Qvortrup, "Inclusion," 803–817.

37. For a discussion of cliques and out-groups in relation to disability, see Hall, "Narrowing the Breach," 144–152.

38. Lisa Delpit, *Other People's Children: Cultural Conflict in the Classroom* (New York: New Press, 2006); Hall, "Narrowing the Breach," 144–152; Vivian Gussin Paley, *You Can't Say You Can't Play* (Cambridge, MA; Harvard University Press, 1993)

Notes to Chapter 5

39. Shernaz B. Garcia and Alba A. Ortiz, "Intersectionality as a Framework for Transformative Research in Special Education," *Multiple Voices for Ethnically Diverse Exceptional Students* 13, no. 2 (2013): 32–47.

40. Lisa M. Bedore and Elizabeth D. Peña, "Assessment of Bilingual Children for Identification of Language Impairment: Current Findings and Implications for Practice," *International Journal of Bilingual Education and Bilingualism* 11 (2008): 1–29; Maria Cioè-Peña, "Disability, Bilingualism and What It Means to Be Normal," *Journal of Bilingual Education Research and Instruction* 19, no. 1 (2017): 138–160.

41. For a discussion of intersectional considerations in the implementation of inclusive service provision for multilingual students with disabilities, see Sara E. N. Kangas, "When Special Education Trumps ESL: An Investigation of Service Delivery for ELLs with Disabilities," *Critical Inquiry in Language Studies* 11, no. 4 (2014): 273–306, and "Why Working Apart Doesn't Work at All: Special Education and English Student Teacher Collaborations," *Intervention in School and Clinic* 54, no. 1 (2018): 31–39.

42. Obiakor et al., "Making Inclusion Work," 477–490; Kangas, "Why Working Apart Doesn't Work at All," 31–39; Bedore and Peña, "Assessment of Bilingual Children," 1–29.

43. Cioè-Peña, "Disability, Bilingualism and What It Means to Be Normal," 138–160; Kangas, "Why Working Apart Doesn't Work at All," 31–39.

44. Russell S. Rosen, "American Sign Language as a Foreign Language in US High Schools: State of the Art," *The Modern Language Journal* 92, no. 1 (2008): 10–38; Melissa DeLana, Anne Mary Gentry, and Jean Andrews, "The Efficacy of ASL/English Bilingual Education: Considering Public Schools," *American Annals of the Deaf* 152, no. 1 (2007): 73–87.

45. Catherine R. Cooper, "Cultural Brokers: How Immigrant Youth in Multicultural Societies Navigate and Negotiate their Pathways to College Identities," *Learning, Culture and Social Interaction* 3, no. 2 (2014): 170–176.

46. Obiakor et al., "Making Inclusion Work," 477–490.

47. Audrey A. Trainor, "Diverse Approaches to Parent Advocacy During Special Education Home–School Interactions: Identification and Use of Cultural and Social Capital," *Remedial and Special Education* 31, no. 1 (2010): 34–47.

48. Prado et al., "Dual-Language Engagement."

Chapter 5

1. For a discussion of sociocultural interrelations between language, literacy, and technology, see Sharin R. Jacob and Mark Warschauer, "Computational Thinking and Literacy," *Journal of Computer Science Integration* 1, no. 1 (2018); James Paul

Gee, "New People in New Worlds: Networks, the New Capitalism and Schools," in *Multiliteracies: Literacy Learning and the Design of Social Futures*, ed. Bill Cope and Mary Kalantzis (London: Routledge, 2000), 43–68; Warschauer, *Electronic Literacies*; Warschauer, *Technology and Social Inclusion*.

2. For a discussion of integration of multiple tools to support scaffolding in classroom contexts integrating students with disabilities, see Yenda Prado, Sharin Jacob, and Mark Warschauer, "Teaching Computational Thinking to Exceptional Students: Lessons from Two Inclusive Classrooms," *Computer Science Education* 32, no. 2 (2022): 188–212, https://doi.org/10.1080/08993408.2021.1914459.

3. For a discussion of inclusive pedagogical supports for learning, see Prado et al., "Teaching Computational Thinking."

4. Ghosh, *Technology for Inclusion*; Anderson and Putman, "Special Education Teachers' Experience," 37–50; Warschauer, *Electronic Literacies* and *Technology and Social Inclusion*.

5. Michael C. McKenna et al., "Reading Attitudes of Middle School Students: Results of a US Survey," *Reading Research Quarterly* 47, no. 3 (2012): 283–306; Stanovich, "Matthew Effects in Reading," 360–407.

6. For discussions of challenges in integrating digital technologies into classroom practice, see Michele Jacobsen, Pat Clifford, and Sharon Friesen, "Preparing Teachers for Technology Integration: Creating a Culture of Inquiry in the Context of Use," *Contemporary Issues in Technology and Teacher Education* 2, no. 3 (2002): 363–388; Hatice Yildiz Durak, "Preparing Pre-Service Teachers to Integrate Teaching Technologies into Their Classrooms: Examining the Effects of Teaching Environments Based on Open-Ended, Hands-On and Authentic Tasks," *Education and Information Technologies* 26, no. 5 (2021): 5365–5387.

7. Asaro-Saddler, "Writing Instruction and Self-Regulation," 266–283; Gillespie and Graham, "A Meta-Analysis of Writing Interventions," 454–473.

8. Asaro-Saddler, "Writing Instruction and Self-Regulation," 266–283; Gillespie and Graham, "A Meta-Analysis of Writing Interventions," 454–473; Fasting and Lyster, "The Effects of Computer Technology," 21–40.

9. Anderson and Putman, "Special Education Teachers' Experience," 37–50; Rosie Flewitt, David Messer, and Natalia Kucirkova, "New Directions for Early Literacy in a Digital Age: The iPad," *Journal of Early Childhood Literacy* 15, no. 3 (2015): 289–310; Cathy Burnett, "Technology and Literacy in Early Childhood Educational Settings: A Review of Research," *Journal of Early Childhood Literacy* 10, no. 3 (2010): 247–270; Blamires, *Enabling Technology for Inclusion*.

10. Yenda Prado, Mark Warschauer, and Penelope Collins, "Promoting Positive Literacy Attitudes in Struggling Readers through Digital Scaffolding." (paper presented at the International Society for Technology in Education, Chicago, Illinois, June 2018).

Notes to Chapter 5

11. Prado et al., "Promoting Positive Literacy Attitudes."

12. Blamires, *Enabling Technology for Inclusion*; Prado et al., "Promoting Positive Literacy Attitudes."

13. Ghosh, *Technology for Inclusion*; Katie Headrick Taylor, Deborah Silvis, and Reed Stevens, "Collecting and Connecting: Intergenerational Learning with Digital Media," in *Children and Families in the Digital Age*, ed. Elisabeth Gee, Lori Takeuchi, and Ellen Wartella (New York: Routledge, 2017), 74–75.

14. Anabella Davila and A. M. Hartman, "Tradition and Modern Aspects of Mexican Corporate Culture," in *Mexican Business Culture: Essays on Tradition, Ethics, Entrepreneurship and Commerce and the State*, ed. Carlos M. Coria-Sánchez and John T. Hyatt (Jefferson, NC: McFarland, 2016), 26–37.

15. Leslie Reese et al., "The Concept of Educación: Latino Family Values and American Schooling," in *Interdisciplinary Perspectives on the New Immigration*, ed. Marcelo M. Suárez-Orozco, Carola Suárez-Orozco, and Desirée Qin-Hilliard (New York: Routledge, 2022), 305–328; Susan Auerbach, "'If the Student Is Good, Let Him Fly': Moral Support for College Among Latino Immigrant Parents," *Journal of Latinos and Education* 5, no. 4 (2006): 275–292.

16. Cranmer, *Disabled Children and Digital Technologies*; Gee, "New People in New Worlds," 43–68; Warschauer, *Technology and Social Inclusion*.

17. Prado et al., "Dual-Language Engagement."

18. Amber M. Levinson and Brigid Barron, "Latino Immigrant Families Learning with Digital Media Across Settings and Generations," *Digital Education Review* 33 (2018): 150–169; Burnett, "Technology and Literacy in Early Childhood," 247–270.

19. For a discussion of accessibility features as a determinant of technology use, see Alper, *Giving Voice*.

20. Ok and Rao, "Digital Tools for the Inclusive Classroom," 205.

21. For a discussion of concerted cultivation practices in diverse families, see Prado et al., "Dual-Language Engagement."

22. Alper, *Giving Voice*.

23. Alper, *Giving Voice*.

24. Kathy Cologon, "Debunking Myths: Reading Development in Children with Down Syndrome," *Australian Journal of Teacher Education* 38, no. 3 (2013): 9.

25. Cologon, "Debunking Myths."

26. Cologon, "Debunking Myths."

27. John Jessel et al., "Different Spaces: Learning and Literacy with Children and their Grandparents in East London Homes," *Linguistics and Education* 22 (2011):

37–50; Susan M. Burns, Peg Griffin, and Catherine E. Snow, *Starting Out Right: A Guide to Promoting Children's Reading Success. Specific Recommendations from America's Leading Researchers on How to Help Children Become Successful Readers* (Washington, DC: National Academy Press, 1999).

28. Cranmer, *Disabled Children and Digital Technologies*; Christine A. Weiland et al., "Advocates in Odd Places: Social Justice for Behaviorally Challenged, Minority Students in a Large Urban School District," *Education, Citizenship and Social Justice* 9, no. 2 (2014): 114–127; Alquaraini and Gut, "Critical Components of Successful Inclusion," 42–59.

29. Burns et al., *Starting Out Right*.

30. Horne and Timmons, "Making it Work," 273–286; Somer Harding, "Successful Inclusion Models for Students with Disabilities Require Strong Site Leadership: Autism and Behavioral Disorders Create Many Challenges for the Learning Environment," *International Journal of Learning* 16, no. 3 (2009): 91–104; Avramidis and Norwich, "Teachers' Attitudes towards Integration/Inclusion," 129–147.

31. Vesa Korhonen, "Dialogic Literacy: A Sociocultural Literacy Learning Approach," in *Practicing Information Literacy: Bringing Theories of Learning, Practice and Information Literacy Together*, ed. Annemaree Lloyd and Sanna Talja (Witney, UK: Chandos, 2010), 211–226.

32. Gunther Kress and Theo Van Leeuwen, *Multimodal Discourse: The Modes and Media of Contemporary Communication* (London: Arnold, 2001).

33. Alper, *Giving Voice*; Peppler and Warschauer, "Uncovering Literacies, Disrupting Stereotypes," 15–41; Blamires, *Enabling Technology for Inclusion*.

34. Flewitt et al., "New Directions for Early Literacy," 289–310; Renee Hobbs and Amy Jensen, "The Past, Present, and Future of Media Literacy Education," *Journal of Media Literacy Education* 1, no. 1 (2009): 1–11.

35. Hobbs and Jensen, "The Past, Present, and Future"; Peppler and Warschauer, "Uncovering Literacies, Disrupting Stereotypes" 15–41.

36. Pennington and Delano, "Writing Instruction for Students with Autism Spectrum Disorders," 158–167; Asaro-Saddler, "Writing Instruction and Self-Regulation," 266–283; Graham and Harris, "Improving the Writing Performance of Young Struggling Writers," 19–33.

37. Englert et al., "Scaffolding the Writing of Students with Disabilities," 9–29; MacArthur et al., "Technology Applications for Students with Literacy Problems," 273–301.

38. Asaro-Saddler, "Writing Instruction and Self-Regulation," 266–283; MacArthur et al., "Technology Applications for Students with Literacy Problems," 273–301.

Notes to Chapter 6

39. Ghosh, *Technology for Inclusion*; Blamires, *Enabling Technology for Inclusion*.

40. Ghosh, *Technology for Inclusion*; Alper, *Giving Voice*.

41. Alper, *Giving Voice*.

42. Alper, *Giving Voice*.

43. Alper, *Giving Voice*.

44. For a discussion of negotiating personhood vis-à-vis assistive technologies, see Alper, *Giving Voice*.

45. Alper, *Giving Voice*, 44.

46. Snaefridur T. Egilson and Rannveig Traustadottir, "Assistance to Pupils with Physical Disabilities in Regular Schools: Promoting Inclusion or Creating Dependency?" *European Journal of Special Needs Education* 24 (2009): 21–36; Stephen M. Broer, Mary B. Doyle, and Michael F. Giangreco, "Perspectives of Students with Intellectual Disabilities about their Experiences with Paraprofessional Support," *Exceptional Children* 71, no. 4 (2005): 415; Karen E. Broomhead, "Acceptance or Rejection? The Social Experiences of Children with Special Educational Needs and Disabilities Within a Mainstream Primary School," *Education 3–13* 47, no. 8 (2019): 877–888.

47. Alper, *Giving Voice*.

48. Cranmer, *Disabled Children and Digital Technologies*; Alper, *Giving Voice*.

49. Ghosh, *Technology for Inclusion*; Blamires, *Enabling Technology for Inclusion*.

50. White et al., "Moving from Independence to Interdependence," 233–240; Stacy M. Branham and Shaun K. Kane, "Collaborative Accessibility: How Blind and Sighted Companions Co-create Accessible Home Spaces," in *Proceedings of the 33rd Annual ACM Conference on Human Factors in Computing Systems* (New York: ACM, 2015), 2373–2382, https://doi.org/10.1145/2702123.2702511.

51. Alper, *Giving Voice*, 121.

Chapter 6

1. Sonali Kohli, "Children with Disabilities Are Regressing: How Much Is Distance Learning to Blame?" *Los Angeles Times*, August 7, 2020, https://www.latimes.com /california/story/2020-08-07/covid-19-distance-learning-weakens-special-education.

2. Howard Blume and Laura Newberry, "California Teacher Unions Fight Calls to Reopen Schools," *Los Angeles Times*, October 16, 2020, https://www.latimes.com /california/story/2020-10-16/state-teacher-unions-push-back-against-calls-to-reopen -k-12-campuses-parents-divided; Sanjay Gupta, "Dr. Sanjay Gupta: Why I Am Not Sending My Kids Back to School," *CNN Health*, August 12, 2020, https://www.cnn

.com/2020/08/12/health/covid-kids-school-gupta-essay/index.html; Kohli, "Children with Disabilities Are Regressing."

3. Dana Goldstein, "Coronavirus is Shutting Schools. Is America Ready for Virtual Learning?" *The New York Times*, March 13, 2020, https://oercommons.s3.amazonaws.com/media/editor/260648/Coronavirus_Is_Shutting_Schools._Is_America_Ready _for_Virtual_Learning__-_The_New_York_Times.pdf; Gupta, "Why I Am Not Sending My Kids Back to School."

4. Kate H. Averett, "Remote Learning, COVID-19, and Children with Disabilities," *AERA Open* 7 (2021), https://doi.org/10.1177/23328584211058471; Ain A. Grooms and Joshua Childs, "'We Need to Do Better by Kids': Changing Routines in US Schools in Response to COVID-19 School Closures," *Journal of Education for Students Placed at Risk (JESPAR)* 26, no. 2 (2021): 135–156, https://doi.org/10.1080/10824669.2021.1906251.

5. Yoree Koh, "Can You Form a School Pod without Fueling Inequality? These Groups Are Trying," *Wall Street Journal*, August 4, 2020, https://www.wsj.com /articles/can-you-form-a-school-pod-without-fueling-inequality-these-groups-are -trying-11596542410.

6. Laura Hamilton and Betheny Gross, "How Has the Pandemic Affected Students' Social-Emotional Well-Being? A Review of the Evidence to Date," https://eric.ed .gov/?id=ED614131; Lana Peterson et al., "A Rapid Response to COVID-19: One District's Pivot from Technology Integration to Distance Learning," *Information and Learning Sciences* 121, no. 5/6 (2020): 461–469, https://doi.org/DOI: 10.1108/ILS-04 -2020-0131.

7. Koh, "Can You Form a School Pod?"; Yenda Prado et al., "Virtual Inclusion: Supporting Exceptional Students' Participation in Remote Learning Environments" (panel discussion, Conference of the American Education Research Association, Orlando, FL, April 2021).

8. Koh, "Can You Form a School Pod?"; Prado et al., "Virtual Inclusion."

9. Cory Turner, "6 Things We've Learned about How the Pandemic Disrupted Learning," *National Public Radio*, June 22, 2022, https://www.npr.org/2022/06/22 /1105970186/pandemic-learning-loss-findings.

10. Grooms and Childs, "We Need to Do Better by Kids," 135–156.

11. Grooms and Childs, "We Need to Do Better by Kids," 135–156.

12. Grooms and Childs, "We Need to Do Better by Kids," 135–156.

13. Peterson et al., "A Rapid Response to COVID-19"; Linda Darling-Hammond and Maria E. Hyler, "Preparing Educators for the Time of COVID . . . and Beyond," *European Journal of Teacher Education* 43, no. 4 (2020): 457–465, https://doi.org/10 .1080/02619768.2020.1816961.

Notes to Chapter 6

14. Colleen McClain et al., "The Internet and the Pandemic," *PEW Research Center*, September 1, 2021, https://www.pewresearch.org/internet/2021/09/01/the-internet-and-the-pandemic/.

15. Turner, "6 Things We've Learned"; McClain et al., "The Internet and the Pandemic."

16. Ashley Abramson, "Capturing the Benefits of Remote Learning," *American Psychological Association* 52, no. 6 (2021): 46, https://www.apa.org/monitor/2021/09/cover-remote-learning.

17. Hibah K. Aladsani, "The Perceptions of Female Breadwinner Parents Regarding their Children's Distance Learning during the COVID-19 Pandemic," *Education and Information Technologies* 27, no. 4 (2022): 4817–4839, https://doi.org/10.1007/s10639-021-10812-9; Rebecca Michelson et al., "Parenting in a Pandemic: Juggling Multiple Roles and Managing Technology Use in Family Life during COVID-19 in the United States," *Proceedings of the ACM on Human–Computer Interaction* 5, no. CSCW2 (2021): 1–39, https://doi.org/10.1145/3479546.

18. Michelson et al., "Parenting in a Pandemic," 1–39.

19. Emma Bowman, "Scanning Students' Rooms during Remote Tests Is Unconstitutional, Judge Rules," *National Public Radio*, August 26, 2022, https://www.npr.org/2022/08/25/1119337956/test-proctoring-room-scans-unconstitutional-cleveland-state-university.

20. Grooms and Childs, "We Need to Do Better by Kids," 135–156; Tyler A. Womack and Elissa M. Monteiro, "Special Education Staff Well-Being and the Effectiveness of Remote Services during the COVID-19 Pandemic," *Psychology in the Schools* 60, no. 5 (2022): 1374–1393, https://doi.org/10.1002/pits.22702.

21. Frank R. Castelli and Mark A. Sarvary, "Why Students Do Not Turn On Their Video Cameras during Online Classes and an Equitable and Inclusive Plan to Encourage Them to Do So," *Ecology and Evolution* 11, no. 8 (2021): 3565–3576, https://doi.org/DOI: 10.1002/ece3.7123; Youki Terada, "The Camera-On/Camera-Off Dilemma," *Edutopia*, February 5, 2021, https://www.edutopia.org/article/camera-oncamera-dilemma.

22. Castelli and Sarvary, "Why Students Do Not Turn On Their Video Cameras," 3565–3576; Terada, "The Camera-On/Camera-Off Dilemma."

23. Turner, "6 Things We've Learned"; Castelli and Sarvary, "Why Students Do Not Turn On Their Video Cameras"; Terada, "The Camera-On/Camera-Off Dilemma."

24. Grooms and Childs, "We Need to Do Better by Kids," 135–156.

25. Kohli, "Children with Disabilities Are Regressing."

26. Kohli, "Children with Disabilities Are Regressing."

27. Womack and Monteiro, "Special Education Staff Well-Being."

28. Womack and Monteiro, "Special Education Staff Well-Being."

29. Alper, *Giving Voice*; Antero Garcia, *Good Reception: Teens, Teachers, and Mobile Media in a Los Angeles High School* (Cambridge, MA: MIT Press, 2017).

30. Vu et al., "Digital Storytelling for Academic Literacy."

31. Tamara Tate and Mark Warschauer, "Equity in Online Learning," *Educational Psychologist* 57, no. 3 (2022): 192–206, https://doi.org/10.1080/00461520.2022.2062597.

32. Michelson et al., "Parenting in a Pandemic," 1–39.

33. Michelson et al., "Parenting in a Pandemic," 1–39.

34. Marcela Almeida et al., "Editorial Perspective: The Mental Health Impact of School Closures during the COVID-19 Pandemic," *Journal of Child Psychology and Psychiatry* 63, no. 5 (2022): 608–612, https://doi.org/10.1111/jcpp.13535; Anne Helen Petersen, "Other Countries Have Social Safety Nets. The US Has Women," *Culture Study*, November 11, 2020, https://annehelen.substack.com/p/other-countries-have-social-safety.

35. Michelson et al., "Parenting in a Pandemic," 1–39.

36. Averett, "Remote Learning, COVID-19, and Children with Disabilities"; Womack and Monteiro, "Special Education Staff Well-Being."

37. Averett, "Remote Learning, COVID-19, and Children with Disabilities."

38. Almeida et al., "Editorial Perspective"; Aladsani, "The Perceptions of Female Breadwinner Parents."

39. Jessica Calarco et al., "'My Husband Thinks I'm Crazy': Covid-19-Related Conflict in Couples with Young Children," *SocArXiv* (2020), https://doi.org/doi:10.31235/osf.io/cpkj6; Almeida et al., "Editorial Perspective"; Michelson et al., "Parenting in a Pandemic," 1–39.

40. Petersen, "Other Countries Have Social Safety Nets."

41. Peterson et al., "A Rapid Response to COVID-19."

42. Grooms and Childs, "We Need to Do Better by Kids," 135–156; Peterson et al., "A Rapid Response to COVID-19."

43. Tate and Warschauer, "Equity in Online Learning," 192–206.

44. Prado et al., "Dual-Language Engagement"; Steve D. Przymus, "Challenging the Monolingual Paradigm in Secondary Dual-Language Instruction: Reducing Language-As-Problem with the 2-1-L2 Model," *Bilingual Research Journal* 39, no. 3–4 (2016): 279–295; Ofelia García and Li Wei, "Language, Bilingualism and Education,"

Notes to Chapter 6

Translanguaging: Language, Bilingualism and Education (New York: Palgrave MacMillan, 2014): 46–62, https://doi.orghttp://dx.doi.org/10.12795/elia.2021.i21.06.

45. Rose et al., *The Universally Designed Classroom.*

46. Prado et al., "Dual-Language Engagement"; Sarah J. Shin, *Bilingualism in Schools and Society: Language, Identity, and Policy* (New York: Routledge, 2017), https://doi.org/10.4324/9781315535579.

47. Hamilton and Gross, "How Has the Pandemic Affected Students' Social-Emotional Well-Being?"

48. Almeida et al., "Editorial Perspective."

49. Prado et al., "Virtual Inclusion."

50. Elizabeth D. Steiner and Ashley Woo, "Job-Related Stress Threatens the Teacher Supply: Key Findings from the 2021 State of the US Teacher Survey," https://www.rand.org/pubs/research_reports/RRA1108-1.html.

51. Steiner and Woo, "Job-Related Stress Threatens the Teacher Supply."

52. Petersen, "Other Countries Have Social Safety Nets"; Aladsani, "The Perceptions of Female Breadwinner Parents."

53. Michelson et al., "Parenting in a Pandemic," 1–39; Averett, "Remote Learning, COVID-19, and Children with Disabilities."

54. "COVID-19 Vaccines," US Department of Health and Human Services, accessed August 31, 2022, https://www.hhs.gov/coronavirus/covid-19-vaccines/index.html; Suzanne C. Smeltzer et al., "Vulnerability, Loss, and Coping Experiences of Health Care Workers and First Responders during the Covid-19 Pandemic: A Qualitative Study," *International Journal of Qualitative Studies on Health and Well-Being* 17, no. 1 (2022), https://doi.org/10.1080/17482631.2022.2066254.

55. Grooms and Childs, "We Need to Do Better by Kids," 135–156; Smeltzer et al., "Vulnerability, Loss, and Coping Experiences of Health Care Workers and First Responders."

56. Smeltzer et al., "Vulnerability, Loss, and Coping Experiences of Health Care Workers and First Responders."

57. Hamilton and Gross, "How Has the Pandemic Affected Students' Social-Emotional Well-Being?"; Steiner and Woo, "Job-Related Stress Threatens the Teacher Supply."

58. Almeida et al., "Editorial Perspective"; Tate and Warschauer, "Equity in Online Learning," 192–206.

59. Michelson et al., "Parenting in a Pandemic," 1–39; Womack and Monteiro, "Special Education Staff Well-Being"; Peterson et al., "A Rapid Response to COVID-19."

60. "Missing Social and Educational Milestones during COVID-19," *Providence*, May 24, 2020, https://www.providence.org/news/uf/614770827; Peterson et al., "A Rapid Response to COVID-19"; Turner, "6 Things We've Learned."

61. McClain et al., "The Internet and the Pandemic"; Abramson, "Capturing the Benefits of Remote Learning."

62. Peterson et al., "A Rapid Response to COVID-19"; Almeida et al., "Editorial Perspective."

63. Tate and Warschauer, "Equity in Online Learning."

Chapter 7

1. Tate and Warschauer, "Equity in Online Learning."

2. Kristen L. Walker et al., "Compulsory Technology Adoption and Adaptation in Education: A Looming Student Privacy Problem," *Journal of Consumer Affairs* 57 (2023): 445–478.

3. Tony Wan, "Google Apps Are Used Widely in K–12. A New Tool ill Show Just How Useful They Are," *EdSurge*, September 24, 2019, https://www.edsurge.com/news/2019-09-24-google-apps-are-used-widely-in-k-12-a-new-tool-will-show-just-how-useful-they-are; Zach Yeskel, "New Meet Features to Improve Distance Learning," *Google for Education*, April 9, 2020, https://www.blog.google/outreach-initiatives/education/meet-for-edu/.

4. Walker et al., "Compulsory Technology Adoption and Adaptation in Education," 445–478.

5. Tate and Warschauer, "Equity in Online Learning"; Walker et al., "Compulsory Technology Adoption and Adaptation in Education": 445–478.

6. Turner, "6 Things We've Learned"; Womack and Monteiro, "Special Education Staff Well-Being."

7. Hamilton and Gross, "How Has the Pandemic Affected Students' Social-Emotional Well-Being?"; Steiner and Woo, "Job-Related Stress Threatens the Teacher Supply"; Peterson et al., "A Rapid Response to COVID-19."

8. Womack and Monteiro, "Special Education Staff Well-Being"; Grooms and Childs, "We Need to Do Better by Kids," 135–156; Peterson et al., "A Rapid Response to COVID-19."

9. Michelson et al., "Parenting in a Pandemic," 1–39.

Chapter 8

1. Bennett et al., "Interdependence as a Frame," 161–173; Mingus, "Access Intimacy"; White et al., "Moving from Independence to Interdependence," 233–240.

Notes to Chapter 8

2. Bennett et al., "Interdependence as a Frame," 161–173; Branham and Kane, "Collaborative Accessibility," 2373–2382.

3. Oliver, "The Individual and Social Models of Disability"; Jennifer Mankoff, Gillian R. Hayes, and Devva Kasnitz, "Disability Studies as a Source of Critical Inquiry for the Field of Assistive Technology," in *ASSETS '10: Proceedings of the 12th International ACM SIGACCESS Conference on Computers and Accessibility* (New York: ACM, 2010), 3–10, https://doi.org/10.1145/1878803.1878807.

4. DeJong, "Independent Living," 435–446; White et al., "Moving from Independence to Interdependence," 233–240.

5. Bennett et al., "Interdependence as a Frame," 161–173; Branham and Kane, "Collaborative Accessibility," 2373–2382.

6. Bennett et al., "Interdependence as a Frame," 161–173; Branham and Kane, "Collaborative Accessibility," 2373–2382; Mingus, "Access Intimacy."

7. Mingus, "Access Intimacy"; Mankoff et al., "Disability Studies," 3–10; Bennett et al., "Interdependence as a Frame," 161–173; Branham and Kane, "Collaborative Accessibility," 2373–2382.

8. Bennett et al., "Interdependence as a Frame," 161–173; Branham and Kane, "Collaborative Accessibility," 2373–2382; Mingus, "Access Intimacy."

9. Alper, *Giving Voice*; Cranmer, *Disabled Children and Digital Technologies*.

10. Alper, *Giving Voice*; Cranmer, *Disabled Children and Digital Technologies*.

11. Alper, *Giving Voice*.

12. Alper, *Giving Voice*.

13. Alper, *Giving Voice*.

14. DeJong, "Independent Living," 435–446; White et al., "Moving from Independence to Interdependence," 233–240.

15. Mankoff et al., "Disability Studies," 3–10.

16. Frieden, "Independent Living Models," 169–173; White et al., "Moving from Independence to Interdependence," 233–240; DeJong, "Independent Living," 435–446.

17. White et al., "Moving from Independence to Interdependence," 233–240; Mia Mingus, "Interdependency (Excerpts from Several Talks)," *Leaving Evidence* (blog), January 22, 2010, https://leavingevidence.wordpress.com/2010/01/22/interdependency-exerpts-from-several-talks/, and "Changing the Framework: Disability Justice," *Leaving Evidence* (blog), February 12, 2011. https://leavingevidence.wordpress.com/2011/02/12/changing-the-framework-disability-justice/.

18. Mingus, "Changing the Framework."

19. Cranmer, *Disabled Children and Digital Technologies*.

20. Cranmer, *Disabled Children and Digital Technologies*, 42.

21. Cranmer, *Disabled Children and Digital Technologies*.

22. Damien Power, Tobias Schoenherr, and Danny Samson. "The Cultural Characteristic of Individualism/Collectivism: A Comparative Study of Implications for Investment in Operations Between Emerging Asian and Industrialized Western Countries," *Journal of Operations Management* 28, no. 3 (2010): 206–222, https://doi.org/10.1016/j.jom.2009.11.002.

23. Eva G. Green, Jean-Claude Deschamps, and Dario Paez, "Variation of Individualism and Collectivism within and between 20 Countries: A Typological Analysis," *Journal of Cross-Cultural Psychology* 36, no. 3 (2005): 321–339, https://doi.org/10.1177%2F0022022104273654.

24. Cranmer, *Disabled Children and Digital Technologies*.

25. Bennett et al., "Interdependence as a Frame," 161–173; Dom Chatterjee, "Independence Is an Ableist Myth: Unlocking the Power of Community in Healing," *The Body Is Not an Apology*, July 4, 2018, https://thebodyisnotanapology.com/magazine/independence-is-an-ableist-myth-unlocking-the-power-of-community-in-healing/; Mingus, "Access Intimacy"; White et al., "Moving from Independence to Interdependence," 233–240.

26. White et al., "Moving from Independence to Interdependence," 233–240.

27. White et al., "Moving from Independence to Interdependence," 233–240; Al Conduci, "Interdependence: A Model for Community-Based Health Information Management Systems," *Topics in Health Information Management* 19, no. 3 (1999): 40–46.

28. White et al., "Moving from Independence to Interdependence," 233–240; John Helliwell, "Social Capital, the Economy and Well-Being," in *The Review of Economic Performance and Social Progress 2001: The Longest Decade: Canada in the 1990s* (Ottawa: Centre for the Study of Living Standards, 2001), 43–60.

29. White et al., "Moving from Independence to Interdependence," 233–240; Condeluci, "Interdependence," 40–46.

30. Mingus, "Interdependency."

31. Mingus, "Interdependency"; White et al., "Moving from Independence to Interdependence," 233–240.

32. Bennett et al., "Interdependence as a Frame," 161–173.

33. Bennett et al., "Interdependence as a Frame," 161–173.

34. Prado et al., "Dual-Language Engagement."

Notes to Chapter 8

35. Prado et al., "Dual-Language Engagement."

36. Bennett et al., "Interdependence as a Frame," 161–173.

37. Bennett et al., "Interdependence as a Frame," 161–173; Branham and Kane, "Collaborative Accessibility," 2373–2382.

38. White et al., "Moving from Independence to Interdependence," 233–240; Mingus, "Interdependency" and "Changing the Framework."

39. Algozzine and Ysseldyke, *The Fundamentals of Special Education*; Hall et al., "SATurated Models of Pupildom," 801–817; Causton-Theoharis and Theoharis, "Creating Inclusive Schools," 24–25; Obiakor et al., "Making Inclusion Work," 477–490; Sailor and Roger, "Rethinking Inclusion," 503–509.

40. Kimberle Crenshaw, "Demarginalizing the Intersection of Race and Sex: A Black Feminist Critique of Antidiscrimination Doctrine, Feminist Theory and Antiracist Politics," *University of Chicago Forum* 1989, no. 1 (1989): 138–167, https://philpapers .org/archive/CREDTI.pdf?ncid=txtlnkusaolp00000603; Olena Hankivsky, "Intersectionality 101" (PhD diss., Institute for Intersectionality Research and Policy, Simon Fraser University, 2014), 1–34, https://www.researchgate.net/profile/Olena_Hankivsky /publication/279293665_Intersectionality_101/links/56c35bda08ae602342508c7f /Intersectionality-101.pdf.

41. Crenshaw, "Demarginalizing the Intersection of Race and Sex," 138–167; Hankivsky, "Intersectionality 101," 1–34.

42. Brittney Cooper, "Intersectionality," in *Oxford Handbook of Feminist Theory*, ed. Lisa Disch and Mary Hawkesworth (Oxford: Oxford Academic, 2016), 385–406, https://doi.org/10.1093/oxfordhb/9780199328581.013.20; Jennifer, C. Nash, *Black Feminism Reimagined: After Intersectionality* (Durnham, North Carolina: Duke University Press, 2018).

43. David Gillborn, "Intersectionality, Critical Race Theory, and the Primacy of Racism," *Qualitative Inquiry* 21, no. 3 (2015): 277–287, https://doi.org/10 .1177%2F1077800414557827; Tina Goethals, Elisabeth De Schauwer, and Geert Van Hove, "Weaving Intersectionality into Disability Studies Research," *DiGeSt. Journal of Diversity and Gender Studies* 2, no. 1–2 (2015): 113–135, https://core.ac.uk/download /pdf/74560235.pdf.

44. Gillborn, "Intersectionality, Critical Race Theory, and the Primacy of Racism," 277–287; Robert A. Shaw, "Employing Universal Design for Instruction," *New Directions for Student Services* 134 (2011): 21–33, https://doi.org/10.1002/ss.392.

45. Goethals et al., "Weaving Intersectionality into Disability Studies Research," 114.

46. Helliwell, "Social Capital, the Economy and Well-Being"; Trainor, "Diverse Approaches to Parent Advocacy," 34–47.

47. Hall, "Narrowing the Breach," 144–152.

48. Nancy Spencer-Cavaliere and E. Jane Watkinson, "Inclusion Understood from the Perspectives of Children with Disability," *Adapted Physical Activity Quarterly* 27, no. 4 (2010): 275–293.

49. Bennett et al., "Interdependence as a Frame," 161–173.

50. Campbell, "An Application of the Theory of Planned Behavior," 235–250.

51. For a discussion of the ecological and relational nature of the practices and customs within diverse school communities, see Prado et al., "Dual-Language Engagement."

52. Adriana Villavicencio, *Am I My Brother's Keeper? Educational Opportunities and Outcomes for Black and Brown Boys* (Cambridge, MA: Harvard Education Press, 2021), 81.

53. Cranmer, *Disabled Children and Digital Technologies*.

54. Cranmer, *Disabled Children and Digital Technologies*.

55. Cranmer, *Disabled Children and Digital Technologies*.

56. Kristine Black-Hawkins, "Understanding Inclusive Pedagogy," in *Inclusive Education: Making Sense of Everyday Practice*, ed. Vicky Plows and Ben Whitburn (Rotterdam: Brill Sense, 2017), 13–28; Roger Slee, "Defining the Scope of Inclusive Education," paper commissioned for the *2020 Global Education Monitoring Report, Inclusion and Education* (2018).

57. Cranmer, *Disabled Children and Digital Technologies*.

58. Qvortrup and Qvortrup, "Inclusion," 803–817.

59. Villavicencio, *Am I My Brother's Keeper?*, 134.

60. Garcia, *Good Reception*; Alper, *Giving Voice*.

61. Garcia, *Good Reception*.

62. Warschauer, *Technology and Social Inclusion*.

Chapter 9

1. Causton-Theoharis and Theoharis, "Creating Inclusive Schools," 24–25; Sailor and Roger, "Rethinking Inclusion," 503–509.

2. Schuelka and Carrington, "Innovative and Global Directions for Inclusive Education," 1–26.

3. Cranmer, *Disabled Children and Digital Technologies*; Schuelka and Carrington, "Innovative and Global Directions for Inclusive Education," 1–26.

Notes to Chapter 9 255

4. Warschauer, *Technology and Social Inclusion*.

5. For a discussion of the need for more research in the areas of inclusion and digital literacy practices, see Cranmer, *Disabled Children and Digital Technologies*; Alper, *Giving Voice*; Livingstone and Sefton-Green, *The Class*.

6. Bennett et al., "Interdependence as a Frame," 161–173.

7. For a discussion of disparities in teacher and student tech utility and use, see Garcia, *Good Reception*.

8. For a discussion of digital technology use to support students' inclusion, critical thinking, and engagement, see Cranmer, *Disabled Children and Digital Technologies*.

9. For a discussion of students' technology use as a source of cultural wealth, see Garcia, *Good Reception*.

10. McClain et al., "The Internet and the Pandemic"; Michelson et al., "Parenting in a Pandemic," 1–39.

11. Grooms and Childs, "We Need to Do Better by Kids," 135–156; Peterson et al., "A Rapid Response to COVID-19."

12. Michelson et al., "Parenting in a Pandemic," 1–39.

13. Joseph A. Maxwell, *Qualitative Research Design* (Thousand Oaks, CA: SAGE, 2013).

14. Cranmer, *Disabled Children and Digital Technologies*; Garcia, *Good Reception*.

15. Morgan G. Ames, *The Charisma Machine: The Life, Death, and Legacy of One Laptop per Child* (Cambridge, MA: MIT Press, 2019); Selwyn (2016) as cited in Cranmer, *Disabled Children and Digital Technologies*.

16. Bennett et al., "Interdependence as a Frame," 161–173; Garcia, *Good Reception*; Cranmer, *Disabled Children and Digital Technologies*.

17. Cranmer, *Disabled Children and Digital Technologies*.

18. Warschauer, *Technology and Social Inclusion*; Cranmer, *Disabled Children and Digital Technologies*.

19. Sonia Livingstone and Tink Palmer, *Identifying Vulnerable Children Online and What Strategies Can Help Them* (London: UK Safer Internet Centre, 2012); Livingstone and Sefton-Green, *The Class*.

20. Alper, *Giving Voice*; Cranmer, *Disabled Children and Digital Technologies*.

21. Garcia, *Good Reception*.

22. Alper, *Giving Voice*; Garcia, *Good Reception*.

256   Notes to Chapter 9

23. Garcia, *Good Reception*; Livingstone and Sefton-Green, *The Class*.

24. Garcia, *Good Reception*; Cranmer, *Disabled Children and Digital Technologies*.

25. Livingstone and Sefton-Green, *The Class*; Garcia, *Good Reception*.

26. Alper, *Giving Voice*; Livingstone and Sefton-Green, *The Class*.

27. Alper, *Giving Voice*; Livingstone and Sefton-Green, *The Class*.

28. Vu et al., "Digital Storytelling for Academic Literacy."

29. Ames, *The Charisma Machine*; Warschauer, *Technology and Social Inclusion*.

30. Vu et al., "Digital Storytelling for Academic Literacy."

31. Cranmer, *Disabled Children and Digital Technologies*; Garcia, *Good Reception*.

32. Livingstone and Sefton-Green, *The Class*, 11.

33. Livingstone and Sefton-Green, *The Class*; Garcia, *Good Reception*.

34. Livingstone and Sefton-Green, *The Class*.

35. Garcia, *Good Reception*; Alper, *Giving Voice*.

36. Livingstone and Sefton-Green, *The Class*, 249–250.

37. Sonia Livingstone and Julian Sefton-Green, *The Class: Living and Learning in the Digital Age* (New York: New York University Press, 2016), 254.

Appendix A

1. Robert K. Yin, *Case Study Research: Design and Methods (Applied Social Research Methods)*, 5th ed. (Thousand Oaks, CA: SAGE, 2014); John W. Creswell and Cheryl N. Poth, *Qualitative Inquiry and Research Design (International Student Edition): Choosing Among Five Approaches*, 4th ed. (Thousand Oaks, CA: SAGE, 2018).

2. J. Amos Hatch, *Doing Qualitative Research in Education Settings* (Albany: State University of New York Press, 2002), https://muse.jhu.edu/book/4583/; Matthew B. Miles, Michael A. Huberman, and Johnny Saldaña, *Qualitative Data Analysis: A Methods Sourcebook* (Thousand Oaks, CA: SAGE, 2013); Hsiu-Fang Hsieh and Sarah E. Shannon, "Three Approaches to Qualitative Content Analysis," *Qualitative Health Research* 15, no. 9 (2005): 1277–1288. https://doi.org/10.1177%2F1049732305276687.

3. For a discussion of challenges relating to the implementation of digital technologies in schools, including one-to-one laptop programs and mobile media, see Mark Warschauer, *Laptops and Literacy: Learning in the Wireless Classroom* (New York: Teachers College Press, 2007); Garcia, *Good Reception*; Ames, *The Charisma Machine*.

4. Yin, *Case Study Research*; Creswell and Poth, *Qualitative Inquiry and Research Design*.

5. Maxwell, *Qualitative Research Design*.

Notes to Appendix B

6. Matthew T. Hora and Joseph J. Ferrare, *The Teaching Dimensions Observation Protocol (TDOP) 2.0* (Madison, WI: University of Wisconsin–Madison, Wisconsin Center for Education Research, 2014).

7. Maxwell, *Qualitative Research Design*.

8. Thomas R. Lindlof and Bryan C. Taylor, *Qualitative Communication Research Methods*, 2nd ed. (Thousand Oaks, CA: SAGE, 2017); Michael Q. Patton, "Two Decades of Developments in Qualitative Inquiry: A Personal, Experiential Perspective," *Qualitative Social Work* 1, no. 3 (2002): 261–283. https://doi.org/10.1177%2F1473325002001003636; Harsh Suri, "Purposeful Sampling in Qualitative Research Synthesis," *Qualitative Research Journal* 11, no. 2 (2011): 63–75, https://doi.org/10.3316/QRJ1102063.

9. For a discussion of remote learning at FVA during the COVID-19 pandemic, see Prado et al., "Virtual Inclusion" and "Organizing to Support Learning Pods across Diverse Family Contexts," symposium presentation at American Education Research Association, Orlando, FL, April 2021.

10. Hatch, *Doing Qualitative Research in Education Settings*.

11. Miles et al., *Qualitative Data Analysis*.

12. Hsieh and Shannon, "Three Approaches to Qualitative Content Analysis," 1277–1288.

13. Creswell and Poth, *Qualitative Inquiry and Research Design*.

14. Miles et al., *Qualitative Data Analysis*; Margarete Sandelowski, "Rigor or Rigor Mortis: The Problem of Rigor in Qualitative Research Revisited," *Advances in Nursing Science* 16, no. 2 (1993): 1–8. https://doi.org/10.1097/00012272-199312000-00002.

15. Robert P. Weber, *Basic Content Analysis* (Thousand Oaks, CA: SAGE, 1990).

16. Tony Long and Martin Johnson, "Rigor, Reliability and Validity in Qualitative Research," *Clinical Effectiveness in Nursing* 4 (2000): 30–37, https://doi.org/10.1054/cein.2000.0106.

17. Kristie Saumure and Lisa M. Given, "Data Saturation," in *The Sage Encyclopedia of Qualitative Research Methods*, ed. Lisa M. Given (Thousand Oaks, CA: SAGE, 2008), 195–196.

18. Ayelet Kuper, Lorelei Lingard, and Wendy Levinson, "Critically Appraising Qualitative Research," *BMJ* 337 (2008): 687–692, https://doi.org/10.1136/bmj.a1035.

Appendix B

1. The Center for AAC and Autism, accessed March 3, 2022, https://www.aacandautism.com/.

2. Pyramid Educational Consultants, accessed March 3, 2022, https://pecsusa.com/.

3. AssistiveWare, accessed March 3, 2022, https://www.assistiveware.com/.

4. "Endless Alphabet," Originator, accessed August 31, 2022, https://www.originatorkids.com/endless-alphabet/.

5. Epic!, accessed August 1, 2022, https://www.getepic.com/educator-resources.

6. Everyday Speech, accessed March 3, 2022, https://everydayspeech.com/.

7. Flip, accessed August 1, 2022, https://info.flip.com/.

8. Google for Education, accessed August 1, 2022, https://edu.google.com/workspace-for-education/classroom/.

9. IXL, accessed August 1, 2022, https://www.ixl.com/.

10. "What is Kahoot!?" Kahoot! accessed August 1, 2022, https://kahoot.com/what-is-kahoot/.

11. Lexia, accessed August 1, 2022, https://www.lexialearning.com/.

12. Prodigy, accessed August 1, 2022, https://www.prodigygame.com/main-en/.

13. ReadWorks, accessed August 1, 2022, https://www.readworks.org/.

14. Seesaw, accessed August 1, 2022, https://web.seesaw.me/lessons.

15. "Turn Young Students into Independent Readers with Smarty Ants," accessed August 1, 2022, https://www.achieve3000.com/products/smarty-ants/.

16. "Use FaceTime with Your iPhone, iPad, or iPod Touch," accessed August 1, 2022, https://support.apple.com/en-us/HT204380.

17. "Google Workspace User Guide to Accessibility," accessed August 1, 2022, https://support.google.com/a/answer/1631886?hl=en.

18. WeVideo, accessed August 2, 2022, https://www.wevideo.com/.

19. YouTube, accessed August 2, 2022, https://www.youtube.com/.

20. "Zoom Is for Everyone," accessed August 2, 2022, https://explore.zoom.us/en/accessibility/.

Bibliography

Abramson, Ashley. "Capturing the Benefits of Remote Learning." *American Psychological Association* 52, no. 6 (2021): 46. https://www.apa.org/monitor/2021/09/cover-remote-learning.

Adams, Marilyn Jager. *Beginning to Read: Thinking and Learning about Print.* Cambridge, MA: MIT Press, 1994.

Aladsani, Hibah K. "The Perceptions of Female Breadwinner Parents Regarding their Children's Distance Learning during the COVID-19 Pandemic." *Education and Information Technologies* 27, no. 4 (2022): 4817–4839. https://doi.org/10.1007/s10639-021-10812-9.

Algozzine, Bob, and James E. Ysseldyke. *The Fundamentals of Special Education: A Practical Guide for Every Teacher.* Thousand Oaks, CA: Corwin Press, 2006.

Almeida, Marcela, Mamatha Challa, Monique Ribeiro, Alexandra M. Harrison, and Marcia C. Castro. "Editorial Perspective: The Mental Health Impact of School Closures during the COVID-19 Pandemic." *Journal of Child Psychology and Psychiatry* 63, no. 5 (2022): 608–612. https://doi.org/10.1111/jcpp.13535.

Alper, Meryl. *Digital Youth with Disabilities.* Cambridge, MA: MIT Press, 2014.

Alper, Meryl. *Giving Voice: Mobile Communication, Disability, and Inequality.* Cambridge, MA: MIT Press, 2017.

Alquraini, Turki, and Dianne Gut. "Critical Components of Successful Inclusion of Students with Severe Disabilities: Literature Review." *International Journal of Special Education* 27, no. 1 (2012): 42–59.

Ames, Morgan G. *The Charisma Machine: The Life, Death, and Legacy of One Laptop per Child.* Cambridge, MA: MIT Press, 2019.

Anderman, Lynley H., and Eric M. Anderman. "Considering Contexts in Educational Psychology: Introduction to the Special Issue." *Educational Psychologist* 35, no. 2 (2000): 67–68. https://citeseerx.ist.psu.edu/viewdoc/download?doi=10.1.1.470.307&rep=rep1&type=pdf.

Anderson, Peggy L. *Case Studies for Inclusive Schools*. Austin, TX: Pro-Ed, 2012.

Anderson, Susan E., and Rebecca S. Putman. "Special Education Teachers' Experience, Confidence, Beliefs, and Knowledge about Integrating Technology." *Journal of Special Education Technology* 35, no. 1 (2020): 37–50.

Angrist, Joshua D., Parag A. Pathak, and Christopher R. Walters. "Explaining Charter School Effectiveness." *American Economic Journal: Applied Economics* 5, no. 4 (2013): 1–27.

Armstrong, Derrick, Ann C. Armstrong, and Ilektra Spandagou. "Inclusion: By Choice or By Chance?" *International Journal of Inclusive Education* 15, no. 1 (2011): 29–39. https://doi.org/10.1080/13603116.2010.496192.

Artiles, Alfredo J., Federico R. Waitoller, and Rebecca Neal. "Grappling with the Intersection of Language and Ability Differences: Equity Issues for Chicano/Latino Students in Special Education." In *Chicano School Failure and Success: Past, Present, and Future*, edited by Richard R. Valencia, 213–234. New York: Routledge, 2010.

Asaro-Saddler, Kristie. "Using Evidence-Based Practices to Teach Writing to Children with Autism Spectrum Disorders." *Preventing School Failure: Alternative Education for Children and Youth* 60, no. 1 (2016): 79–85.

Asaro-Saddler, Kristie. "Writing Instruction and Self-Regulation for Students with Autism Spectrum Disorders." *Topics in Language Disorders* 36, no. 3 (2016): 266–283.

Assistive Technology Act, US Code 29 (1998), §§ 3002 et seq.

AssistiveWare. Accessed March 3, 2022. https://www.assistiveware.com/.

Auerbach, Susan. "'If the Student Is Good, Let Him Fly': Moral Support for College Among Latino Immigrant Parents." *Journal of Latinos and Education* 5, no. 4 (2006): 275–292.

Averett, Kate H. "Remote Learning, COVID-19, and Children with Disabilities." *AERA Open* 7 (2021). https://doi.org/10.1177/23328584211058471.

Avramidis, Elias, and Brahm Norwich. "Teachers' Attitudes towards Integration/ Inclusion: A Review of the Literature." *European Journal of Special Needs Education* 17, no. 2 (2002): 129–147.

Baines, AnnMarie D. *(Un)Learning Disability: Recognizing and Changing Restrictive Views of Student Ability*. New York: Teachers College Press, 2014.

Banotai, A. "Classroom Collaboration Offers Benefits to Students, Teachers and Clinicians." *Advance Online Edition for Speech–Language Pathologists and Audiologists* 16, no. 33 (2006): 6.

Barker, Theodore A., and Joseph K. Torgesen. "An Evaluation of Computer-Assisted Instruction in Phonological Awareness with Below Average Readers." *Journal of Educational Computing Research* 13, no. 1 (1995): 89–103.

Bibliography

Bauer, Kellie L., Suneeti Nathani Iyer, Richard T. Boon, and Cecil Fore. "20 Ways for Classroom Teachers to Collaborate with Speech–Language Pathologists." *Intervention in School and Clinic* 45, no. 5 (2010): 333–337.

Bedore, Lisa M., and Elizabeth D. Peña. "Assessment of Bilingual Children for Identification of Language Impairment: Current Findings and Implications for Practice." *International Journal of Bilingual Education and Bilingualism* 11, no. 1 (2008): 1–29.

Beltrán, Elina V., Chris Abbott, and Jane Jones, eds. *Inclusive Language Education and Digital Technology*, Vol. 30. Bristol: Multilingual Matters, 2013.

Bennett, Cynthia L., Erin Brady, and Stacy M. Branham. "Interdependence as a Frame for Assistive Technology Research and Design." In *Proceedings of the 20th International ACM SIGACCESS Conference on Computers and Accessibility*. New York: ACM, 2018, 161–173. https://doi.org/10.1145/3234695.3236348.

Bickenbach, Jerome E., Somnath Chatterji, Elizabeth M. Badley, and Tevfik B. Üstün. "Models of Disablement, Universalism and the International Classification of Impairments, Disabilities and Handicaps." *Social Science and Medicine* 48, no. 9 (1999): 1173–1187. https://doi.org/10.1016/S0277-9536(98)00441-9.

Biklen, Douglas. *Achieving the Complete School: Strategies for Effective Mainstreaming.* New York: Teachers College Press, 1985.

Biklen, Douglas. *Autism and the Myth of the Person Alone.* New York: New York University Press, 2005.

Biklen, Douglas, and Jamie Burke. "Presuming Competence." In *Beginning with Disability: A Primer*, edited by Lennard J. Davis, 269–288. New York: Routledge, 2018.

Black-Hawkins, Kristine. "Understanding Inclusive Pedagogy." In *Inclusive Education: Making Sense of Everyday Practice*, edited by Vicky Plows and Ben Whitburn, 13–28. Rotterdam: Brill Sense, 2017.

Blamires, Mike, ed. *Enabling Technology for Inclusion.* Thousand Oaks, CA: SAGE, 1999.

Blum, Grace, Megan Wilson, and Yelena Patish. "Moving Toward a More Socially Just Classroom through Teacher Preparation for Inclusion." *Catalyst: A Social Justice Forum* 5, no. 1 (2015): article 4.

Blume, Howard, and Laura Newberry. "California Teacher Unions Fight Calls to Reopen Schools." *Los Angeles Times*, October 16, 2020. https://www.latimes.com/california/story/2020-10-16/state-teacher-unions-push-back-against-calls-to-reopen-k-12-campuses-parents-divided.

Boone, Randall, and Kyle Higgins. "The Role of Instructional Design in Assistive Technology Research and Development." *Reading Research Quarterly* 42, no. 1 (2007): 135–140.

Boroson, Barbara. "Inclusive Education: Lessons from History." *Educational Leadership* 74, no. 7 (2017): 18–23.

Bowman, Emma. "Scanning Students' Rooms during Remote Tests Is Unconstitutional, Judge Rules." *National Public Radio*, August 26, 2022. https://www.npr.org/2022/08/25/1119337956/test-proctoring-room-scans-unconstitutional-cleveland-state-university.

Branham, Stacy M., and Shaun K. Kane. "Collaborative Accessibility: How Blind and Sighted Companions Co-Create Accessible Home Spaces." In *Proceedings of the 33rd Annual ACM Conference on Human Factors in Computing Systems*, 2373–2382. New York: ACM. https://doi.org/10.1145/2702123.2702511.

Broer, Stephen M., Mary B. Doyle, and Michael F. Giangreco. "Perspectives of Students with Intellectual Disabilities about their Experiences with Paraprofessional Support." *Exceptional Children* 71, no. 4 (2005): 415.

Broomhead, Karen E. "Acceptance or Rejection? The Social Experiences of Children with Special Educational Needs and Disabilities within a Mainstream Primary School." *Education 3–13* 47, no. 8 (2019): 877–888.

Bunch, Gary, and Kevin Finnegan. "Values Teachers Find in Inclusive Education." In *Proceedings of the 5th International Special Education Conference*. Manchester, UK: University of Manchester, 2000.

Burgstahler, Sheryl. "The Role of Technology in Preparing Youth with Disabilities for Postsecondary Education and Employment." *Journal of Special Education Technology* 18, no. 4 (2003): 7–19.

Burnett, Cathy. "Technology and Literacy in Early Childhood Educational Settings: A Review of Research." *Journal of Early Childhood Literacy* 10, no. 3 (2010): 247–270.

Burns, M. Susan, Peg Griffin, and Catherine E. Snow. *Starting Out Right: A Guide to Promoting Children's Reading Success. Specific Recommendations from America's Leading Researchers on How to Help Children Become Successful Readers*. Washington, DC: National Academy Press, 1999.

Byrnes, James P., and Barbara A. Wasik. *Language and Literacy Development: What Educators Need to Know*. New York: Guilford Press, 2019.

Calarco, Jessica M., Emily V. Meanwell, Elizabeth Anderson, and Amelia Knopf. "'My Husband Thinks I'm Crazy': Covid-19-Related Conflict in Couples with Young Children." *SocArXiv* (2020). https://doi.org/10.31235/osf.io/cpkj6.

Campbell, Michael. "An Application of the Theory of Planned Behavior to Examine the Impact of Classroom Inclusion on Elementary School Students." *Journal of Evidence-Based Social Work* 7, no. 3 (2010): 235–250.

Cardona Moltó, María Cristina. "Teacher Education Students' Belief of Inclusion and Perceived Competence to Teach Students with Disabilities in Spain." *International Journal of Special Education* 10 (2009): 33–41.

Bibliography

Carnegie Corporation of New York. *The Opportunity Equation: Transforming Mathematics and Science Education for Citizenship and Global Economy.* Princeton, NJ: Institute for Advanced Study, 2009.

Castelli, Frank R., and Mark A. Sarvary. "Why Students Do Not Turn On Their Video Cameras during Online Classes and an Equitable and Inclusive Plan to Encourage Them to Do So." *Ecology and Evolution* 11, no. 8 (2021): 3565–3576. https://doi.org /10.1002/ece3.7123.

Causton-Theoharis, Julie, and George Theoharis. "Creating Inclusive Schools for All Students." *School Administrator* 65, no. 8 (2008): 24–25. https://www.aasa.org /SchoolAdministratorArticle.aspx?id=4936.

The Center for AAC and Autism. Accessed March 3, 2022. https://www.aacandautism .com/.

Center for Applied Special Technology. Accessed September 8, 2022. https://www .cast.org/.

Chamberlain, Brandt, Connie Kasari, and Erin Rotheram-Fuller. "Involvement or Isolation? The Social Networks of Children with Autism in Regular Classrooms." *Journal of Autism and Developmental Disorders* 37, no. 2 (2007): 230–242.

Chaparro, Sofía. "School, Parents, and Communities: Leading Parallel Lives in a Two-Way Immersion Program." *International Multilingual Research Journal* 14, no. 1 (2020): 41–57.

Chatterjee, Dom. "Independence Is an Ableist Myth: Unlocking the Power of Community in Healing." *The Body Is Not an Apology*, July 4, 2018. https:// thebodyisnotanapology.com/magazine/independence-is-an-ableist-myth-unlocking -the-power-of-community-in-healing/.

Chen, Weiqin. "Multitouch Tabletop Technology for People with Autism Spectrum Disorder." *Procedia Computer Science* 14 (2012): 198–207. https://doi.org/10.1016/j .procs.2012.10.023.

Cheng, Albert, Collin Hitt, Brian Kisida, and Jonathan N. Mills. "'No Excuses' Charter Schools: A Meta-Analysis of the Experimental Evidence on Student Achievement." *Journal of School Choice* 11, no. 2 (2017): 209–238.

Chun, Dorothy, Richard Kern, and Bryan Smith. "Technology in Language Use, Language Teaching, and Language Learning." *The Modern Language Journal* 100, no. S1 (2016): 64–80.

Cioè-Peña, Maria. "Disability, Bilingualism and What It Means to Be Normal." *Journal of Bilingual Education Research and Instruction* 19, no. 1 (2017): 138–160.

Closing the Gap. Accessed April 21, 2023. https://www.closingthegap.com/con ference/.

Coben, Sharon S., and Naomi Zigmond. "The Social Integration of Learning Disabled Students from Self-Contained to Mainstream Elementary School Settings." *Journal of Learning Disabilities* 19, no. 10 (1986): 614–618.

Coiro, Julie, Michele Knobel, Colin Lankshear, and Donald J. Leu. "Central Issues in New Literacies and New Literacies Research." *Handbook of Research on New Literacies*, edited by Julie Coiro, Michele Knobel, Clin Lankshear, and Donald J. Leu, 1–21. New York: Routledge, 2008.

Cole, Michael. *Cultural Psychology: A Once and Future Discipline*. Cambridge, MA: Harvard University Press, 1998.

Cologon, Kathy. "Debunking Myths: Reading Development in Children with Down Syndrome." *Australian Journal of Teacher Education* 38, no. 3 (2013): 9.

Condeluci, Al. "Interdependence: A Model for Community-Based Health Information Management Systems." *Topics in Health Information Management* 19, no. 3 (1999): 40–46.

Connelly, Vince, and Julie Dockrell. "Writing Development and Instruction for Students with Learning Disabilities: Using Diagnostic Categories to Study Writing Difficulties." In *Handbook of Writing Research*, edited by Charles A. MacArthur, Steve Graham, and Jill Fitzgerald, 349–363. New York: Guilford Press, 2016.

Cooper, Brittney. "Intersectionality." In *Oxford Handbook of Feminist Theory*, edited by Lisa Disch and Mary Hawkesworth, 385–406. Oxford: Oxford Academic, 2016. https://doi.org/10.1093/oxfordhb/9780199328581.013.20.

Cooper, Catherine R. "Cultural Brokers: How Immigrant Youth in Multicultural Societies Navigate and Negotiate their Pathways to College Identities." *Learning, Culture and Social Interaction* 3, no. 2 (2014): 170–176.

"COVID-19 Vaccines." US Department of Health and Human Services. Accessed August 31, 2022. https://www.hhs.gov/coronavirus/covid-19-vaccines/index.html.

Coyne, Peggy, Bart Pisha, Bridget Dalton, Lucille A. Zeph, and Nancy C. Smith. "Literacy by Design: A Universal Design for Learning Approach for Students with Significant Intellectual Disabilities." *Remedial and Special Education* 33, no. 3 (2012): 162–172. https://doi.org/10.1177/0741932510381651.

Crane, Eric, Brian Edwards, and Noli Brazil. *California's Charter Schools: Measuring their Performance*. Mountain View, CA: EdSource, 2007. https://www.wested.org/resources/californias-charter-schools-measuring-their-performance/#.

Cranmer, Sue. *Disabled Children and Digital Technologies: Learning in the Context of Inclusive Education*. London: Bloomsbury Academic, 2020.

Crenshaw, Kimberle. "Demarginalizing the Intersection of Race and Sex: A Black Feminist Critique of Antidiscrimination Doctrine, Feminist Theory and Antiracist

Bibliography

Politics." *University of Chicago Forum* 1989, no. 1 (1989): 138–167. https://philpapers .org/archive/CREDTI.pdf?ncid=txtlnkusaolp00000603.

Creswell, John W., and Cheryl N. Poth. *Qualitative Inquiry and Research Design (International Student Edition): Choosing Among Five Approaches.* 4th ed. Thousand Oaks, CA: SAGE, 2018.

Cullen, Jennifer, Stephen B. Richards, and Catherine Lawless Frank. "Using Software to Enhance the Writing Skills of Students with Special Needs." *Journal of Special Education Technology* 23, no. 2 (2008): 33–44.

Daniel, Larry G., and Debra A. King. "Impact of Inclusion Education on Academic Achievement, Student Behavior and Self-Esteem, and Parental Attitudes." *The Journal of Educational Research* 91, no. 2 (1997): 67–80.

Daniels-Mayes, Sheelagh, Gary Fry, and Karen Sinclair. "Is Inclusive Education Enough for Australian Aboriginal Students? Making the Case for Belonging Education to Disrupt the Normalised Agenda of Assimilation." In *Global Directions in Inclusive Education*, edited by Matthew J. Schuelka and Suzanne Carrington, 99–115. London: Routledge, 2021.

Darling-Hammond, Linda, and Maria E. Hyler. "Preparing Educators for the Time of COVID . . . and Beyond." *European Journal of Teacher Education* 43, no. 4 (2020): 457–465. https://doi.org/10.1080/02619768.2020.1816961.

Davila, Anabella, and A. M. Hartman. "Tradition and Modern Aspects of Mexican Corporate Culture." In *Mexican Business Culture: Essays on Tradition, Ethics, Entrepreneurship and Commerce and the State*, edited by Carlos M. Coria-Sánchez and John T. Hyatt, 26–37. Jefferson, NC: McFarland, 2016.

Davis, Lennard J. *The Disability Studies Reader.* Abingdon, UK: Routledge, 1997.

Davis, Lennard J. *The Disability Studies Reader.* 2nd ed. Abingdon, UK: Routledge, 2006.

DeJong, Gerben M. "Independent Living: From Social Movement to Analytic Paradigm." *Archives of Physical Medical Rehabilitation* 60 (1979): 435–446. http://citeseerx .ist.psu.edu/viewdoc/download?doi=10.1.1.879.20&rep=rep1&type=pdf.

DeLana, Melissa, Anne Mary Gentry, and Jean Andrews. "The Efficacy of ASL/ English Bilingual Education: Considering Public Schools." *American Annals of the Deaf* 152, no. 1 (2007): 73–87.

Delpit, Lisa. *Other People's Children: Cultural Conflict in the Classroom.* New York: New Press, 2006.

Dudley-Marling, Curt, and Mary B. Burns. "Two Perspectives on Inclusion in the United States." *Global Education Review* 1, no. 1 (2014): 14–31. https://files.eric.ed .gov/fulltext/EJ1055208.pdf.

Edyburn, Dave L. "2003 in Review: A Synthesis of the Special Education Technology Literature." *Journal of Special Education Technology* 19, no. 4 (2004): 57–80. https://doi.org/10.1177/016264340401900407.

Edyburn, Dave L. "Critical Issues in Advancing the Special Education Technology Evidence Base." *Exceptional Children* 80, no. 1 (2013): 7–24. https://doi.org/10.1177/001440291308000107.

Egilson, Snaefridur T., and Rannveig Traustadottir. "Assistance to Pupils with Physical Disabilities in Regular Schools: Promoting Inclusion or Creating Dependency?" *European Journal of Special Needs Education* 24 (2009): 21–36.

Englert, Carol S., Yong Zhao, Kailonnie Dunsmore, Natalia Yevgenyevna Collings, and Kimberly Wolbers. "Scaffolding the Writing of Students with Disabilities through Procedural Facilitation: Using an Internet-Based Technology to Improve Performance." *Learning Disability Quarterly* 30, no. 1 (2007): 9–29.

Epic! Accessed August 1, 2022. https://www.getepic.com/educator-resources.

Everyday Speech. Accessed March 3, 2022. https://everydayspeech.com/.

Fasting, Rolf B. and Solveig-Alma Halaas Lyster. "The Effects of Computer Technology in Assisting the Development of Literacy in Young Struggling Readers and Spellers." *European Journal of Special Needs Education* 20, no. 1 (2005): 21–40.

Ferri, Beth A. "Undermining Inclusion? A Critical Reading of Response to Intervention (RTI)." *International Journal of Inclusive Education* 16, no. 8 (2012): 863–880.

Fisher, Pamela, and Dan Goodley. "The Linear Medical Model of Disability: Mothers of Disabled Babies Resist with Counter-Narratives." *Sociology of Health and Illness* 29 (2007): 66–81. https://doi.org/10.1111/j.1467-9566.2007.00518.x.

Fitch, Frank. "Inclusion, Exclusion, and Ideology: Special Education Students' Changing Sense of Self." *The Urban Review* 35, no. 3 (2003): 233–252.

Flewitt, Rosie, David Messer, and Natalia Kucirkova. "New Directions for Early Literacy in a Digital Age: The iPad." *Journal of Early Childhood Literacy* 15, no. 3 (2015): 289–310.

Flip. Accessed August 1, 2022. https://info.flip.com/.

Fox, Norman E., and James E. Ysseldyke. "Implementing Inclusion at the Middle School Level: Lessons from a Negative Example." *Exceptional Children* 64 (1997): 81–98.

Frankenberg, Erica. "NEPC Review: *Segregation, Race, and Charter Schools: What Do We Know?*" Boulder, CO: National Education Policy Center, 2016.

Freeman, Stephanny F. N., and Marvin C. Alkin. "Academic and Social Attainments of Children with Mental Retardation in General Education and Special Education Settings." *Remedial and Special Education* 21, no. 1 (2000): 3–18.

Bibliography

Frieden, Lex. "Independent Living Models." *Rehabilitation Literature* 41, no. 7–8 (1980): 169–173.

Friend, Marilyn, Lynne Cook, DeAnna Hurley-Chamberlain, and Cynthia Shamberger. "Co-Teaching: An Illustration of the Complexity of Collaboration in Special Education." *Journal of Educational and Psychological Consultation* 20, no. 1 (2010): 9–27.

Garcia, Antero. *Good Reception: Teens, Teachers, and Mobile Media in a Los Angeles High School*. Cambridge, MA: MIT Press, 2017.

García, Ofelia, and Li Wei. "Language, Bilingualism and Education." In *Translanguaging: Language, Bilingualism and Education*, 46–62. New York: Palgrave MacMillan, 2014.

Garcia, Shernaz B., and Alba A. Ortiz. "Intersectionality as a Framework for Transformative Research in Special Education." *Multiple Voices for Ethnically Diverse Exceptional Students* 13, no. 2 (2013): 32–47.

Garrison, Donn R., and Terry Anderson. *E-Learning in the 21st Century: A Framework for Research and Practice*. London: Routledge, 2003.

Gee, James P. "The New Literacy Studies: From 'Socially Situated' to the Work of the Social." In *Situated Literacies: Theorising Reading and Writing in Context*, edited by David Barton, Mary Hamilton, and Roz Ivanic, 180–196. Abingdon, UK: Routledge, 2000.

Gee, James Paul. *Social Linguistics and Literacies: Ideology in Discourses*. 2nd ed. Bristol, PA: Falmer Press, 1996.

Gee, James Paul. "New People in New Worlds: Networks, the New Capitalism and Schools." In *Multiliteracies: Literacy Learning and the Design of Social Futures*, edited by Bill Cope and Mary Kalantzis, 43–68. London: Routledge, 2000.

Gergen, Kenneth J. "Social Understanding and the Inscription of Self." In *Cultural Psychology: Essays on Comparative Human Development*, edited by James W. Stigler, Richard A. Schweder, and Gilbert Herdt, 569–606. Cambridge, UK: Cambridge University Press, 1990.

Ghosh, Sumita C. *Technology for Inclusion: Special Education, Rehabilitation, for All*. Ronkonkoma, NY: Linus Learning, 2017.

Gillborn, David. "Intersectionality, Critical Race Theory, and the Primacy of Racism: Race, Class, Gender, and Disability in Education." *Qualitative Inquiry* 21, no. 3 (2015): 277–287. https://doi.org/10.1177%2F1077800414557827.

Gillespie, Amy, and Steve Graham. "A Meta-Analysis of Writing Interventions for Students with Learning Disabilities." *Exceptional Children* 80, no. 4 (2014): 454–473.

Goethals, Tina, Elisabeth De Schauwer, and Geert Van Hove. "Weaving Intersectionality into Disability Studies Research: Inclusion, Reflexivity and Anti-Essentialism."

DiGeSt. Journal of Diversity and Gender Studies 2, no. 1–2 (2015): 113–135. https://core.ac.uk/download/pdf/74560235.pdf.

Goldstein, Dana. "Coronavirus is Shutting Schools. Is America Ready for Virtual Learning?" *The New York Times*, March 13, 2020. https://oercommons.s3.amazonaws.com/media/editor/260648/Coronavirus_Is_Shutting_Schools._Is_America_Ready_for_Virtual_Learning__-_The_New_York_Times.pdf.

Goodenow, Carol. "School Motivation, Engagement, and Sense of Belonging among Urban Adolescent Students." Paper published in Education Resources Information Center (ERIC), Washington D.C., 1992. https://eric.ed.gov/?id=ED349364

Goodman, Hollace, Jay Gottlieb, and Robert H. Harrison. "Social Acceptance of EMRS Integrated into a Non-Graded Elementary School." *American Journal of Mental Deficiency* 76, no. 4 (1972): 412–417.

Google for Education. Accessed August 1, 2022. https://edu.google.com/workspace-for-education/classroom/.

Google Workspace Admin Help. "Google Workspace User Guide to Accessibility." Accessed August 1, 2022. https://support.google.com/a/answer/1631886?hl=en.

Graham, Steve, and Karen R. Harris. "Writing Instruction." In *Learning About Learning Disabilities*, 3rd ed., edited by B. Wong, 281–313. San Diego, CA: Elsevier Science, 2004.

Graham, Steve, and Karen R. Harris. "Improving the Writing Performance of Young Struggling Writers: Theoretical and Programmatic Research from the Center on Accelerating Student Learning." *The Journal of Special Education* 39, no. 1 (2005): 19–33.

Graham, Steve, Karen R. Harris, and Lynn Larsen. "Prevention and Intervention of Writing Difficulties for Students with Learning Disabilities." *Learning Disabilities Research and Practice* 16, no. 2 (2001): 74–84.

Green, Eva G., Jean-Claude Deschamps, and Dario Paez. "Variation of Individualism and Collectivism within and between 20 Countries: A Typological Analysis." *Journal of Cross-Cultural Psychology* 36, no. 3 (2005): 321–339. https://doi.org/10.1177%2F0022022104273654.

Green, Laura, Paula Chance, and Melissa Stockholm. "Implementation and Perceptions of Classroom-Based Service Delivery: A Survey of Public School Clinicians." *Language, Speech, and Hearing Services in Schools* 50, no. 4 (2019): 656–672.

Grooms, Ain A., and Joshua Childs. "'We Need to Do Better by Kids': Changing Routines in US Schools in Response to COVID-19 School Closures." *Journal of Education for Students Placed at Risk (JESPAR)* 26, no. 2 (2021): 135–156. https://doi.org/10.1080/10824669.2021.1906251.

Bibliography

Gupta, Sanjay. "Dr. Sanjay Gupta: Why I Am Not Sending My Kids Back to School." *CNN Health*, August 12, 2020. https://www.cnn.com/2020/08/12/health/covid-kids-school-gupta-essay/index.html.

Hall, Jean P. "Narrowing the Breach: Can Disability Culture and Full Educational Inclusion Be Reconciled?" *Journal of Disability Policy Studies* 13, no. 3 (2002): 144–152.

Hall, Kathy, Janet Collins, Shereen Benjamin, Melanie Nind, and Kieron Sheehy. "SATurated Models of Pupildom: Assessment and Inclusion/Exclusion." *British Educational Research Journal* 30, no. 6 (2004): 801–817. https://doi.org/10.1080/0141192042000279512.

Hamilton, Laura, and Betheny Gross. "How Has the Pandemic Affected Students' Social-Emotional Well-Being? A Review of the Evidence to Date." https://eric.ed.gov/?id=ED614131.

Hamilton-Jones, Bethany M., and Cynthia O. Vail. "Preparing Special Educators for Collaboration in the Classroom: Pre-Service Teachers' Beliefs and Perspectives." *International Journal of Special Education* 29, no. 1 (2014): 76–86.

Hankivsky, Olena. "Intersectionality 101." PhD diss., Institute for Intersectionality Research and Policy, Simon Fraser University, 2014. https://www.researchgate.net/profile/Olena_Hankivsky/publication/279293665_Intersectionality_101/links/56c35bda08ae602342508c7f/Intersectionality-101.pdf.

Harding, Somer. "Successful Inclusion Models for Students with Disabilities Require Strong Site Leadership: Autism and Behavioral Disorders Create Many Challenges for the Learning Environment." *International Journal of Learning* 16, no. 3 (2009): 91–104.

Harris, Karen R., and Steve Graham. "Self-Regulated Strategy Development in Writing: Premises, Evolution, and the Future." *British Journal of Educational Psychology* 6 (2009): 113–135.

Harris, Karen R., Steve Graham, Amber B. Chambers, and Julia D. Houston. "Turning Broccoli into Ice Cream Sundaes." In *Write Now! Empowering Writers in Today's K–6 Classroom*, edited by Kathy Ganske, 87–108. Newark, DE: International Reading Association, 2014.

Hatch, J. Amos. *Doing Qualitative Research in Education Settings*. Albany: State University of New York Press, 2002. https://muse.jhu.edu/book/4583/.

Helliwell, John. "Social Capital, the Economy and Well-Being." In *The Review of Economic Performance and Social Progress 2001: The Longest Decade: Canada in the 1990s*, 43–60. Ottawa: Centre for the Study of Living Standards, 2001.

Herold, Benjamin. "Technology in Education: An Overview." *Education Week* 20, no. 7 (2016): 129–141.

Higashida, Naoki. *The Reason I Jump: The Inner Voice of a Thirteen-Year-Old Boy with Autism.* Toronto, CA: Knopf Canada, 2013.

Hitchcock, Chuck, and Skip Stahl. "Assistive Technology, Universal Design, Universal Design for Learning: Improved Learning Opportunities." *Journal of Special Education Technology* 18, no. 4 (2003): 45–52.

Hobbs, Renee, and Amy Jensen. "The Past, Present, and Future of Media Literacy Education." *Journal of Media Literacy Education* 1, no. 1 (2009): 1–11.

Hopkins, Janet. "Assistive Technology: 10 Things to Know." *Library Media Connection* 25, no. 1 (2006): 12–14.

Hora, Matthew T., and Joseph J. Ferrare, *The Teaching Dimensions Observation Protocol (TDOP) 2.0.* Madison, WI: University of Wisconsin–Madison, Wisconsin Center for Education Research, 2014.

Horne, Phyllis E., and Vianne Timmons. "Making It Work: Teachers' Perspectives on Inclusion." *International Journal of Inclusive Education* 13, no. 3 (2009): 273–286.

Hsieh, Hsiu-Fang, and Sarah E. Shannon. "Three Approaches to Qualitative Content Analysis." *Qualitative Health Research* 15, no. 9 (2005): 1277–1288. https://doi.org/10.1177%2F1049732305276687.

Idol, Lorna. "Key Questions Related to Building Collaborative and Inclusive Schools." *Journal of Learning Disabilities* 30, no. 4 (1997): 384–394.

Individuals With Disabilities Act, US Code 20 (2004), §§ 1401 et seq.

IXL. Accessed August 1, 2022. https://www.ixl.com/.

Jacob, Sharin R., and Mark Warschauer. "Computational Thinking and Literacy." *Journal of Computer Science Integration* 1, no. 1 (2018).

Jacobsen, Michele, Pat Clifford, and Sharon Friesen. "Preparing Teachers for Technology Integration: Creating a Culture of Inquiry in the Context of Use." *Contemporary Issues in Technology and Teacher Education* 2, no. 3 (2002): 363–388.

Januszewski, Al, and Michael Molenda, eds. *Educational Technology: A Definition with Commentary.* New York: Routledge, 2013.

Jessel, John, Charmian Kenner, Eve Gregory, Mahera Ruby, and Tahera Arju. "Different Spaces: Learning and Literacy with Children and their Grandparents in East London Homes." *Linguistics and Education* 22 (2011): 37–50.

John-Steiner, Vera, and Holbrook Mahn. "Sociocultural Approaches to Learning and Development: A Vygotskian Framework." *Educational Psychologist* 31, no. 3–4 (1996), 191–206. https://doi.org/10.1080/00461520.1996.9653266.

Jorgensen, Cheryl M., Michael McSheehan, and Rae M. Sonnenmeier. "Presumed Competence Reflected in the Educational Programs of Students with IDD before and after the Beyond Access Professional Development Intervention." *Journal of Intellectual and Developmental Disability* 32, no. 4 (2007): 248–262.

Kalenga, Rosemary Chimbala, and Elsa Fourie. "Trekking Back to Mainstream for Inclusive Education, Is It There?" *Educational Studies* 38, no. 2 (2012): 175–187.

Kangas, Sara E. N. "When Special Education Trumps ESL: An Investigation of Service Delivery for ELLs with Disabilities." *Critical Inquiry in Language Studies* 11, no. 4 (2014): 273–306.

Kangas, Sara E. N. "Why Working Apart Doesn't Work At All: Special Education and English Student Teacher Collaborations." *Intervention in School and Clinic* 54, no. 1 (2018): 31–39.

Kauffman, James M., Daniel P. Hallahan, Paige C. Pullen, and Jeanmarie Badar. *Special Education: What It Is and Why We Need It*. New York: Routledge, 2018.

Kemp, Coral, and Mark Carter. "The Social Skills and Social Status of Mainstreamed Students with Intellectual Disabilities." *Educational Psychology* 22, no. 4 (2002): 391–411.

Kennedy, Michael J., and Donald D. Deshler. "Literacy Instruction, Technology, and Students with Learning Disabilities: Research We Have, Research We Need." *Learning Disability Quarterly* 33, no. 4 (2010): 289–298. https://doi.org/10.1177/073194871003300406.

Klingner, Janette K., and Sharon Vaughn. "Students' Perceptions of Instruction in Inclusion Classrooms: Implications for Students with Learning Disabilities." *Exceptional Children* 66, no. 1 (1999): 23–37.

Koh, Yoree. "Can You Form a School Pod without Fueling Inequality? These Groups Are Trying." *Wall Street Journal*, August 4, 2020. https://www.wsj.com/articles/can-you-form-a-school-pod-without-fueling-inequality-these-groups-are-trying-11596542410.

Kohli, Sonali. "Children with Disabilities Are Regressing. How Much Is Distance Learning to Blame?" *Los Angeles Times*, August 7, 2020. https://www.latimes.com/california/story/2020-08-07/covid-19-distance-learning-weakens-special-education.

Kollia, Betty, and Christopher Mulrine. "Collaborative Practice Patterns for Included Students among Elementary Educators and Speech and Language Pathologists." *Journal of Education and Human Development* 3, no. 4 (2014): 33–44.

Korhonen, Vesa. "Dialogic Literacy: A Sociocultural Literacy Learning Approach." In *Practicing Information Literacy: Bringing Theories of Learning, Practice and Information Literacy Together*, edited by Annemaree Lloyd and Sanna Talja, 211–226. Witney, UK: Chandos, 2010.

Koster, Marloes, Han Nakken, Sip Jan Pijl, and Els Van Houten. "Being Part of the Peer Group: A Literature Study Focusing on the Social Dimension of Inclusion in Education." *International Journal of Inclusive Education* 13, no. 2 (2009): 117–140.

Koster, Marloes, Sip Jan Pijl, Els van Houten, and Han Nakken. "The Social Position and Development of Pupils with SEN in Mainstream Dutch Primary Schools." *European Journal of Special Needs Education* 22, no. 1 (2007): 31–46.

Kress, Gunther, and Theo Van Leeuwen. *Multimodal Discourse: The Modes and Media of Contemporary Communication.* London: Arnold, 2001.

Krishnan, Jenell, Soobin Yim, Alissa Wolters, and Andrew Cusimano. "Supporting Online Synchronous Collaborative Writing in the Secondary Classroom." *Journal of Adolescent and Adult Literacy* 63, no. 2 (2019): 135–145.

Kuhne, Michael, and Judith Wiener. "Stability of Social Status of Children with and without Learning Disabilities." *Learning Disability Quarterly* 23 (2000): 64–75.

Kuper, Ayelet, Lorelei Lingard, and Wendy Levinson. "Critically Appraising Qualitative Research." *BMJ* 337 (2008): 687–692. https://doi.org/10.1136/bmj.a1035.

Ladau, Emily. *Demystifying Disability: What To Know, What To Say, and How To Be an Ally.* Berkeley, CA: Ten Speed Press, 2021.

Lanear, John, and Elise Frattura. "Getting the Stories Straight: Allowing Different Voices to Tell an 'Effective History' of Special Education Law in the United States." *Education and the Law* 19, no. 2 (2007): 87–109.

Lankshear, Colin, and Michele Knobel. *New Literacies.* London: McGraw-Hill Education, 2011.

Lave, Jean, and Etienne Wenger. *Situated Learning: Legitimate Peripheral Participation* Cambridge University Press, 1991.

Leu, Donald J., Charles K. Kinzer, Julie Coiro, Jill Castek, and Laurie A. Henry. "New Literacies: A Dual-Level Theory of the Changing Nature of Literacy, Instruction, and Assessment." *Journal of Education* 197, no. 2 (2017): 1–18. https://doi.org/10.1177%2F002205741719700202.

Levinson, Amber M., and Brigid Barron. "Latino Immigrant Families Learning with Digital Media Across Settings and Generations." *Digital Education Review* 33 (2018): 150–169.

Lexia. Accessed August 1, 2022. https://www.lexialearning.com/.

Lima, Clarisse O., and Scott W. Brown. "Global Citizenship and New Literacies Providing New Ways for Social Inclusion." *Psicologia Escolar e Educacional* 11 (2007): 13–20. https://doi.org/10.1590/S1413-85572007000100002.

Lindlof, Thomas R., and Bryan C. Taylor. *Qualitative Communication Research Methods.* 2nd ed. Thousand Oaks, CA: SAGE, 2017.

Liu-Gitz, Lan, and Devender R. Banda. "A Replication of the RIRD Strategy to Decrease Vocal Stereotypy in a Student with Autism." *Behavioral Interventions: Theory*

Bibliography

and Practice in Residential and Community-Based Clinical Programs 25, no. 1 (2010): 77–87.

Livingstone, Sonia, and Julian Sefton-Green. *The Class: Living and Learning in the Digital Age*. New York: New York University Press, 2016.

Livingstone, Sonia, and Tink Palmer. *Identifying Vulnerable Children Online and What Strategies Can Help Them*. London: UK Safer Internet Centre, 2012.

Long, Tony, and Martin Johnson. "Rigor, Reliability and Validity in Qualitative Research." *Clinical Effectiveness in Nursing* 4 (2000): 30–37. https://doi.org/10.1054/cein.2000.0106.

MacArthur, Charles A., Ralph P. Ferretti, Cynthia M. Okolo, and Albert R. Cavalier. "Technology Applications for Students with Literacy Problems: A Critical Review." *The Elementary School Journal* 101, no. 3 (2001): 273–301.

MacArthur, Charles A., Steve Graham, Jacqueline B. Haynes, and Susan DeLaPaz. "Spelling Checkers and Students with Learning Disabilities: Performance Comparisons and Impact on Spelling." *The Journal of Special Education* 30 (1996): 35–57.

Manetti, Mara, Barry H. Schneider, and Gary Siperstein. "Social Acceptance of Children with Mental Retardation: Testing the Contact Hypothesis with an Italian Sample." *International Journal of Behavioral Development* 25, no. 3 (2001): 279–286.

Mankoff, Jennifer, Gillian R. Hayes, and Devva Kasnitz. "Disability Studies as a Source of Critical Inquiry for the Field of Assistive Technology." In *ASSETS '10: Proceedings of the 12th International ACM SIGACCESS Conference on Computers and Accessibility*. 3–10. New York: ACM, 2010. https://doi.org/10.1145/1878803.1878807.

Margalit, Malka, and Meira Efrati. "Loneliness, Coherence and Companionship among Children with Learning Disorders." *Educational Psychology* 16 (1996): 69–79.

Marin, Elena. "Are Today's General Education Teachers Prepared to Face Inclusion in the Classroom?" *Procedia Social and Behavioral Sciences* 142 (2014): 702–707.

Marino, Matthew T. "Defining a Technology Research Agenda for Elementary and Secondary Students with Learning and Other High-Incidence Disabilities in Inclusive Science Classrooms." *Journal of Special Education Technology* 25 (2010): 1–27.

Matthewman, Steve. *Technology and Social Theory*. London: Macmillan International Higher Education, 2011.

Maxwell, Joseph A. *Qualitative Research Design*. Thousand Oaks, CA: SAGE, 2013.

McClain, Colleen, Emily A. Vogels, Andrew Perrin, Stella Secholpoulos, and Lee Rainie. "The Internet and the Pandemic." *PEW Research Center*, September 1, 2021. https://www.pewresearch.org/internet/2021/09/01/the-internet-and-the-pandemic/.

McCutchen, Deborah. "Cognitive Factors in the Development of Children's Writing." In *Handbook of Writing Research*, edited by C. MacArthur, S. Graham, and J. Fitzgerald, 115–130. New York: Guilford Press, 2003.

McDermott, Ray, and Hervé Varenne. "Culture as Disability." *Anthropology and Education Quarterly* 26, no. 3 (1995): 324–348.

McDonnell, John, and Pam Hunt. "Inclusive Education and Meaningful School Outcomes." In *Equity and Full Participation for Individuals with Severe Disabilities: A Vision for the Future*, edited by Martin Agran, Fredda Brown, Carolyn Hughes, Carol Quirk, and Diane Ryndak, 155–176. Baltimore, MD: Paul H. Brookes, 2014.

McKenna, Michael C., Kristin Conradi, Camille Lawrence, Bong Gee Jang, and J. Patrick Meyer. "Reading Attitudes of Middle School Students: Results of a US Survey." *Reading Research Quarterly* 47, no. 3 (2012): 283–306.

Michelson, Rebecca, Akeiylah DeWitt, Ria Nagar, Alexis Hiniker, Jason Yip, Sean A. Munson, and Julie A. Kientz. "Parenting in a Pandemic: Juggling Multiple Roles and Managing Technology Use in Family Life during COVID-19 in the United States." *Proceedings of the ACM on Human–Computer Interaction* 5, no. CSCW2 (2021): 1–39. https://doi.org/10.1145/3479546.

Miles, Matthew B., Michael A. Huberman, and Johnny Saldaña. *Qualitative Data Analysis: A Methods Sourcebook*. Thousand Oaks, CA: SAGE, 2013.

Miller, Lynda. *What We Call Smart: A New Narrative for Intelligence and Learning. School-Age Children Series*. San Diego, CA: Singular Publishing Group, 1993.

Mingus, Mia. "Access Intimacy, Interdependence and Disability Justice." *Leaving Evidence* (blog), April 12, 2017. https://leavingevidence.wordpress.com/2017/04/12/access-intimacy-interdependence-and-disability-justice/.

Mingus, Mia. "Interdependency (Excerpts from Several Talks)." *Leaving Evidence* (blog), January 22, 2010. https://leavingevidence.wordpress.com/2010/01/22/interdependency-exerpts-from-several-talks/.

Mingus, Mia. "Changing the Framework: Disability Justice." *Leaving Evidence* (blog), February 12, 2011. https://leavingevidence.wordpress.com/2011/02/12/changing-the-framework-disability-justice/.

"Missing Social and Educational Milestones During COVID-19." *Providence*, May 24, 2020. https://www.providence.org/news/uf/614770827.

Moore, Caroline, Debra Gilbreath, and Fran Maiuri. "Educating Students with Disabilities in General Education Classrooms: A Summary of the Research." Paper published in Education Resources Information Center (ERIC), Washington D.C., 1998. https://eric.ed.gov/?id=ED419329

Bibliography

Mueller, Tracy Gershwin, and Anna Moriarity Vick. "An Investigation of Facilitated Individualized Education Program Meeting Practice: Promising Procedures that Foster Family–Professional Collaboration." *Teacher Education and Special Education* 42 (2019): 67–81.

Mundy, Peter, and Ann Mastergeorge. *Educational Interventions for Students with Autism.* UC Davis MIND Institute Autism for Educators Series. Hoboken, NJ: Jossey Bass, 2012.

Naraian, Srikala, and Mark Surabian. "New Literacy Studies: An Alternative Frame for Preparing Teachers to Use Assistive Technology." *Teacher Education and Special Education* 37, no. 4 (2014): 330–346.

Nash, Jennifer C. *Black Feminism Reimagined: After Intersectionality.* Durham, North Carolina: Duke University Press, 2018.

National Alliance for Public Charter Schools. Accessed April 21, 2023. https://www.publiccharters.org/.

National Council on Disability. *IDEA Series: The Segregation of Students with Disabilities.* Washington, DC: National Council on Disability, 2018. https://ncd.gov/sites/default/files/NCD_Segregation-SWD_508.pdf.

Obiakor, Festus E., Mateba Harris, Kagendo Mutua, Anthony Rotatori, and Bob Algozzine. "Making Inclusion Work in General Education Classrooms." *Education and Treatment of Children* 35, no. 3 (2012): 477–490. https://doi.org/10.1353/etc.2012.0020.

Official Apple Support. "Use FaceTime with your iPhone, iPad, or iPod touch." Accessed August 1, 2022. https://support.apple.com/en-us/HT204380.

Ok, Min Wook, and Kavita Rao. "Digital Tools for the Inclusive Classroom: Google Chrome as Assistive and Instructional Technology." *Journal of Special Education Technology* 34, no. 3 (2019): 204–211.

Okolo, Cynthia M., and Emily C. Bouck. "Research about Assistive Technology: 2000–2006. What Have We Learned?" *Journal of Special Education Technology* 22, no. 3 (2007): 19–33.

Oliver, Mike. "The Individual and Social Models of Disability." Paper presented at the Joint Workshop of the Living Options Group and the Research Unit of the Royal College of Physicians, London, UK, July 1990.

Oliver, Mike. *Understanding Disability: From Theory to Practice.* New York: St Martin's Press, 1996.

Originator. "Endless Alphabet." Accessed August 31, 2022. https://www.originatorkids.com/endless-alphabet/.

Paley, Vivian Gussin. *You Can't Say You Can't Play*. Cambridge, MA: Harvard University Press, 1993.

Palincsar, A. Sullivan. "Social Constructivist Perspectives on Teaching and Learning." *Annual Review of Psychology* 49 (1998): 345–375.

Palmer, Deborah, Kathryn Henderson, Dorothy Wall, Christian E. Zúñiga, and Stefan Berthelsen. "Team Teaching among Mixed Messages: Implementing Two-Way Dual Language Bilingual Education at Third Grade in Texas." *Language Policy* 15, no. 4 (2016): 393–413.

Palmer, Susan B., Jean Ann Summers, Mary Jane Brotherson, Elizabeth J. Erwin, Susan P. Maude, Vera Stroup-Rentier, Hsiang-Yi Wu, et al. "Foundations for Self-Determination in Early Childhood: An Inclusive Model for Children with Disabilities." *Topics in Early Childhood Special Education* 33, no. 1 (2013): 38–47.

Patton, Michael Q. "Two Decades of Developments in Qualitative Inquiry: A Personal, Experiential Perspective." *Qualitative Social Work* 1, no. 3 (2002): 261–283. https://doi.org/10.1177%2F1473325002001003636.

Peña, Edlyn V., Lissa D. Stapleton, and Lenore M. Schaffer. "Critical Perspectives on Disability Identity." *New Directions for Student Services* 2016, no. 154 (2016): 85–96. https://doi.org/10.1002/ss.20177.

Pennington, Robert C., Melinda Jones Ault, John W. Schuster, and Ann Sanders. "Using Simultaneous Prompting and Computer-Assisted Instruction to Teach Story Writing to Students with Autism." *Assistive Technology Outcomes and Benefits* 7 (2011): 24–38.

Pennington, Robert C., and Monica E. Delano. "Writing Instruction for Students with Autism Spectrum Disorders: A Review of Literature." *Focus on Autism and Other Developmental Disabilities* 27, no. 3 (2012): 158–167.

Peppler, Kylie A., and Mark Warschauer. "Uncovering Literacies, Disrupting Stereotypes: Examining the (Dis)Abilities of a Child Learning to Computer Program and Read." *International Journal of Learning and Media* 3, no. 3 (2011): 15–41.

Petersen, Anne Helen. "Other Countries Have Social Safety Nets. The US Has Women." *Culture Study*, November 11, 2020. https://annehelen.substack.com/p/other-countries -have-social-safety.

Peterson, Lana, Cassie Scharber, Amy Thuesen, and Katie Baskin. "A Rapid Response to COVID-19: One District's Pivot from Technology Integration to Distance Learning." *Information and Learning Sciences* 121, no. 5/6 (2020): 461–469. https://doi.org /10.1108/ILS-04-2020-0131.

Paley, Vivian Gussin. *You can't say you can't play*. Harvard University Press, 1993.

Bibliography

Power, Damien, Tobias Schoenherr, and Danny Samson. "The Cultural Characteristic of Individualism/Collectivism: A Comparative Study of Implications for Investment in Operations Between Emerging Asian and Industrialized Western Countries." *Journal of Operations Management* 28, no. 3 (2010): 206–222. https://doi.org/10.1016/j.jom.2009.11.002.

Prado, Yenda, Sharin R. Jacob, and Mark Warschauer. "Teaching Computational Thinking to Exceptional Students: Lessons from Two Inclusive Classrooms." *Computer Science Education* 32, no. 2 (2022): 188–212. https://doi.org/10.1080/08993408.2021.1914459.

Prado, Yenda, Michelle Ramos, Elizabeth Peña, and Jenny Zavala. "Dual-Language Engagement: Concerted Cultivation of Spanish use among Students, Teachers, and Parents." *Bilingual Research Journal* 45, no. 2 (2022): 159–179.

Prado, Yenda, Jessica Tunney, Tamara Tate, and Mark Warschauer. "Virtual Inclusion: Supporting Exceptional Students' Participation in Remote Learning Environments." Panel discussion at the American Education Research Association, Orlando, FL, April 2021.

Prado, Yenda, Mark Warschauer, and Penelope Collins. "Promoting Positive Literacy Attitudes in Struggling Readers through Digital Scaffolding." Paper presented at the International Society for Technology in Education, Chicago, Illinois, June 2018.

Prado, Yenda, Taffeta Wood, Dorond Zinger, and June Ahn, "Organizing to Support Learning Pods Across Diverse Family Contexts." Symposium presentation at American Education Research Association, Orlando, FL, April 2021.

Prodigy. Accessed August 1, 2022. https://www.prodigygame.com/main-en/.

Przymus, Steve Daniel. "Challenging the Monolingual Paradigm in Secondary Dual-Language Instruction: Reducing Language-as-Problem with the 2-1-L2 Model." *Bilingual Research Journal* 39, no. 3–4 (2016): 279–295.

Pyramid Educational Consultants. Accessed March 3, 2022. https://pecsusa.com/.

Qvortrup, Ane, and Lars Qvortrup. "Inclusion: Dimensions of Inclusion in Education." *International Journal of Inclusive Education* 22, no. 7 (2018): 803–817.

Ramdoss, Sathiyaprakash, Austin Mulloy, Russell Lang, Mark O'Reilly, Jeff Sigafoos, Giulio Lancioni, Robert Didden, and Farah El Zein. "Use of Computer-Based Interventions to Improve Literacy Skills in Students with Autism Spectrum Disorders: A Systematic Review." *Research in Autism Spectrum Disorders* 5, no. 4 (2011): 1306–1318.

ReadWorks. Accessed August 1, 2022. https://www.readworks.org/.

Reese, Leslie, Silvia Balzano, Ronald Gallimore, and Claude Goldenberg. "The Concept of Educación: Latino Family Values and American Schooling." In *Interdisciplinary*

Perspectives on the New Immigration, edited by Marcelo M. Suárez-Orozco, Carola Suárez-Orozco, and Desirée Qin-Hilliard, 305–328. New York: Routledge, 2022.

Richey, Rita C. "Reflections on the 2008 AECT Definitions of the Field." *TechTrends* 52 (2008): 24–25. https://doi.org/10.1007/s11528-008-0108-2.

Rojewski, Jay W., In Heok Lee, and Noel Gregg. "Causal Effects of Inclusion on Post-secondary Education Outcomes of Individuals with High-Incidence Disabilities." *Journal of Disability Policy Studies* 25, no. 4 (2015): 210–219.

Rose, David H., and Anne Meyer. *A Practical Reader in Universal Design for Learning.* Cambridge, MA: Harvard Education Press, 2006.

Rose, David H., and Anne Meyer. *Teaching Every Student in the Digital Age: Universal Design for Learning.* Alexandria, VA: Association for Supervision and Curriculum Development, 2002.

Rose, David H., Anne Meyer, and Chuck Hitchcock, eds. *The Universally Designed Classroom: Accessible Curriculum and Digital Technologies.* Cambridge, MA: Harvard Education Press, 2005.

Rosen, Russell S. "American Sign Language as a Foreign Language in US High Schools: State of the Art." *The Modern Language Journal* 92, no. 1 (2008): 10–38.

Roser, Max, and Esteban Ortiz-Ospina. "Global Education." *Our World in Data* (2016). https://ourworldindata.org/global-education.

Rubin, Julia S., and Mark Weber. "Charter Schools' Impact on Public Education: Theory versus Reality." In *The Risky Business of Education Policy*, edited by Christopher H. Tienken and Carol A. Mullen, 72–87. New York: Routledge, 2021.

Ryan, James. "Establishing Inclusion in a New School: The Role of Principal Leadership." *Exceptionality Education International* 20, no. 2 (2010): 6–24.

Sailor, Wayne, and Blair Roger. "Rethinking Inclusion: School Wide Applications." *Phi Delta Kappan* 86, no. 7 (2005): 503–509. https://doi.org/10.1177/003172170508600707.

Samborski, Zoe E. "Educator Perceptions of the Social Benefits from Peer to Peer Interactions between General and Special Education Students." PhD diss., California State University, Sacramento, CA, 2021.

Sandelowski, Margarete. "Rigor or Rigor Mortis: The Problem of Rigor in Qualitative Research Revisited." *Advances in Nursing Science* 16, no. 2 (1993): 1–8. https://doi.org/10.1097/00012272-199312000-00002.

Sanderson, Catherine A. *Social Psychology.* Hoboken, NJ: Wiley, 2010.

Saumure, Kristie, and Lisa M. Given. "Data Saturation." In *The Sage Encyclopedia of Qualitative Research Methods*, edited by Lisa M. Given, 195–196. Thousand Oaks, CA: SAGE, 2008.

Bibliography

Scanlon, David, and Diana Baker. "An Accommodations Model for the Secondary Inclusive Classroom." *Learning Disability Quarterly* 35, no. 4 (2012): 212–224.

Schuelka, Matthew J., and Suzanne Carrington, eds. *Global Directions in Inclusive Education*. London: Routledge, 2021.

Schuelka, Matthew J., and Suzanne Carrington. "Innovative and Global Directions for Inclusive Education in the 21st Century." In *Global Directions in Inclusive Education*, edited by Matthew J. Schuelka and Suzanne Carrington, 1–26. London: Routledge, 2021.

Scruggs, Thomas E., and Margo A. Mastropieri. "Teacher Perceptions of Mainstreaming/Inclusion, 1958–1995: A Research Synthesis." *Exceptional Children* 63, no. 1 (1996): 59–74.

Seesaw. Accessed August 1, 2022. https://web.seesaw.me/lessons.

Shaw, Robert A. "Employing Universal Design for Instruction." *New Directions for Student Services* 134 (2011): 21–33. https://doi.org/10.1002/ss.392.

Shin, Sarah J. *Bilingualism in Schools and Society: Language, Identity, and Policy*. New York: Routledge, 2017. https://doi.org/10.4324/9781315535579.

Silberman, Steve. *NeuroTribes: The Legacy of Autism and the Future of Neurodiversity*. New York: Penguin, 2015.

Sinclair Broadcast Group. "Teacher Pulls Mic from Boy with Autism at Thanksgiving Performance." *Local12*, November 18, 2016. https://local12.com/news/nation-world/teacher-pulls-mic-from-boy-with-autism-at-thanksgiving-performance.

Skårbrevik, Karl J. "The Quality of Special Education for Students with Special Needs in Ordinary Classes." *European Journal of Special Needs Education* 20, no. 4 (2005): 387–401.

Slee, Roger. "Defining the Scope of Inclusive Education." Paper commissioned for the *2020 Global Education Monitoring Report, Inclusion and Education* (2018).

Slee, Roger. *The Inclusive Education Workbook: Teaching, Learning and Research in the Irregular School*. Abingdon, UK: Routledge, 2017.

Smeltzer, Suzanne C., Linda C. Copel, Patricia K. Bradley, Linda T. Maldonado, Christine D. Byrne, Jennifer D. Durning, Donna S. Havens, Heather Brom, Janell L. Mensinger, and Jennifer Yost. "Vulnerability, Loss, and Coping Experiences of Health Care Workers and First Responders During the Covid-19 Pandemic: A Qualitative Study." *International Journal of Qualitative Studies on Health and Well-Being* 17, no. 1 (2022). https://doi.org/10.1080/17482631.2022.2066254.

Snow, Catherine E., M. Susan Burns, and Peg Griffin, eds. *Preventing Reading Difficulties in Young Children*. Washington, DC: National Research Council, National Academy Press, 1998.

Solis, Michael, Sharon Vaughn, Elizabeth Swanson, and Lisa McCulley. "Collaborative Models of Instruction: The Empirical Foundations of Inclusion and Co-Teaching." *Psychology in the Schools* 49, no. 5 (2012): 498–510. https://doi.org/10.1002/pits.21606.

Spencer-Cavaliere, Nancy, and E. Jane Watkinson. "Inclusion Understood from the Perspectives of Children with Disability." *Adapted Physical Activity Quarterly* 27, no. 4 (2010): 275–293.

Stanovich, Keith E. "Matthew Effects in Reading: Some Consequences of Individual Differences in the Acquisition of Literacy." *Reading Research Quarterly* 21, no. 4 (1986): 360–407.

Steiner, Elizabeth D., and Ashley Woo, "Job-Related Stress Threatens the Teacher Supply: Key Findings from the 2021 State of the US Teacher Survey." https://www.rand.org/pubs/research_reports/RRA1108-1.html.

Strayhorn, Joseph M., and Philip S. Strain. "Social and Language Skills for Preventive Mental Health: What, How, Who and When." In *Children's Social Behavior: Development, Assessment and Modifications*, edited by P. S. Strain, M. J. Guralnick and H. Walker, 287–330. New York: Academic Press, 1996.

Street, Brian V. "Introduction: The New Literacy Studies." In *Cross Cultural Approaches to Learning*, edited by Brian V. Street, 1–21. Cambridge University Press, 1993.

Street, Brian V. *Social Literacies: Critical Approaches to Literacy in Development, and Education*. London: Longman, 1995.

Suri, Harsh. "Purposeful Sampling in Qualitative Research Synthesis." *Qualitative Research Journal* 11, no. 2 (2011): 63–75. https://doi.org/10.3316/QRJ1102063.

Tate, Tamara, and Mark Warschauer. "Equity in Online Learning." *Educational Psychologist*, 57, no. 3 (2022): 192–206. https://doi.org/10.1080/00461520.2022.2062597.

Taylor, Katie Headrick, Deborah Silvis, and Reed Stevens. "Collecting and Connecting: Intergenerational Learning with Digital Media." In *Children and Families in the Digital Age*, edited by Elisabeth Gee, Lori Takeuchi, and Ellen Wartella, 74–75. New York: Routledge, 2017.

Technology-Related Assistance Act for Individuals with Disabilities, US Code 29 (1988).

Terada, Youki. "The Camera-On/Camera-Off Dilemma." *Edutopia*, February 5, 2021. https://www.edutopia.org/article/camera-oncamera-dilemma.

Thomas, Gary, and Mark Vaughan. *Inclusive Education: Readings and Reflections*. Columbus: McGraw-Hill Education, 2004.

Trainor, Audrey A. "Diverse Approaches to Parent Advocacy during Special Education Home–School Interactions: Identification and Use of Cultural and Social Capital." *Remedial and Special Education* 31, no. 1 (2010): 34–47.

Bibliography

"Turn Young Students into Independent Readers with Smarty Ants." Accessed August 1, 2022. https://www.achieve3000.com/products/smarty-ants/.

Turner, Cory. "6 Things We've Learned about How the Pandemic Disrupted Learning." *National Public Radio*, June 22, 2022. https://www.npr.org/2022/06/22/1105970186/pandemic-learning-loss-findings.

UNESCO. "The Salamanca Statement and Framework for Action on Special Needs Education." Adopted by the World Conference on Special Needs Education: Access and Quality, Salamanca, Spain, June 7–10, 1994.

UNESCO. *EFA Global Monitoring Report 2015—Education for All 2000–2015: Achievements and Challenges.* Paris: UNESCO, 2015.

UNESCO. *A Guide for Ensuring Inclusion and Equity in Education.* Paris: UNESCO, 2017. https://unesdoc.unesco.org/ark:/48223/pf0000248254.

UNESCO. *Global Education Monitoring Report 2020—Inclusion and Education: All Means All.* Paris: UNESCO, 2020. https://unesdoc.unesco.org/ark:/48223/pf0000373718.

Ur, Penny. *A Course in Language Teaching: Practice and Theory* Cambridge University Press, 1996.

Vaughn, Sharon, Jeanne Shay Schumm, and Maria Elena Arguelles. "The ABCDEs of Co-Teaching." *Teaching Exceptional Children* 30, no. 2 (1997): 4–10.

Villavicencio, Adriana. *Am I My Brother's Keeper? Educational Opportunities and Outcomes for Black and Brown Boys.* Cambridge, MA: Harvard Education Press, 2021.

Vu, Viet, Yenda Prado, Soobin Yim, and Phuong Nghi Ngoc Le. "Digital Storytelling for Academic Literacy: Culturally Responsive Multimodal Composition Course Design." In *Learning Critical Thinking Skills Beyond the 21st Century for Multidisciplinary Courses,* edited by Zehilia B. Wilhite, 172–190. San Diego, CA: Cognella, 2021.

Vygotsky, Lev S. *Mind in Society: The Development of Higher Psychological Processes.* Cambridge, MA: Harvard University Press, 1978.

Waitoller, Federico R. *Excluded by Choice: Urban Students with Disabilities in the Education Marketplace.* New York: Teachers College Press, 2020.

Walker, Kristen L., Kiya Bodendorf, Tina Kiesler, Georgie de Mattos, Mark Rostom, and Amr Elkordy. "Compulsory Technology Adoption and Adaptation in Education: A Looming Student Privacy Problem." *Journal of Consumer Affairs* 57 (2023): 445–478.

Walpole, Sharon, and Michael C. McKenna. *Differentiated Reading Instruction: Strategies for the Primary Grades.* New York: Guilford Press, 2007.

Wan, Tony. "Google Apps Are Used Widely in K–12. A New Tool Will Show Just How Useful They Are." *EdSurge.* September 24, 2019. https://www.edsurge.com

/news/2019-09-24-google-apps-are-used-widely-in-k-12-a-new-tool-will-show-just -how-useful-they-are.

Warschauer, Mark. *Electronic Literacies: Language, Culture, and Power in Online Education.* New York: Routledge, 1998.

Warschauer, Mark. "Information Literacy in the Laptop Classroom." *Teachers College Record* 109, no. 11 (2007): 2511–2540.

Warschauer, Mark. *Laptops and Literacy: Learning in the Wireless Classroom.* New York: Teachers College Press, 2007.

Warschauer, Mark. *Technology and Social Inclusion: Rethinking the Digital Divide.* Cambridge, MA: MIT Press, 2004.

Weber, Robert P. *Basic Content Analysis.* Thousand Oaks, CA: SAGE, 1990.

Weiland, Christine A., Elizabeth T. Murakami, Evangeline Aguilera, and Michael G. Richards. "Advocates in Odd Places: Social Justice for Behaviorally Challenged, Minority Students in a Large Urban School District." *Education, Citizenship and Social Justice* 9, no. 2 (2014): 114–127.

Weimer, Larry. *Crossroads: Harrison A. Williams, Jr. and Great Society Liberalism, 1959– 1981: An Exhibition.* New Brunswick, NJ: Rutgers University Libraries, 2009. https://doi .org/10.7282/T3GX48H9.

West, Jessica A. "Using New Literacies Theory as a Lens for Analyzing Technology-Mediated Literacy Classrooms." *E-Learning and Digital Media* 16, no. 2 (2019): 151–173. https://doi.org/10.1177%2F2042753019828355.

WeVideo. Accessed August 2, 2022, https://www.wevideo.com/.

"What is Kahoot!?" Kahoot! Accessed August 1, 2022. https://kahoot.com/what-is -kahoot/.

White, Glen W., Jamie L. Simpson, Chiaki Gonda, Craig Ravesloot, and Zach Coble. "Moving from Independence to Interdependence: A Conceptual Model for Better Understanding Community Participation of Centers for Independent Living Consumers." *Journal of Disability Policy Studies* 20, no. 4 (2010): 233–240. https://doi.org /10.1177%2F1044207309350561.

Wiener, Judith. "Do Peer Relationships Foster Behavioral Adjustment in Children with Learning Disabilities?" *Learning Disability Quarterly* 27 (2004): 21–30.

Williams, David, and Alisha Ebrahimji. "Cheerleading Manager with Down Syndrome Left out of Team Photo in Junior High Yearbook." *CNN*, June 18, 2021. https://www .cnn.com/2021/06/18/us/utah-cheerleader-down-syndrome-yearbook-trnd/index .html.

Bibliography

Womack, Tyler A., and Elissa M. Monteiro. "Special Education Staff Well-Being and the Effectiveness of Remote Services during the COVID-19 Pandemic." *Psychology in the Schools* 60, no. 5 (2022): 1374–1393. https://doi.org/10.1002/pits.22702.

Wong, Alice, ed. *Disability Visibility: First-Person Stories from the Twenty-First Century.* New York: Vintage, 2020.

World Health Organization. *International Classification of Impairments, Disabilities, and Handicaps: A Manual of Classification Relating to the Consequences of Disease.* Geneva: World Health Organization, 1980. https://apps.who.int/iris/handle/10665/41003.

Yeskel, Zach. "New Meet Features to Improve Distance Learning." *Google for Education.* April 9, 2020. https://www.blog.google/outreach-initiatives/education/meet-for-edu/.

Yildiz Durak, Hatice. "Preparing Pre-Service Teachers to Integrate Teaching Technologies into Their Classrooms: Examining the Effects of Teaching Environments Based on Open-Ended, Hands-On and Authentic Tasks." *Education and Information Technologies* 26, no. 5 (2021): 5365–5387.

Yin, Robert K. *Case Study Research: Design and Methods (Applied Social Research Methods).* 5th ed. Thousand Oaks, CA: SAGE, 2014.

YouTube. Accessed August 2, 2022. https://www.youtube.com/.

Zambo, Debby, and Carter Davidson. "Ostracism and Adolescents with Learning and Behavioral Disabilities: Preventing and Lessening its Effects." *Intervention in School and Clinic* 48, no. 3 (2013): 178–183.

Zashchirinskaia, Oksana V. "Modern Ideas about Intellectual Disability in Medical Psychology in the Context of Non-Verbal Communication of Primary School Children." *Journal of Intellectual Disability-Diagnosis and Treatment* 8, no. 4 (2020): 594–601.

Zigmond, Naomi. "Where Should Students with Disabilities Receive Special Education Services? Is One Place Better than Another?" *The Journal of Special Education* 37, no. 3 (2003): 193–199.

Zigmond, Naomi, Amanda Kloo, and Victoria Volonino. "What, Where, and How? Special Education in the Climate of Full Inclusion." *Exceptionality* 17, no. 4 (2009): 189–204.

Zoom. "Zoom is for Everyone." Accessed August 2, 2022. https://explore.zoom.us/en/accessibility/.

Index

Page numbers followed by *t* indicate tables and *f* indicate figures.

AAC. *See* Augmented and alternative (AAC) technologies
Abbott, Chris, 8
Abnormal brain, 22
Absent audiences, 35
Accessibility features as determinant of technology, 243n19
Accessible mainstream technologies, 42–44, 218–219
Achieving the Complete School: Strategies for Effective Mainstreaming (Biklen), 23
ADHD. *See* Attention deficit/ hyperactivity disorder (ADHD)
Adjustable font size, 42
Affect, 42
Agency and voice, 175, 176, 193
Alper, Meryl
  accessibility features as determinant of technology, 243n19
  diverse media affording alternative avenues for communication, 103
  embracing fluidity between bodies and device, 110
  Giving Voice, 7
  "liminal space" of multiple bodies, 111
  negotiating personhood vis-a-vis assistive technologies, 245n44

  surveying and conversing early on in school year, 189
  using digital technologies expands communicative possibilities, 114
Alphabetic principle, 33
Alternative teaching, 25
American Sign Language (ASL), 75–76
Am I My Brother's Keeper? Educational Opportunities and Outcomes for Black and Brown Boys (Villavicencio), 172, 176
Anticipatory planning, 35
ASL. *See* American Sign Language (ASL)
Assistive technologies. *See also* Technology use
  assistive technology devices, 38–39
  assistive technology services, 39
  challenges relating to implementation, 256n3
  defined, 38
  digital features, 200*t*
  digital technologies, 82
  environmental modifications, 200*t*
  feasibility and ease of use, 98
  linguistic expression, 107–113
  mismatch between various interests in using digital technologies, 92
  mobility aids, 200*t*
  physical technologies, 82

Index

Assistive technologies (cont.)
  software/hardware, 200t
  technologies designed to create
    access, 38–40, 215
  technologies used at FVA, 215–219
    (see also Technologies used at FVA)
  uses, 114
Assistive technology devices, 38–39
Assistive technology services, 39
Attending to language, 35
Attention deficit/hyperactivity disorder
  (ADHD)
  attending to language, 35
  self-regulation, 36
Audio voice-over, 42
Augmented and alternative (AAC)
  technologies, 108–113, 175,
  181
Autism
  absent audiences, 35
  attending to language, 35
  autonomy and choice, 68
  handwriting fatigue, 43
  institutional support, 68
  literal thinking, 35
  non-preferred topics, 35
  self-regulation, 36
  teacher mindset, 68
Automaticity, 33
Autonomy and choice, 63–68
  active appointments for leadership,
    65–66
  allowing students to share work in
    multiple ways, 67
  autonomy, defined, 63
  classroom placements, 67–68
  independence movement, 63
  interdependence, 174–175
  nonspeaking forms of
    communication, 66
  peer-directed leadership, 65–66
  self-expression, 66–67

  self-regulation exercise, 64–65
  special education teachers, 64–65
  student expression, 66–67
  teacher and student agency, 64–65
  transparent approach, 65

Baines, AnnMarie, 8
Behavior chart, 39
"Being in this together," 171
Beltrán, Elina, 8
Bennett, Cynthia, 165, 166
Biklen, Douglas, 23
Black feminist theory, 168
Book. See Voices on the Margins (Prado/
  Warschauer)
Breakout rooms, 121, 122, 124
Brown v. Board of Education, 4, 18–19

Captioning, 43
Carrington, Suzanne. See Schuelka,
  Matthew J., and Suzanne
  Carrington
CAST. See Center for Applied Special
  Technology (CAST)
Cellular technologies used to address
  engagement barriers, 123
Center for Applied Special Technology
  (CAST), 41
Charter schools, 50–51, 238n3
Chatterjee, Dom, 163
Child assent protocol, 206
Choral reading, 83
Civil rights movement (1960s), 23
Class: Living and Learning in the Digital
  Age, The (Livingston/Sefton-Green),
  8, 11
Classroom and school observations, 64,
  207–209
Classroom engagement, 200t
Cliques, 240n37
Closed captioning, 42
Coffee chats, 142

Index

Collaboration, 173

Collaboration meetings, 113

Collaborative peer communication, 110–111

Combo-grade configurations, 52, 53

Community Education Fellows initiative, 118

Community of care, 172. *See also* Culture of care

Community tutor, 99

Condeluci, Al, 163, 164

Constant comparative method of analysis, 213

Content modification, 58

Controlled learning environment, 34

Convention on the Rights of Persons with Disabilities, 4, 20

Co-teaching
  alternative teaching, 25
  one teach, one assist, 25, 199*t*
  parallel teaching, 25, 199*t*
  station teaching, 25, 199*t*
  team teaching, 25–26, 199*t*

COVID-19 pandemic
  Community Education Fellows initiative, 118
  expansive shift in use of digital technologies, 84
  mid-pandemic period (*see* Returning to hybrid and in-person instruction)
  returning to hybrid and in-person instruction, 14
  shifting to remote learning (*see* Pandemic-related remote learning)
  upending social contract between home and school, 124–125
  violating social boundaries between home and school as separate places, 126
  weakness and blind spots in emergency preparedness, 155

Cranmer, Sue
  current policy on inclusion undermined by individualism within wider society, 164
  digital technology use to support student's inclusion and critical thinking, 255n8
  Disabled Children and Digital Technologies, 181
  need for more research in areas of inclusion and digital literacy practices, 255n5
  policy enabling society to understand its values, 164
  technology use in schools tends toward the pedestrian, 181
  understanding technology as mechanism for access, 184

Creativity and innovation
  FVA, 53–63
  IEP development process, 55–56
  instructional leadership, 60–62
  interdependence, 172–174
  presumed competence, 57–59
  push-in services, 56–57
  recruitment and onboarding of staff, 62–63
  team teaching, 54–55

Crenshaw, Kimberle, 167

Critical disability theory, 223n21

Cultural brokers, 76–77

Cultural wealth, 181, 255n9

Culture of care, 141–145. *See also* Community of care

Culture of kindness
  acceptance of student's verbal exclamation as legitimate communication, 69
  "contagious" nature of inclusivity and kindness, 73
  developing kindness being incremental process, 71–72

Culture of kindness (cont.)
"doing friendship," 72
empathy and care, 72
helpful prompting behaviors, 70–71
inclusive schoolyard behaviors, 73
interdependence, 176
normalization of neurodiverse
behaviors, 71
pandemic-related remote learning,
141
paraprofessionals, 69–70
peer-to-peer modeling, 70
perception of kindness at FVA, 71–73
protective factors, 72
social capital, 70
wider lens of acceptance, 73
Curricular adjustments, 79

Decoding, 37
Deficit-based beliefs, 27, 28
Demonstration equipment, 200*t*
Demystifying Disability (Ladau), 9
Desktop publishing, 44
Details of FVA study. *See* Research
methodology
Determinist perspectives, 10
Differentiated instruction, 78
Differentiated technology use, 97, 98
Digital alarm, 82, 83
Digital cloud tools, 154
Digital equity gap, 94
Digital inclusion, 186
Digital storytelling, 132, 190–191
Digital technologies, 82. *See also*
Assistive technologies; Mainstream
technologies; Technology use
Digital writing, 92
Digital Youth with Disabilities (Alper), 7
Directed content analysis, 213
Disability justice movement, 22
Disability rights movements, 22
Disability studies, 7
Disability Visibility (Wong), 9

*Disabled Children and Digital
Technologies: Learning the Context
of Inclusive Education* (Cranmer), 7,
9, 181
Disabled students. *See* Students with
disabilities
Distractibility, 36
"Doing friendship," 72
Down syndrome
autonomy and choice, 68
defined, 100
embodiment of voice, 108–110
misconceptions about literacy
practices, 100
protected under IDEA, 100
self-regulation, 36

EBP. *See* Evidence-based practices (EBPs)
Ecological and relational nature of
practices and customs, 172,
254n51
Ecological perspectives in education
program implementation, 239n20
EdTech. *See* Educational technology
(EdTech)
Education
access to, 20
ecological perspectives in education
program implementation, 239n20
inclusive pedagogical supports for
learning, 242n3
invasion of privacy, 124–127
"mismatch" between teaching
population and diverse student
populations, 126
Educational anthropology, 8
Educational game apps, 87
Educational technology (EdTech), 40
Education anthropology, 8
Education for All Handicapped Children
Act, 4, 20, 22
Electronic keyboard, 43
Elmo, 151

Index

Embedded case-study approach, 196

Embodiment of voice, 108–110

Empathy, 111

Empathy and care, 72

Empirical studies, 31

Endless Alphabet, 188, 216

Environmental modifications, 200t

Epic
  brief description, 216
  grounded in principles of universal design for learning (UDL), 41
  reading, 90
  "read to me" function, 106

Equity and social justice, 17

Ethnographic approach, 197

Everyday Speech
  brief description, 216
  digital social communication and socio-emotional skills video, 112f
  social skills video about empathy, 111

Evidence-based practices (EBPs), 19

Excluded by Choice: Urban Students with Disabilities in the Education Marketplace (Waitoller), 8

Existential crisis, 119

Eye tracking, 37, 44

FaceTime
  acceptable form of communication between staff, 122
  assisting families with their home Internet connectivity, 123
  brief description, 218
  mitigating isolation, 142
  staff connecting with each other and offering care, 142

Feasibility and ease of use, 98

Feminism, 168

First-cycle of coding, 212

First-responder families, 143–145, 156

Flip
  audio recording, 132
  brief description, 216

Flipgrid, 216. *See also* Flip

Full inclusion environments, 18

"Full inclusion mindset," 61

Future Visions Academy (FVA), 13, 49–79
  all forms of communication being equally valued, 111
  American Sign Language (ASL), 75–76
  autonomy and choice, 63–68 (*see also* Autonomy and choice)
  charter school, 50
  collaboration as ecosystem, 54–55
  collaboration meetings, 113
  combo-grade configurations, 52, 53
  content modification, 58
  creativity and innovation, 53–63
  cultural brokers, 76–77
  curricular adjustments, 79
  differentiated instruction, 78
  "doing friendship," 72
  family perspectives on intersectionality, 77–79
  focus of FVA's piloting years, 86
  founder and executive director (Dr. Tully), 54–55, 60–61, 189
  "full inclusion mindset," 61
  general description (overview), 205–206
  IEP development process, 55–56
  instructional leadership, 60–62
  instructional philosophy, 52
  integration of service providers into classroom, 53
  interdependent approach to inclusion, 54, 170–177
  intersectional vision of inclusive education, 73–79
  investigating inclusive education (*see* Research methodology)
  kindness, 69–73 (*see also* Culture of kindness)
  meeting children at their "level," 78
  mismatch between various interests in using digital technologies, 92

Future Visions Academy (cont.)
modeling social skills, 58
multilingual language support, 74–79, 241n41
multiple identities, 74, 75
normalization of neurodiverse behaviors, 71
paraprofessionals, 52 (*see also* Paraprofessionals)
peer-to-peer modeling, 56, 70
positioning of student achievement, 61
presumed competence, 57–59
"progress is progress," 62
provision of service, 57
push-in services, 56
recruitment, 62–63, 205–206
school demographics, 202, 202t
school handbook, 52, 74
school's mission, 52
"starting over," 62–63
team teaching, 51–52, 53, 54–55
technologies used at FVA, 215–219 (*see also* Technologies used at FVA)
tension between adherence and letting go, 61
two campus sites, expansion to, 157
very close-knit community of caring, 158
FVA. *See* Future Visions Academy (FVA)
FVA Parent Handbook, 52, 74

Garcia, Antero, 8, 181, 255n7, 255n9
Ghosh, Sumita, 8
Giving Voice: Mobile Communication, Disability and Inequality (Alper), 7, 9, 11. See also Alper, Meryl
Global Directions in Inclusive Education (Schuelka/Carrington), 8, 9
Global Monitoring Report (UNESCO, 2015), 20
Global problems, 178

Good Reception: Teens, Teachers, and Mobile Media in a Los Angeles School (Garcia), 8, 181, 255n7, 255n9
Google Classroom
increased number of users in schools, 149
observing asynchronous classroom practice, 115
responding to questions regarding assignments, 131
two teachers granting author remote access to their platforms, 209
Google Docs
brief description, 218
editing and revision, 44, 107
speech-to-text functions, 105
spell checking, 105
transitioning to writing using Chromebook, 106
very good skill to have, 154
writing, 43
Google Slides
brief description, 218
used to anchor all of FVA's lessons, 154
very good skill to have, 154
Google Suite, 43
Google Translate, 138
Google Workspace, 84, 91, 218
Graham, Steve, 34
Great Society, 23
G Suite, 218. *See also* Google Workspace
Guiding research questions, 197–198

Hand-over-hand approach, 110
Handwriting fatigue, 43, 44
Harris, Karen, 34
Hearing impairment, 43
Helpful prompting behaviors, 70–71
Higashida, Naoki, 22
High-tech tools, 39, 108
Historical overview, 18–20, 22–23
Hobbies and interests, 133
Holding spaces, 84

Index

"How" of learning, 41
Humanizing education movement, 119

IDEA. *See* Individuals with Disabilities Education Act (IDEA)
Identity-first language, 9–10
IEP. *See* Individualized education plan (IEP)
If You Give a Mouse a Cookie (Numeroff), 64
Inclusion models
  co-teaching, 25–26 (*see also* Co-teaching)
  wide range of possibilities, 24
"inclusion" vs. "inclusive," 18, 166
Inclusive classrooms, 10, 167
Inclusive education, 12, 17–30
  additional personnel (i.e., school psychologists, supplemental aides), 19
  barriers to teacher professional development and support, 29–30
  Brown v. Board of Education, 18–19
  burden of, shared at school, district, state, and national levels, 24
  challenges to overcome, 26–30
  co-teaching, 25–26
  deficit-based beliefs, 27, 28
  defined, 17, 18
  differentiated instruction, 78
  equity and social justice, 17
  evidence-based practices (EBPs), 19
  feasibility of fully inclusive environment, 28–29
  framework for understanding inclusive digital pedagogy across contexts, 185*f*
  full inclusion environments, 18
  historical overview, 18–20, 22–23
  importance, 17–18
  "inclusion" vs. "inclusive," 18
  inclusive instructional supports, 17
  inclusive technology use across disability, 169*f*
  independence movement, 21–22
  individualized education plan (IEP), 19, 24
  Individuals with Disabilities Education Act (IDEA), 19
  integration of paraprofessionals into curriculum planning and implementation, 173
  interdependence, 170
  key principles of inclusive schools, 23
  lack of institutional resources, infrastructure, and support, 30
  least restrictive environment (LRE), 19
  mainstreaming movement, 23
  medical model of disability, 20–21
  methods of investigation (*see* Research methodology)
  models of, 24–26
  moral question/moral imperative, 23
  normalizing use of assistive features in digital technologies to support students' LLT practices, 187
  other social justice movements, 22
  parent perceptions of inclusion, 28
  protective spaces, 176
  questions of equity and access, 26
  reform based on restructuring school environment, not remediation of students, 27
  Salamanca Statement, 20
  social models of disability, 21
  student perceptions of inclusion, 28–29
  teacher perceptions of inclusion, 29
  teachers designing lessons to be more inclusive, rather than building inclusion after the fact, 174
  "ungraded classrooms," 22
  US counterpoint to discussion of inclusiveness in international context, 18

Inclusive education (cont.)
variability in implementation resulting in affordances and challenges, 26
vulnerability and inter-reliance, 171
Inclusive instructional practices, 10
Inclusive instructional supports, 17
Inclusive Language Education and Digital Technology (Beltrán et al.), 8
Inclusive schoolyard behaviors, 73
Inclusive supports for literacy, 5
Independence movement, 21–22, 63, 163–164
Individualism, 164
Individualized education plan (IEP)
collaboration across various members of IEP teams, 174
defined, 19
district and state reporting requirements, 131
IDEA requirements, 19
IEP development process, 55–56
implementation of inclusive practices, 24
prioritizing IEP goals that could be supported at home, 130
Individuals with Disabilities Education Act (IDEA), 4, 19, 22, 34, 100
Information recall (working memory), 34
Innovation. *See* Creativity and innovation
In-person classroom observations, 64, 207–209
In-person LLT practices, 79. *See also* LLT practices at FVA
Instant messaging, 122–123
Instructional leadership, 60–62
Instructional technology, 200t
Instructional videos, 129, 139
Intentional cultivation of literacy practices, 92–96, 99

Interdependence, 14–15, 161–178
assessing participant moves to support inclusion, 166–167
autonomy and choice, 174–175
"being in this together," 171
commitment to intentionally work, play and learn together, 170
community of care, 172
creativity and innovation, 172–174
culture of kindness, 176
defined, 161
empowerment framework for acknowledging work done by disabled people, 166
global problems, 178
heuristic for how accessible a situation is with regard to contextual factors, 165
independence movement, 163–164
interaction of personal contingencies across multiple axes of difference, 168
intersectionality, 167–168, 177
marrying "inclusion as act" with "interdependence as engagement," 167
medical model of disability, 162
multiple simultaneous actions and practices with classroom environment, 170
multiple types of access support, 165
negotiating social encounters with each other, 71
relational and contextual nature of people's engagement with each other, 180
relational nature of simultaneous actions and behaviors, 165
relationship building, 164, 165
sharing burden of problem solving together, 171
social capital (*see* Social capital)
social models of disability, 162–163

Index

293

technology use across disability, 168–169

understanding ways that inclusion occurs in school communities, 67

using interdependence as framework for assessing, adopting, and exploring, 166

vulnerability and inter-reliance, 171

"Interdependency (Excerpts from Several Talks)" (Mingus), 164

Intersectionality, 73–79, 167–168, 177

iPad, 108

Isolation, 142

IXL

brief description, 217

grounded in principles of universal design for learning (UDL), 41

Jamboard, 218

Johnson, Lyndon B., 23

Jones, Jane, 8

Just-in-time messaging, 122–123

Kahoot

brief description, 217

fun to use and highlight of student's day, 88

working memory/information recall, 87

Kindness. *See* Culture of kindness

Ladau, Emily, 9, 22

LAMP

AAC applications, 39

augmentative and alternative (AAC) applications, 39

brief description, 215

embodiment of voice, 108–110, 162

speech-to-text software, 40

text-to-speech software, 39

using LAMP in small-group settings to engage with classmates, 108–110, 162

Language, literacy, and technology (LLT)

FVA (*see* LLT practices at FVA)

inclusive LLT practices at schools - success and challenges, 180–181

LLT practices, defined, 81, 179

practical questions, 183–184

research questions, 183

sociocultural interrelations, 81, 241n1

Language Acquisition through Motor Planning. *See* LAMP

Leap of faith, 102

Learning. *See* Education

Learning hubs, 117

Learning pods, 118

Learning to read, 32

Least restrictive environment (LRE), 19

Lexia

brief description, 217

grounded in principles of universal design for learning (UDL), 41

literacy skills at home, 96

phonological awareness, 88

rhyming words, 88

supporting early language and literacy goals, 83

working memory/information recall, 87

Library, 93, 94

"Liminal space" of multiple bodies, 111

Linguistic expression, 39, 107–113

Literacy activities, 199t

Literacy apps, 188

Literacy studies, 7

Literal thinking, 35

Little Mermaid storybook, 75

Livingstone, Sonia, 8

LLT practices at FVA, 13–14, 81–114

AAC interventions, 108–113

choral reading, 83

classroom use of LLT tools, 82–90

collaborative peer communication, 110–111

LLT practices at FVA (cont.)
community tutor, 99
concerted cultivation practices, 92–96, 243n21
descriptive overview, 82–85
differentiated technology use, 97, 98
digital alarm, 82, 83
digital equity gap, 94
digital writing, 92
disabled children (creators and writers), 102–107
disabled children (LLT practices at home), 98–100
disabled children (misconceptions about skills), 100–102
educational game apps, 87
embodiment of voice, 108–110
feasibility and ease of use, 98
Google Workspace, 91
hand-over-hand approach, 110
holding spaces, 84
home use of assistive technologies, 92–100
intentional cultivation of literacy practices, 92–96, 99
keeping portion of class autonomously occupied, 84
leap of faith, 102
limited financial resources, 95
linguistic expression, 107–113
LLT practices, defined, 81
LLT preferences, 85–92
making agency and participation visible, 111–113, 114
multimodality to support expression, 103–105
peer modeling, 100
physical/digital technologies, defined, 82
physical manipulatives, 82
productivity, 94, 97
promoting joy of reading, 99
public library, 93, 94
reading physical books, 91
rhyming words, 88
self-guided literacy skills review, 83–84
structured routines, 93
student perspectives, 87–92
teacher preferences, 85–87
typing, 86
video gaming, 97
writing proficiency, 86
writing with pencil and paper, 86, 89
Loneliness and disconnect, 146–147
Low-tech tools, 39, 108
LRE. *See* Least restrictive environment (LRE)

Mainstreaming movement, 23
Mainstream technologies, 42–44. *See also* Technology use
academic instruction, 43
FaceTime, 218
facilitating writing production, 43–44
Google Workspace, 218
reading comprehension and fluency, 44
WeVideo, 219
YouTube, 219
Zoom, 219
Marketization, 164
Matthew effect, 33
Medical model of disability, 20–21, 162
Meeting children at their "level," 78
Mental health, 135, 141, 143
Methods of investigating inclusive education. *See* Research methodology
Mexican culture, 94
Meyer, Anne, 41
Mid-pandemic period. *See* Returning to hybrid and in-person instruction
Mid-tech tools, 39
Mingus, Mia, 9, 22, 163, 164–165, 166
"minimally speaking," 66

Index

Mobility aids, 200t

Modeling social skills, 58

Moral question/moral imperative, 23

Morning meetings, 141–142

Morning recess, 152

Multilingual students
American Sign Language (ASL), 75–76
comfort using English during in-person vs. online instruction, 140
cultural brokers bridging language gaps between student and parents, 76
cultural push to socialize children as helpers, 1441
family perspectives on intersectionality, 77–78
framing and valuation of English as dominant language, 138
Google Translate, 138
intersecting needs across language and disability, 74–79, 241n41
major of student population at FVA being of Latino descent, 137
older students helping their younger siblings, 140–141
remote learning, 137–141

Multimodality, 103–105

Multiple identities, 74, 75

Multiple means of action and expression, 42

Multiple means of engagement, 42

Multiple means of representation, 41–42

Multiple types of access support, 165

Nash, Jennifer C., 168

National Alliance for Public Charter Schools, 50–51

National Council on Disability (NCD), 4

National Longitudinal Transition Study-2, 17

National Research Council, 32

NCD. *See* National Council on Disability (NCD)

Neoliberalism, 164

Neurodiversity movement, 22

No Child Left Behind Act, 19

Non-inclusive classrooms, 10

Non-preferred topics, 35

"nonspeaking," 66

Nonspeaking forms of communication, 66

Non-text content, 42

"nonverbal," 66

Normalization of neurodiverse behaviors, 71

Occupational therapy, 199t

One teach, one assist, 25, 199t

One-to-one Chromebooks, 117, 152

One-to-one laptop programs, 256n3

Open-ended play, 42

Out-groups, 240n37

Pandemic-related remote learning, 14, 115–147. *See also* COVID-19 pandemic
affordances/challenges made visible in eye of camera, 124
awareness of students' personal circumstances and barriers to access, 125–126
breakout rooms, 121, 122, 124
cancellation of significant celebrations and events, 145
cellular technologies used to address engagement barriers, 123
children's perspectives of schooling, 145–147
coffee chats, 142
communication at FVA becoming more fluid, just-in-time, and informal, 122
connection at FVA, 115–116
creating proper learning environment at home, 137
culture of care, 141–145

Pandemic-related remote learning (cont.)
culture of kindness, 141
digital storytelling, 132
disappearance of social peer-to-peer interaction, 147
establishing expectations online schooling being in fact "real school," 128
existential crisis, 119
first-responder families, 143–145
forced revisioning of role of digital technology, 117
increased visibility of students' lives and homes, 125–126
increased visibility of teacher practice, 124–125
in-depth discussion of remote learning at FVA, 257n9
just-in-time emergency measures, 117
just-in-time messaging, 122–123
lack of guidance from state/federal levels regarding provision of services, 131
loneliness and disconnect, 146–147
mental health, 135, 141, 143
morning meetings, 141–142
multilingual students, 137–141 (*see also* Multilingual students)
one-to-one Chromebooks, 117
opportunities for connection and relationship building, 132–133
parents as teachers in remote learning, 133–137
physical space needed for remote learning, 137
professional work obligations vs. managing children's behavior while attending "school," 134
provider-created instructional videos, 129
"reformed" parents who were initially ambivalent about value of technologies, 136
reprioritizing essential learning goals, 119
school meetups, 142
shifting range of acceptable remote school behaviors, 128
shifting staff attitudes as to possible uses of technology, 131
shifting what it means to be inclusive, 129
shifting what it means to be in school, 127–129
shifts in boundaries and roles, 117
Spring Jam talent show, 145
staff who were also parents, 142–143
stories of families who benefited from remote learning, 122
students' hobbies and interests, 133
students' socio-emotional states, 118
students turning off camera at "sensitive" times, 127
synchronous and asynchronous technologies, 120–122
tutoring and enrichment programs, 117–118
virtual check-in, 123
virtual one-to-one sessions with students and small groups, 130
willingness to return to in-person schooling, 145
Parallel teaching, 25, 199t
Paraprofessionals
collaboration with, preemptively being built into teacher and staff preparation time, 174
cultural brokers, 76–77
incorporating digital tools into students' writing practices, 107
integration of, into curriculum planning and implementation, 173
making asynchronous video content, 139
pivoting to meet school community needs, 129

Index

positive reception vis-a-vis digital technologies, 189
shifting what it means to provide services, 129–131
station teaching, 52
universal design for learning (UDL), 139
work experience, 205
PECS
brief description, 215
collaborative peer communication, 110–111
goal, 40
mid-tech tool, 39, 108
Pedagogy. *See* Education
Peer-directed discussion, 65
Peer-to-peer modeling (peer modeling), 56, 70, 101, 170
Person-first language, 10
Perspective taking, 35
Phonological awareness, 33, 44, 88
Phonological processing, 33
Physical manipulatives, 82
Physical technologies, 82
Picture Exchange Communication System. *See* PECS
Play, 73
Playground, 152
Playground culture studies, 73
Positioning of student achievement, 61
Prado, Yenda, 8–9. *See also Voices on the Margins* (Prado/Warschauer)
Presumption of competence, 27, 57–59, 114, 174
Preventing Reading Difficulties in Young Children, 32
Processes of social reproduction, 192
Prodigy
brief description, 217
literacy skills at home, 96
Productivity, 94, 97
Professional development, 30, 31, 61, 174, 189–191

"Progress is progress," 62
Proloquo2Go
AAC applications, 39
amplifying student's voice within classroom community, 175
augmentative and alternative (AAC) applications, 39
brief description, 215
centering disabled students as agentive participants, 113
impacting how staff viewed student's competencies, 114
interview of Madeline, 188
making agency and participation visible, 111–113
speech-generating device, 40
synthetic speech feedback software, 40
text-to-speech software, 39
Protective factors, 72
Protective spaces, 176
Provision of service, 57
Psychiatric survivors movement, 22
Public library, 93, 94
Pullout services, 56
Push-in services, 56

Reading
alphabetic principle, 33
automaticity, 33
challenging features of academic reading, 32
decoding, 37
eye tracking, 37, 44
learning to read, 32
mainstream technologies, 43, 44
Matthew effect, 33
needs of students with disabilities, 32–34
NRC landmark report, 32
phonological processing, 33
physical books, 91
promoting joy of reading, 99

Reading (cont.)
  reading to learn, 32
  successful readers, characteristics of, 32–33
  technology use, 37
  text comprehension, 37
  word identification, 37
  working memory, 34
Reading to learn, 32
Reading/writing intervention, 199t
"Read to me" function, 43, 106
ReadWorks, 217
Receptive language needs, 35
Recruitment, 62–63, 205–206
Relationship building, 164, 165
Remote learning. See Pandemic-related remote learning
Research methodology, 195–213
  analysis, 213–213
  analytic memos, 213
  audio recording, transcribing, and anonymizing, 197
  child assent protocol, 206
  constant comparative method of analysis, 213
  content analysis, 213
  data sources collected using protocols, 206
  de-identification using pseudonyms, 197
  embedded case-study approach, 196
  embedded units of analysis, 197t
  ethnographic approach, 197
  family interview participants, 202–203, 203t
  family interviews, 211–212
  first- and second-cycle coding, 212
  follow-up interviews, 210, 212
  Google Classroom platforms, 209
  guiding research questions, 197–198
  interview protocol items, 201
  modified application of Weber protocol, 213

observation protocol items, 199–200t
participants, 202–205
piloting observation protocol, 198
protocol development, 198–202
recruitment, 205–206
reliability and validity concerns, 213
researcher bias, 213
research-practice partnership, 196
respondent validation, 213
school and classroom observations, 207–209
school demographics, 202, 202t
selection of FVA as study site, 195–213
shifting to remote fieldwork (spring 2020), 115 (see also Pandemic-related remote learning)
sources of data, 206–212
staff interviews, 209–211
staff participants, 203–205
study design, 196–197
TDOP, 198
triangulation, 213
trustworthiness of study, 213
truthfulness and validity, 213
Research-practice partnership, 115, 189, 196
Restrictive reporting requirements, 30
Returning to hybrid and in-person instruction, 14, 149–158
  actual mechanics of hybrid classroom instruction, 150
  digital cloud tools, 154
  Elmo, 151
  families and instructional staff who chose to leave FVA, 152, 153
  family expectations for 2021–2022 year, 156–157
  hybrid instruction at FVA, 150–152
  mixed feelings, 155
  morning recess, 152

Index

parental concerns about physical and socio-emotional well-being of children, 156

physical layout of hybrid classroom, 151

planned expansion to two campus sites, 157

planned intervention-focused after-school program, 158

playground, 152

weakness and blind spots in emergency preparedness, 155

Rhyming words, 88

Roger, Blair, 23

Rose, David, 41

SAI. *See* Structured academic instruction (SAI)

Sailor, Wayne, 23

Salamanca Statement, 4, 20

School and classroom observations, 64, 207–209

School meetups, 142

Schuelka, Matthew J., and Suzanne Carrington

analysis of UNESCO's 2015 Global Monitoring Report, 20

education anthropology, 8

professional development, 31

reimagining of schools as ecosystems, 10

universal human right, 3

Screen readability, 44

Second cycle of coding, 212

Seesaw

brief description, 218

putting in your voice, 131

Sefton-Green, Julian, 8

Segregation of Students with Disabilities (NCD), 4

Self-advocacy movement, 22

Self-expression, 66–67

Self-guided literacy skills review, 83–84

Self-regulation, 36, 64

Silberman, Steve, 22

Smarty Ants

brief description, 218

home desktop computer, 97

supporting early language and literacy goals, 83

"Snug as a bug," 113

Social acceptance, 29

Social capital

considerate behaviors, 70

defined, 175

full inclusion education programs, 175

independence movement, 163

interdependence, 170

interdependent approach to technology use, 169, 169*f*

more successful lives, 164

relationship and skill building, 165

Social collaboration and inclusion, 40

Social constructivist theory

challenging all students with rich, engaging content, 27

educational environment needing to adapt to the child, 23

in depth discussion, 223n22

knowledge constructed from human experience, 41

knowledge dependent on processes that position school as cultural process, 9

knowledge informed by cultural psychology and anthropology, 41

presumption of competence, 27

use of frameworks and systems that build on competencies of all students, 41

Social justice movements, 21–22

Social models of disability, 21, 162–163

Social safety net, 137, 143

Social shaping of technologies, 11

Social skills/behavioral supports, 199*t*

Social use approach, 10–11
Sociocultural theories of education, learning, and literacy, 6
Sound-effect modifications, 42
Spanish lessons, 139
Special education services, 199t
Special education teachers, 64–65
Speech feedback, 39, 40, 44
Speech therapy, 199t
Speech-to-text software, 39, 43. *See also* Google Docs
Spell checking, 42–44, 105. *See also* Google Docs
Spring Jam talent show, 145
Sprouting shoot, 72
"Starting over," 62–63
Station teaching, 25, 199t
Structured academic instruction (SAI), 199t
Structured routines, 93
Student agency and voice, 175, 176, 193
Student autonomy. *See* Autonomy and choice
Student-centered, assets-based approach, 7
Student expression, 66–67
Students with disabilities
  being at risk of being teased and rejected, 29
  centering disabled students as agentive participants, 113
  cliques and out-groups, 240n37
  creators and writers, 102–107
  hand-drawn picture of student's daddy, 104f
  integration of multiple tools to support scaffolding in classroom, 242n2
  language and literacy needs—reading, 32–34 (*see also* Reading)
  language and literacy needs—writing, 34–36 (*see also* Writing)
  LLT practices at home, 98–100

misconceptions about their skills, 100–102
  myths regarding their emotional worlds, 105
  receptive language needs, 35
  shared history with assistive technologies, 4–5
  social acceptance, 29
  systemic structures, practices, and attitudes preventing full integration, 172
Study particulars. *See* Research methodology
Synchronous and asynchronous technologies, 120–122
Synthetic speech feedback software, 39, 40, 44

TDOP. *See* Teaching Dimensions Observation Protocol (TDOP)
Teachers
  attitude toward education uses of technology, 37
  perceptions of inclusion, 29
  preferences regarding LLT practices at FVA, 85–87
  professional development, 30
Teaching Dimensions Observation Protocol (TDOP), 198
Team teaching, 25–26, 51–52, 53, 54–55, 199t
Tech Act. *See* Technology-Related Assistance Act for Individuals with Disabilities (Tech Act)
Technologies used at FVA, 215–219
  Endless Alphabet, 216
  Epic, 216
  Everyday Speech, 216
  FaceTime, 218
  Flip, 216
  Google Workspace, 218
  IXL, 217
  Kahoot, 217

Index

301

LAMP, 215

Lexia, 217

mainstream technologies with accessible features, 218–219

PECS, 215

Prodigy, 217

Proloquo2Go, 215

ReadWorks, 217

Seesaw, 218

Smarty Ants, 218

technologies designed to create access, 215

universally designed educational technologies, 216–218

WeVideo, 219

YouTube, 219

Zoom, 219

Technology as connection, 115–147. *See also* Pandemic-related remote learning

Technology for Inclusion: Special Education, Rehabilitation, for All (Ghosh), 8

Technology-Related Assistance Act for Individuals with Disabilities (Tech Act), 38

Technology-supported language and literacy, 12–13, 31–45

assistive technologies designed to create access, 38–40, 215

assistive technology devices, 38–39

assistive technology services, 39

digital technology to support language and literacy, 36–38

future of LLT research, 44–45

high-tech tools, 39

low-tech tools, 39

mainstream technologies with accessible features, 42–44, 218–219

mid-tech tools, 39

multiple means of action and expression, 42

multiple means of engagement, 42

multiple means of representation, 41–42

social collaboration and inclusion, 40

universally designed educational technologies, 40–42, 216–218

use of specific tool aimed at supporting specific academic components, 36

use of technology primarily focussing on supporting functions of classroom, 37

Technology use. *See also* Assistive technologies; Mainstream technologies

affordances of digital technologies offering power access and connection, 192

assessing attitudes of school community members being of critical importance, 189

barriers to adoption of digital technologies, 186–187

digital inclusion, 186

digital storytelling, 190–191

disconnects between home and school in uses of digital technologies, 188

disparities in teacher and student tech utility and use, 255n7

impacts of screens on students' attention and retention, 189

inclusive use of technology, defined, 184

inconsistencies, related to competing priorities in staff uptake and training, 186

interdependent approach, 168–169

"processes of social reproduction," 192

remote and hybrid uses to support connection, 182–183

students' technology use as source of cultural wealth, 255n9

Technology use (cont.)
use of technology in schools tending toward the pedestrian, 181
Text comprehension, 37
Text highlighting, 43
Texting, 122–123
Text-to-speech software, 39, 42–44
Transcription process, 35–36
Transparent approach, 65
Tully, founder and executive director of FVA, 54–55, 60–61, 189
Tutoring and enrichment programs, 117–118
Typing, 86

UDL. *See* Universal design for learning (UDL)
UNESCO. *See* United Nations Educational, Scientific and Cultural Organization (UNESCO)
"Ungraded classrooms," 22
Ungrading movement, 119
United Nations Educational, Scientific and Cultural Organization (UNESCO), 4, 20
Universal design for learning (UDL), 41, 139
Universal design principles, 5, 17
Universal human right, 3
Universally designed educational technologies, 40–42, 216–218
(Un)Learning Disability (Baines), 8

Variable-oriented questions, 198
Video gaming, 97
Villavicencio, Adriana, 172, 176
Virtual check-in, 123
Visual animations, 42
Visual calendar, 39
Voices on the Margins (Prado/Warschauer)
approach to disability, language, and inclusion, 9–10
approach to intersectionality and diversity, 10–11
approach to investigating digital technologies, 10–11
argument, 7–8
author positionality, 8–9
book engaged in research on both formal and informal learning, 191
book written in response to call for more research and policy suggestions, 179
central themes, 6
definitions, 10
details of FVA study (*see* Research methodology)
equity and social justice, 17
examining ways in which digital technologies can support inclusive LLT practices, 192
foundational texts, 7–8
identity-first language, 9–10
illuminating kinds of social organization that allow for inclusive schools to thrive, 193
in-depth assets-based approach, 7
moral question/moral imperative, 23
narrative organization (chapter map), 12–15
person-first language, 10
purpose of book, 5–7
purposes of FVA study, 195
social use approach, 10–11
student-centered, assets-based approach, 7
technologies studied, 11, 215–219
Vulnerability and inter-reliance, 171

Waitoller, Federico, 8, 50
Warschauer, Mark, 8–9. *See also Voices on the Margins* (Prado/Warschauer)
Weber protocol, 213
WeVideo, 132, 219
"What" of learning, 41

Index

White, Glen, 163, 164
"Why" of learning, 41
Wong, Alice, 9, 22
Word identification, 37
Word prediction, 42
Word processing software, 43, 44
Work ethic, 94
Working memory, 34
World Conference on Special Needs
    Education (1994), 20
Writing
  absent audiences, 35
  attending to language, 35
  digital tools (disabled students),
    105–107
  fine- and gross-motor coordination,
    36
  mainstream technologies, 43–44
  non-preferred topics, 35
  pencil and paper, 86, 89
  physically laborious and potentially
    demotivating task, 36
  planning and writing a story, 35
  proficiency, 86
  self-regulation, 36
  technology use, 37–38
  transcription process, 35–36

YouTube
  brief description, 219
  increased use of YouTube in US
    classrooms, 43
  putting lessons up, 132
  Spanish lessons, 139

Zoom
  birthday party, 146
  brief description, 219
  digital forum for remote classroom
    instruction, 182
  general and breakout rooms, 121, 122
  increased use of YouTube in US
    classrooms, 43

special education teachers' weekly
    meetings, 129
student using Zoom platform, 120*f*
synchronous and asynchronous
    digital communications, 121